An Empty Chair

An Empty Chair

Living in the Wake of a Sibling's Suicide

Sara Swan Miller

Writers Club Press
San Jose New York Lincoln Shanghai

An Empty Chair
Living in the Wake of a Sibling's Suicide

Published by Writers Club Press
an imprint of iUniverse.com, Inc.

For information address:
iUniverse.com, Inc.
620 North 48th Street
Suite 201
Lincoln, NE 68504-3467
www.iuniverse.com

ISBN: 0-595-09523-2

Printed in the United States of America

Contents

Preface

I have been practicing as a clinical psychologist for more than thirty years. During that time, I have met many, certainly dozens of patients who were significantly touched by suicide, either because they were survivors of suicides by loved ones, or because they had contemplated or had even attempted suicide for themselves. Perhaps at least in part because of my intervention, or possibly because of dumb luck, in no instance did any of the people I treated actually consummate a suicide, so that I have the satisfaction of believing that I might very well have played a major part in preventing so tragic an end to many good lives. In fact, there was only one instance in my life where someone I knew actually committed suicide, and where I soon thereafter had the sense that I might have helped to prevent that death, if only I had acted more wisely, more quickly, more forcefully…if only I had recognized the signs…if only I had known. That event was outside of my practice, but it was very much a part of my own life. It was the death, by suicide, of my future sister-in-law Ann, the very suicide that was the reason for this book.

I was there that early evening in September of 1990, barely a month before our wedding, when Sara, my wife to be, received the phone call from Ann's husband giving her the terrible news. I saw Sara's response, the mix of anguish, confusion, and anger that she writes about so eloquently in this book. I had been there the days before when there were other phone calls that hinted at what was to come, (but those hints were so much better recognized in retrospect.) I had met Ann only a few weeks earlier, and there were signs of disturbance that I noted, (my vanity, at least, tells me that I noted those signs, but again, the signs were so much more clear when I looked back and remembered them.) When I learned that Ann had been to see several mental health specialists only days before she took her own life, righteous anger welled up inside of me. Why didn't they recognize, know, act as they should have? (As I would have done? Or, would I have responded any more sharply in their place?)

All of this was happening to someone who should "know better," who was only a future brother-in-law, who had barely known the ostensive victim. That is how suicide works: it tears the survivors to shreds, like no other kind of dying. I can testify to that both professionally and personally. It is a testimony about which I wish I were far less expert.

This book is written about and primarily for survivors of suicide in the family. It is in fact much more than that, and I will note some of those additional attributes below. But it is not a book about suicide. There is no attempt made here to look into the dynamics of those who commit suicide, to reflect on the magnitude of the problem, to check the validity of the accounts that their sibling survivors provide, or to advise on prevention. There are excellent texts on these issues, including a recent and remarkable book, Night Falls Fast, by Kay Redfield Jamison, herself a survivor, one who had also attempted suicide in her own life, and still further, a mental health professional who is deeply knowledgeable about the subject. And, as recently as 1999, the U.S. Surgeon General issued a report and a set of recommendations on suicide that places it high on the list of preventable tragedies. These and many related writings are readily available to any interested reader, and I hope that there are many such interested readers.

This book is mainly about a unique subset of survivors of suicide: brothers and sisters, who tell their stories to yet another sibling survivor. In this regard alone, it fills a very significant void. Kay Jamison tells us that "the impact of a suicide on the lives of brothers and sisters has been almost entirely ignored in the clinical research literature, an omission made the more remarkable by the closeness of emotional ties between siblings and the possibility that they may be more likely to kill themselves because of shared genes and environment." (p. 297). Jamison mentions only one relevant reference, and only one other article that directly bears on sibling survivors is mentioned in a bibliography accompanying the Surgeon General's report. But this book gives in-depth accounts by more than 30 such survivors, from all over the United States, whose experiences range from those as young children to those who were adults when their brothers or sisters took their own lives. And those accounts are straightforward, unadorned by jargon: from a scientist's perspective, they are "raw data", retrospective to be sure, but nevertheless rich and compelling. From any reader's perspective, these accounts are moving, often surprising or even startling revelations. Each is a "novel", and each, except for names and related details, is true.

More than that, these are more than thirty stories about relationships among siblings from many cuts of life: some loving, some superficial, some full of hate. This is hardly a random sample of such relationships because all are ultimately defined by the suicide that provides the basis for the story's presence in this book. Nevertheless, there is a richness of detail in many of the stories that helps any reader to understand the extraordinary range of relationships that are possible among siblings.

This is also a book about reactions to a significant death and the bereavement that follows for more than thirty individuals. If literature is sparse about sibling survivors of suicide, this is also the case with regard to the more general question of how brothers and sisters deal with a sibling's death. Self-help books on grief rarely address the special needs of siblings, and several accounts in this book note that solicitude from others is rarely forthcoming to a bereaved brother or sister. It is as though it is typically assumed that life relationships between siblings are relatively trivial, even inconsequential, except for stereotypical notions about sibling rivalry, so that loss of a sibling should be likewise relatively inconsequential. But many stories in this book suggest otherwise.

Finally, as a book where many individuals reflect on their bereavement, this is a source of important information about variations in the way people grieve. It will soon be evident to the reader that despite much literature to the contrary, there is little that fits a given formula for the way that the survivors in this book grieve their losses. The variations in bereavement shown here provide a wealth of information to students of that question.

Above all, this is a book of touching stories, eloquently told. It should enrich, and help, many lives.

Martin B. Miller, Ph.D.
High Falls, NY

Introduction

There are two photographs on my husband's bureau, a matched pair. They were taken the summer my parents took my sister, Ann, and me along on a business trip to Europe, when I was five and my sister was seven. My mother tells me we were standing in front of a French chateau, but I have no memory of the chateau, or, indeed, of much else we saw or did on what was, I suppose, meant to be an educational trip. One thing I do remember was the way my sister typically posed for pictures. She stands firmly, smiling pleasantly, if somewhat gravely in this picture, with her left hand raised in a salute. Ann had a method for everything, and the raised hand was her idea of the correct way to pose for pictures. Later on, I learned the Correct Photo Pose Method myself and emulated her, but apparently these pictures were taken early in the trip. Although my mother has dressed us identically, as I believe she frequently did, our demeanor is utterly different. Unlike my sister, I stand awkwardly, twisting in embarrassment, grinning from ear to ear, eyes squinted shut, with no outward composure at all.

My sister killed herself in September 1990. Afterwards, my mother searched out many, many pictures of her and displayed them around the house. She had the paired shots from the Europe trip enlarged, and set them out in the living room. I have always felt embarrassed by the picture of me—I always thought I looked like an idiot compared to my composed sister—but when my fiance saw it in my parents' house, he fell in love with it, and asked my mother for a copy. Such was my mother's state of mind that she gave him both of the pictures, instead of just the one he loved, as if, surely, he would want the picture of her dead (and favorite?) daughter as well as the one of his wife-to-be.

I look at those two pictures often since they have come to live on my husband's bureau, and I think and wonder. For a long time I asked myself, "Could you tell? Could you tell that one of these little girls would grow up to be an apparently successful and reasonably happy person only to kill herself at the age of 45? Can you see it in Ann's clenched right hand? In that stiff posture? Or would you more likely suspect that, if one of them were going to kill herself, it would be the wimpy, awkward little sister who seems so ill-at-ease in life?"

The why's can never truly be answered, although it is my feeling that if anyone understands what happened to Ann, I am the one. I was her sister. In the months after my sister's death, I began wondering if other siblings of suicides shared that feeling. I asked myself, "*Does a sibling understand it best?*" And I wondered, too, if other siblings experienced other thoughts and feelings that went through me, feelings that I began to think might be unique to a sibling. I understood her suicide on one level, and felt the pain that had driven her to it, but I felt, at the same time, both angry at what she had done and scornful at the stupidity of it. I had been suicidal myself years before for, I believe, very similar reasons, yet I felt superior to her that I had survived and she had not had the means, herself, to work through her pain. I knew how hard it was for either one of us to ask for help, yet I despised her for not seeking it. Perhaps the hardest thing for me to acknowledge, though, was that anger, scorn, resentment, and a sense of superiority were my strongest feelings after her death. Although I saw her suicide as a terrible and unnecessary tragedy, particularly for my parents and my sister's husband and children, I did not feel a very great sense of loss myself. I did not miss her very much, and I felt somewhat ashamed of myself for not feeling greater grief beyond a quiet sadness and regret.

Mulling over my thoughts and feelings in the wake of my sister's suicide, I began to think that a sibling's experience of suicide must be different in many ways from a parent's, husband's, child's, or friend's. Sibling relationships are so varied, and often so laden with rivalry and competition, that siblings' experiences and feelings after the suicide must be similarly varied, complex, and perhaps conflicted. I looked for books on the subject, but found very little that dealt with siblings' experiences after suicide. There are a few books written for suicide survivors, but they pay little attention to the reactions of brothers and sisters. I would find, at most, some mention that siblings may grieve deeply, but feel their sorrow is not taken seriously. I thought that, yes, that may well be true, but surely there is more to siblings' feelings after the suicide than that. Their relationship is bound to be complicated and their reactions more complex than pure and simple grief.

Finally, I decided to write this book, to fill that void in some small way. I wanted to interview a variety of men and women who had lost sisters or brothers to suicide, to find common threads in their experiences as siblings, as well as to explore the gamut of feelings the suicide brought up for them. I wanted to know how their early relationship with their sister or brother affected their feelings after the suicide. I wondered how the experience of losing a sibling to suicide at a young age would be different from that experience as an adult, and how losing a sibling of the same sex might be different from losing one of the opposite sex. I wanted to know how losing one's only sibling might be different from losing one out of a larger family. I was interested, too, in how the suicide had affected people in the context of the rest of the family. Does the family dynamic change? Did the suicide divide the family or bring them together? Would a sibling's suicide have an effect on one's relationships with other people? There were also "sibling" issues I wanted to explore. How often does a sibling's death lead the survivors to consider suicide as an option for themselves? What do people think their part in the sibling's decision might have been? Did they feel responsible on some level? Did they feel their brother's or sister's act was directed at them? Do they feel it was their role, as a sibling, to try to prevent the suicide? And—my original question—can a sibling understand a suicide best?

It was not easy, at first, to find people to interview. I knew only one person in the beginning, a woman whose brother had killed himself some years before. She, in turn, put me in touch with a handful of other people who had lost siblings. Contacting the leader of a suicide survivor's group helped me find a few more people who wanted to talk about their experiences, but the town where I live is too small to yield a very large, or varied, number of potential interviewees. Finally, I printed an author's query in the New York Times Book Review section, and letters poured in from all over the country from people anxious to talk about their experiences. With over a hundred responses, I could pick and choose among them to find a spectrum of men and women of different ages, different backgrounds, and different family configurations. Some had been young when the sibling died and some middle-aged. Some had lost an older sibling, some a younger one, and two had lost a twin. Some had other surviving siblings, while some were now the only one left.

I tried to get a balanced mix of different kinds of people to talk to, and traveled to various far-flung places around the country in order to be able to talk face-to-face with people who seemed to have something special to share. But this was never intended to be a scientific survey aimed at providing a complete and statistically balanced range of experiences. It is an exploration of some of the ways suicide can affect surviving siblings and of the ways their experiences may be different from other people's, by virtue of their sibling-ness, but it is certainly not complete. Many more women responded to the author's query than men, for instance, which did not surprise me, given the fact that women still find it easier to talk about their feelings, and I ended up talking to more women than men. Also, most of the people who contacted me wanted to talk about losing a brother, and I am not entirely sure why, except for the fact that men more frequently succeed at killing themselves, while women may attempt it as frequently, but do not succeed so often. I would have liked to have found more people, particularly men, who wanted to share the experience of losing a sister.

This book is based on interviews with eighteen women and fifteen men. Twenty-six had lost a brother, while six had lost a sister. Eighteen were in their late twenties or older at the time of the suicide, twelve were in their teens or early twenties, and two had been young children. One person I interviewed had not actually lost her sister yet, but her sister had attempted suicide several times over many years and did, I learned, kill herself a few months after our interview. Six had lost a sibling within the last three years, seven within the last three to ten years, and nineteen had lost their sibling more than ten years before we talked. I had also sent pre-interview questionnaires to most of the people who wrote me, in order to help me decide whom to interview in depth, and I referred to those, also, although I do not quote from them often in this book.

If any good came of my sister's death, it was having the opportunity to meet and talk with these thirty-three people. I was very moved by their willingness to share with me their experiences and feelings. That they would trust me, a virtual stranger, with their often very personal thoughts touched me deeply, and I will probably always feel a special warmth for all of them. All of the people who contacted me were eager to talk about their brother's or sister's life and death and their own feelings afterwards, even though the suicide may have happened many years before. For many, losing their sibling was a defining event in their lives that had far-reaching reverberations down through the years. Most of them told me that they wanted very much to know how other people's lives had been affected by their sibling's suicide, and whether other people had experienced feelings similar to theirs.

One of the many truths that emerged in the course of the interviews is that people do need to know that they are not alone, and that other people share their feelings and experiences. They want to hear other people's stories, as well as tell their own. In the first part of this book,

"The Gamut of Feelings", several of the people I talked with tell about their experience and share their feelings about it in their own words. I had to re-organize, to some extent, what they told me in our interviews, since oral stories are rarely told in a completely coherent way, but I tried as much as possible to use people's own language and follow their flow of thought as they shared their stories.

In the second part, "Family, Friends, Strangers, Relationships", these and other people I interviewed share their thoughts about how their sibling's suicide affected them in the context of the whole family, how family dynamics changed, their fears for their own children, the level of support they received after their brother's or sister's death, and some of the ways the suicide affected their relationships with other people later. Part Three, "Sibling Issues", addresses some of the questions particular to siblings: Did suicide become an option for the surviving sibling? What part did they feel they played in their brother's or sister's decision? What responsibility does a sibling bear for another? Can a sibling understand the suicide better than other people? How is a sibling's experience different from other people's?

Several people asked me not to use their names, not necessarily because of a sense of shame or fear of stigma, although that was sometimes the case, but mostly because of a need for privacy around such personal issues. For the sake of protecting everyone's privacy, therefore, I have changed all the names of people in this book and altered other identifying circumstances, but their thoughts and feelings are as they told me.

Many of the people I interviewed asked me why I was writing this book. Was it because I needed to come to terms with my own feelings about my sister's suicide? That may, in part, be true, although I feel I have been aware of my feelings as they arose and accepted them for what they are. I do not feel I have unresolved issues in that regard, although writing this book does give a feeling of closure. My real reason for writing it, though, is to let other sibling survivors know that, whatever their experience has been and whatever their thoughts and feelings, others have shared it. The gamut of feelings is various and long, but not inexhaustible, and I think others who read the stories here will find their own mirrored in at least one. Often, people experience thoughts or feelings that they are ashamed of—the "unbidden thoughts" in Chapter Nine. They may feel that they shouldn't have such thoughts, and hide them from other people or even from themselves. But those thoughts and feelings are natural, and I hope hearing other sibling survivors express some of those unbidden thoughts and feelings can help people realize that, even here, they are not alone.

Losing my Sister

Someone said that a suicide is both a shock and shocking. My sister's suicide was both, and yet, in retrospect, I should have seen it coming. Should have.

In the last years before her death, I saw my sister only rarely. She lived out in Houston and used to come east with her two boys in the summer to visit our parents for a week, and I would come, too, with my two children. Usually, we would all spend the week together at my parents' summer house on Cape Cod. But that summer my father was too old and frail to chance being so far away from his doctors, so my parents stayed home, and Ann brought her boys there for her annual visit. My own relationship with my parents was in upheaval that summer. I was about to remarry, to a man they, for various reasons, had decided they disapproved of. He was Jewish. He was fifteen years older than I. Why didn't he marry "one of his own kind"? They refused to meet him. I, in turn, decided not to visit them that summer, and my sister came up to visit me with her kids for a day, instead.

I knew things were not going well for Ann, but only because my mother had told me about it. Ann had said nothing to me about her difficulties with her new job or her problems with her marriage, and I didn't know how to bring any of it up. We all behaved as if nothing was wrong. She and Marty and I, and her two boys, actually had a fun day together. She seemed to like Marty, and she appeared happier and more relaxed than usual. We took her boys to the County Fair and had a good time visiting the side shows, riding on the rides, laughing over the Racing Pigs, and feasting on hot dogs while her kids told us all about the Teen-age Mutant Ninja Turtles. We laughed a lot that day. The only thing that seemed odd was her evasiveness when I asked her about her new job. Instead of answering my questions about what she did, she spun a long, supposedly amusing story about how everyone there spent all their working time having coffee breaks, and long lunches, and more coffee breaks, and never actually did any work at all.

Apparently, she spent the rest of the time at my parents' house cleaning out and organizing her things stored in their attic. It seemed a normal thing to do at the time, but looking back I wonder if she was already thinking about suicide—tying up loose ends, putting things in order so my mother wouldn't have to cope with it after she was dead. I also found out, talking to my mother on the phone after she left, that my sister had said some things to her about me that I could only take as "mean" sibling digs. My son, who was eighteen and legally, at least, permitted to do so, had got a sizable tattoo a few months before, something I completely disapproved of and felt that his grandparents didn't need to know about. There was nothing they could do about it, and it would only disturb them, so I insisted that he keep it covered while he was around them. But Ann, of course, had to tell my mother about my son's tattoo. She also hinted to my mother that my daughter was sleeping with her boyfriend. It wasn't true, in fact, but, even so, I was disturbed that Ann felt she had to mention the possibility to my mother. To what end? It seemed to me that she was acting out of some kind of sibling rivalry that ought to have been over long ago.

Meanwhile, my own relationship with my parents became even more difficult. I made a special visit to them to talk about my upcoming marriage and to try to get them to at least meet my future husband, but my mother insisted that she would not meet him and, in fact, would have nothing to do with any of it if I married him. I interpreted what she said to mean she would have nothing to do with me, and left immediately. I called my sister later, wanting some kind of support from someone in my family, but she offered none. Instead, she told me that she had not liked Marty at all, and had told my mother that he seemed "devious". I was both shocked and angry. How could she be saying these nasty things after the great day we had spent together? Part of her disapproval of Marty, I thought, had to do with her own unhappy marriage and her anger at her husband. Of course she would view my upcoming marriage in a sour light, as she probably would any marriage at that point, but I was still upset by what looked to me like "sibling stuff".

Our relationship had always been tinged with competition. It was never spoken, never confronted, but it was always there lurking in the background. Looking back, I can see that Ann's feelings of rivalry with me were more pronounced that summer. She was not doing well in her own life, and the fact that I, apparently, was must have given an edge to her jealousy. In the weeks after my sister's visit, my parents and I had more or less patched up our relationship, and my mother began calling me to talk about my sister's troubles. Ann was calling her often, worrying over her marriage and, more particularly, her new job. She was having a lot of difficulty adjusting to it, and, in fact, didn't understand what was expected of her or how to accomplish it. She was feeling increasingly anxious over her performance. I called her once during this period, feeling somewhat awkward about bringing any of this up, since she hadn't talked to me directly about it. We did talk a little about her problems with her husband, but when

I suggested marital counseling, she dismissed the idea. I also remember telling her how well my son was doing and how eager he was to begin college, which, in retrospect, I wish I had kept quiet about. It was just that he had always been so difficult that I was feeling pleased that he seemed to be turning around, but no doubt it only made my sister feel worse about how badly things were going for her. She seemed both down and distant, and her voice had a deadened quality. Toward the end of our fairly brief conversation, I told her how much I had enjoyed being with her kids, and what delightful boys they were. Ann just sighed, and said in a tired voice, "Well, I've tried. I've tried." If only my antennae had been up, I should have heard the resignation and defeat, and the sense of finality in her using the past tense. Hindsight, as they say, is 20-20.

Over the next couple of weeks, my mother called me more and more often, saying, "I'm so worried about your sister." Ann was calling her every day, anguished and in tears, to talk for literally hours about her increasing inability to cope with the demands of her job. She was failing, and for Ann failure was unthinkable, especially in her professional life. She was someone who had to do everything, and do everything perfectly, and to fail at anything was simply intolerable. I understood what she was feeling, I thought. I had been in a similar condition some years before, unable to cope with the demands of my job, along with being pregnant and having a child at home. I had felt that despair at failing at life, and I had nearly given up altogether. I felt I should call my sister. I felt I could have helped, because I had been there and come out the other side. But my mother told me that Ann had instructed her not to tell me that anything was wrong. I was stunned that, even in her desperation, my sister continued to compete with me.

I felt that my hands were tied. I felt I should reach out, but I wasn't supposed to know that anything was wrong. I thought that, with everything falling apart in her life, my sister was headed for a nervous breakdown, but what could I do? I wasn't even supposed to know.

Eventually, I did pick up the phone and call, but her husband made some excuse—I don't even remember what—and I never did get to talk to her.

My mother decided that the best thing would be for my sister to take a leave of absence from her job, leave her children with their father, and come home to her parents for a rest. I thought it was a terrible idea. Coming home to mother would certainly be an admission of complete defeat, but my sister seemed to be agreeing to the plan, at least according to my mother. My husband and I set to work to find a therapist near my parents' home, and my mother began setting the wheels in motion for my sister to "come home". She decided that my sister was in no condition to fly home alone, and that I would fly out to get her. I'm not sure if my mother told Ann about my part in her plan, but I can imagine that knowing that her little sister was coming out to save her would only have made her sense of failure and despair worse.

But the plan was not to be consummated. Before we had even bought the tickets, my brother-in-law called and broke the news. Ann had made sure her boys were off playing with neighbors, while her husband was outside fixing the roof. She locked all the doors of the house, went into the bathroom, and shot herself in the mouth with a shotgun she had secretly bought the day before. She had left a suicide note addressed to her husband, her boys, and her parents (not her sister), saying "I love all of you. I can't cope anymore. It's not your fault. It's mine, within me. I just couldn't keep up and keep on going…" I saw the note when we went out for the funeral. It was written in a calm, clear hand. It looked like a thank-you note, not the last expression of a desperate person, except that she had appended two post scripts, and her handwriting on the second began to look shaky as she listed the financial assets the family could use to "carry on with."

I was stunned and shocked at the news. Yet, when I got off the phone, I felt, "Yes. It makes perfect sense." It was all foreshadowed in everything that had happened in the last few weeks, but we had all been too illiterate to read the book she had written so plainly.

Then I had to do the hardest task I had ever faced. I had to call my mother and tell her that her daughter was dead.

Part One

The Gamut of Feelings

Chapter One
"I wanted to die, too"

Too often, when there is a suicide, friends of the family assume that the surviving siblings are not much affected. They focus on the grief of the parents, spouse, and children, and minimize the feelings of brothers and sisters. But for siblings who are overcome with grief and loss, their pain becomes even greater when it is not acknowledged.

Many of the people I talked to experienced a depth of grief after the suicide as profound as any spouse's or parent's. For several of them, their sibling's death was the most significant event in their lives, one they felt they would never fully get over. It left a void that could not ever be filled. As they talked to me, many of them wept as they relived their brother's or sister's suicide, and experienced again the flood of grief that they had felt then.

I was not prepared, at first, for the intense feelings of loss that several of the people I talked to expressed. Because my own relationship with my sister was not a very close one, my sense of loss was not at all as powerful as theirs, and it was difficult at first to imagine feeling that loss so deeply. For me, my husband's death four years before was the worst thing that could ever happen, and everything else, including my sister's suicide, paled in comparison. But having experienced that devastating loss allowed me to empathize with people who grieved deeply for their sibling.

Their grief was very real and very moving. All of them had shared the kind of close bond with their sibling that is evoked by phrases like, "He was like a brother to me," or "We were just like sisters." Some of them came from a very loving family that encouraged close relationships among all its members. Very often, though, they came from troubled families, and they had drawn closer to each other in the face of their difficulties. The adversity they shared, whether it was physical abuse, a parent's alcoholism or mental illness, or other family problems, had paradoxically made them allies.

It was striking to see how very close brothers and sisters could be, and I found myself envying their relationship. For many of them, their brother or sister had been their best friend—someone they shared their deepest feelings with and turned to in times of trouble. Besides their common childhood, they also shared similar interests and values with their siblings, and they communicated with each other easily and openly. That their siblings had purposefully killed themselves and abandoned them left them feeling betrayed and angry as well as grief-stricken.

Some of the women, in particular, seemed to mourn for their brothers as if they had lost a husband. Only one of the women I talked to discussed freely her feelings of sexual attraction toward her brother, but there was an underlying current of near-sexual love in the stories of several of the men or women who had lost a sibling of the opposite sex.

Most of these siblings felt a deep need to share their experience with other people, and to tell their stories over and over, yet often found that it was hard to find people who wanted to listen. The three people who share their stories next all experienced their loss in their own individual ways, yet there is a universality in each of their stories, as there is both a singularity and a universality about all loss and bereavement.

Joe

Joe lost his younger brother Matt eight years before our interview, when he was thirty-four and Matt was thirty. Joe had an older sister, as well, but it was Matt he was bonded to. Matt was his best friend and soul-mate, and they had always been extremely close. Although Joe felt that Matt's suicide was inevitable, that his many years of deep depression would finally become unbearable, the finality of it was shocking. Joe still feels devastated by his loss, but relieved, as well, that his brother's years of pain are over, and his own desperate feelings of wanting to save him no longer drain his own life.

Our family is unusual because it's been a very tormented family, but we've been very close emotionally. We were all pretty much able to talk to each other to varying degrees. My brother Matt and I always had a line of communication, and I've always tried to have one with my parents. Our home life was extremely tempestuous. My mother, I think, has been severely mentally ill for much of our lives, without being treated or really understood, and, particularly by the time I went to college, she had really gone off the deep end. Matt spent his late adolescent years with her in that state. Our family was tormented and O'Neill-like, but there's always been a curious bonding emotionally, particularly between my mother and father and Matt and me. My sister quite early on disengaged herself from the family, but the other four of us were very locked into each other. We all love each other so much we can't leave each other, and yet there's the feeling of, "If I could, I'd kill you."

The last ten years of Matt's life were a long journey. Before the onset of his depression there was never any indication that Matt had any problems. When it started, Matt came to visit me out West, where I was acting in the theater, and, two or three days later, told me that he had admitted himself into a hospital back East a little while before. He said, "I don't know what happened. I just knew something was wrong." It devastated me emotionally, because my mother has had some form of manic depression, although it was never treated, and her brother and three of her aunts had killed themselves. Matt wanted to stay with me out there, so he lived with me for two years.

They were really tortuous years and great years at the same time. We had some wonderful times visiting different places and different cities. But his illness hadn't been diagnosed, and Matt didn't know what it was, and it was sometimes very difficult to live with him. I was working in a repertory company at the time, rehearsing during the day and doing a show at night, and when I'd get home at night Matt would be up, unable to sleep. He and I would walk the streets until four o'clock in the morning, or go play pool or something, because he was in such pain that he had to talk and had to walk, and he couldn't sleep. It was exhausting. And there were times when he would just snap. Because of his pain he would lose patience and yell at me or smash a glass or something. But I always understood that it was just him reaching a breaking point. I rarely felt that it was directed at me.

Matt's form of depression wasn't bipolar. He never had the feeling of flying high and then crashing. It was a constant depression that increasingly turned into a self-lacerating depression. Every now and then the depression would lift, and he would feel relatively normal. But they were brief, brief periods. The longest period was about a nine month stretch. It just went away. He kept pinching himself every day—he couldn't believe it. Then one day we were crossing a street—one of those moments I'll never forget—and he said, "I can feel it all coming back. It's starting all over again." From that time it never appreciably lifted.

Matt used to describe it as actual physical pain. He would say, "I hurt so much." He continued to work and be active, but there were periods of time when he just couldn't manage to do much. Matt's pain was almost palpable when it was at its worst. You could walk into a room, and the skin would be pulled taut on his face over his cheekbones. You could see him just enduring minute by minute to get through the day.

The hardest thing for me to deal with was being haunted by how much pain I knew he was in. Being with him was difficult in the sense that I knew I couldn't help him. Wherever I was, there was a shadow on my own being all the time. Whether I was on stage in a comedy or in London seeing a play I loved, there was always a part of me that seemed like a black cloud, because I thought Matt was probably at home unable to get out of bed. It was just the helplessness of not being able to do anything.

Over the next years, after the two years of living together, he and I spoke virtually every day. I spent long periods of time with him. He was extremely articulate and verbal. We talked about suicide and what suicide was. I always tell everybody the same thing: Matt was my best friend as well as my brother, and I think he would say the same thing about me. We were extremely close in every way.

I have to admit that there were moments when I felt resentful, and I would get angry with my parents because all the focus would be on Matt. There was a period during the eighties when I had to be hospitalized and had four operations. I was down in my parents' home afterwards, and they started talking about what we had to do for Matt—drive three hours to take care of him, and fix up his apartment, and so forth. And I let them know that I just wasn't going to do that right then. But the feelings of resentment would pass. It wasn't a lasting thing.

In our discussions about suicide, I didn't try to dissuade him in a Pollyanna-ish way, saying, "Oh, everything will be all right." That wouldn't have passed muster with him, anyway. I would say, "I can't really imagine what you're feeling, and there's nothing I can do to take it away, but at the same time try to imagine how much we love you. Try to know you'll never be abandoned. Even though it's hard to do after ten years of being on various medicines that don't work, you don't know what's around the corner."

After ten years of seeing his pain, his desire to seek escape or seek peace seemed very valid to me and seemed very possible. Right before he died I told several of my friends here that I would not be surprised if he committed suicide, because he just sounded so exhausted. He was visiting my parents, and my sister was there, and they didn't pick up on it because they were seeing him being very active. He was in school at the time getting a degree, and he was giving programs to elementary school children on Indians. But I was only talking to him on the phone, and he sounded so completely exhausted that the timing didn't shock me as much as it shocked the people at home.

I think Matt killed himself when he did because he knew he was surrounded by family at that time. I think he knew people would be on hand when it happened. But it's the ultimate mystery. What is the final weight of a feather that pushed him? He had finished up his work and had all his papers ready to be turned in, and he didn't even wait for his grades. He was awarded his degree posthumously.

He had everything meticulously planned, so there would be no possible chance that he would survive. He took one of his antique pistols and took the bullet apart and put double gunpowder in the casing, so that when he fired it, it would go with double the force. He rigged up a vice in the basement and had the pistol on a pole so that it wouldn't pull up when he fired it. He lay down right next to it and aimed it right at his temple. My parents heard the shot and rushed down and found him. They said his face was completely composed and calm. The only sign of anything being wrong was that even by the time they ran downstairs there was a pool of blood that just kept getting bigger behind his head.

When they called me, I was shocked at the reality of the timing, but I wasn't shocked at the inevitability of it. It was hearing something I had expected for so long. I felt a commingled sadness and relief. The relief, in a purely selfish sense, was being out from under the yoke of trying to help and help him get better and feeling so helpless and so sad about it. I knew there was nothing I could do, and, regardless of where I was, there was always the weight of, "How is Matt doing today?". And there was the pain, too, of having seen him in pain for so long. It was like seeing someone dying of AIDS or cancer and knowing he can't recover.

I really didn't give in much to emotion at that time or throughout the weekend. I instantly felt I had to be in control and sort of see through the weekend, because things would be very bad at home. I was very controlled and businesslike and matter-of-fact throughout much of the weekend. I arranged the service, and read the service, and helped clean out the room and rarely gave in to much emotion then. I think a lot of that came from loving Matt so much and really wanting to give him a good send-off, a funeral service that I felt was reflective of him and would mean something to people who knew him. My parents and sister were just obliterated, and they were willing to let me handle it, knowing how close we were and seeing that I was able to. Maybe it's big brother syndrome, but I felt I very much wanted to finish this final act and do it in the best way, and I'd have the rest of my life to deal with the aftermath.

The difficult part for me has been since all of that—the acceptance of it, and the absence of him, which is getting worse and worse for me as more time goes on. I just miss Matt so much that as a longer time elapses since he died, it just seems so strange. I think initially in some ways it didn't seem so extreme because we didn't live together. There were big blocks of time when I didn't see him. We had such a shared history, and we had very similar tastes and reactions to things, so I'll see something, or hear a song, or read something, and there's still the impulse to share it with him. There's the sense that I'll never be able to connect that particular feeling or reaction with any other person in the same way. It's just an absence. It's very mysterious to me. It's the mystery of wondering what was the final thing that made Matt do it that day as opposed to another time. And it's just the mystery of a presence, a personality, a life, that's just gone, vanished.

What has helped me is the thing that helped me from the very instant I heard it, and continues to reverberate and help me to this day. It's the fact that, while Matt and I were in each other's lives, we loved each other so much, and we told each other that all the time. The quality and the amount of time we spent together, which was the best time for both of us, was always expressed and understood, so in that sense I have no regrets. I have the regret that he's not here, but there was never anything left unsaid. There was never a sense that he didn't know how much I cherished him and vice versa. And that has been a sustaining thing for me, the fact that that was so strongly understood and felt between both of us. Whether he'd died at thirty or eighty, our feelings would not have been more intense, and we always expressed them. That's my main bedrock.

Morna

Morna's brother Simon, one year younger than she, shot himself twelve years before we talked. The two youngest of four children, they had always been very close. They felt almost like twins, a team of two pitted against their older sibling oppressors. Simon had not appeared mentally ill or depressed, and despite their closeness, Morna had no inkling that he was suicidal. His death completely upset the natural order of things—she had assumed that he would always be there for her, and she for him. Suddenly there were no guarantees. She felt betrayed, and robbed of certainty, as if she had suddenly lost her innocence.

I always considered Simon my closest sibling. I was never close to my oldest siblings, and I'm still not, but Simon and I were absolutely close, a team. We were somehow wilier and more street smart than the other two, so most of the time we "beat" them. We were both really popular and had lots of friends. We knew how to fit in. And we were really friends, the way siblings are "supposed" to be. We were like twins, and we were taken for twins a lot growing up. There were a couple of years when we were the same height and wore the same size. I'd give him jeans and he'd break them in, and then he'd give them to me and I'd buy him a new pair. He liked them new and I liked them broken in.

We kind of drifted apart a bit in our early twenties. I was in college, but he would come up to visit sometimes. Then I got married, and he was getting into the hippy-dippy kind of thing. There was a physical distance, too, and we didn't see each other all that much. But it was always that when he was in trouble, or I was in trouble, we went to each other. I wish I knew where I was the night he killed himself. He called my brother Ronald that night, but Ronald was in the midst of something and asked if he could call him back. Maybe he tried calling me that night, too, and I wasn't there. I have no memory of where I was, and that bothers me.

That Saturday morning my father called, saying that Simon was in a bad accident and didn't survive. Of course, I thought it was a car accident, but when we got down to the city, we found out the worst. He was found shot in the mouth in a motel room. The police found a sawed-off shotgun, but his i.d. was gone, and his jacket and a necklace were missing. The police believed it was suicide, but we thought maybe he had been murdered, and it was set up to look like suicide. At the funeral we were all in complete shock, and we didn't know still whether it was homicide or suicide.

After the funeral my father was obsessed with finding out what had really happened, and finally, two weeks later, the police convinced him that Simon had shot himself. The day I found out that it was suicide I had an appointment with a gynecologist, because I was having infertility problems. I waited in the waiting room for two hours, and it was sinking in, the fact of it. Then in the examining room it suddenly hit me, and I began to cry hysterically. The doctor just continued with his examination, never once stopping to ask what was wrong. He just finished and walked out of the room. Only the nurse seemed concerned.

I thought I couldn't be hurt any more at the time, but when I found out it was suicide, my whole world collapsed. I was a basket case for two or three years. I would function. I would go to work and come home and do what I was supposed to do. But I couldn't enjoy myself. I felt that at any moment I would collapse and start crying. There were all kinds of everyday things that I wanted to do that were suddenly so difficult, like going to the movies. About six months after he died I went to see "An Officer and a Gentleman". I thought it was supposed to be a love story. But in the movie a man hangs himself in the shower, and it was just horrible. Every time I heard a gun go off in the movies I just couldn't tolerate it, because of the association.

I didn't feel whole. I felt as though my arm were lost, or my guts removed. I really felt as though I had physically lost a part of my body when Simon died. At the time, I was just beginning infertility treatments, and I ached for something to fill that gap, and I couldn't do it. Each doctor would say he knew the problem and that I was going to get pregnant, but none of them knew.

My husband understood to a certain extent, but it was very hard to talk to him because he was so angry at Simon for what he did and the way he did it. He was very angry because of what it did to his wife. I needed to talk and talk, and there was just so much he could listen to it. When I look back, though, I think he did wonderfully. Most people would have walked out, and he never walked out.

I felt very angry for a while. He wasn't supposed to die first. He was my younger brother. He was supposed to bury me! It destroyed any notion I had that there was justice in the world, that if you did the right things, things would end up the way they're supposed to be. Shortly after he died we were all in his apartment, going through his things. My father kept saying, "How could he do this? How could he do this?" And finally I screamed, "He took a gun and he put it in his mouth and he pulled the damned trigger!" I look back on that and wonder how I could have said that to my father. But I was furious. I felt, "How could you do this to me? How could you leave me?" And I still sometimes feel angry that he betrayed me, walked out on me, and that he's not around to see my kids—he would have been a good uncle.

Then one night I woke up at midnight. It was six months to the day after he died. I don't know whether this was a dream or whether it was real, but in some way I thought he was trying to get a message to me. I saw him under the El tracks. We lived about a block away from the El train in the city where we grew up. We were under the big steel girders that hold the tracks up, and he was shooting a B-B gun. I ducked behind the girders and said, "Simon! You almost shot me!" He turned around and said, "How could you think that?" He had an expression on his face that he used to get when you'd really hurt his feelings. "He said, "How could you think I wanted to hurt you? I would never do anything to hurt you." And I understood then that he didn't do this, kill himself, to hurt me. He wasn't thinking of me or anyone else. He felt tremendous pain, just intense pain to do something like this.

About three years after Simon died I met someone who had lost a brother to suicide eight years before. I felt a great sense of relief, because it meant that I would be able to see what changes time would make. I wouldn't feel alone. We talked about what we'd been through and about our feelings, and for the first time I felt that my reactions were normal, that it was okay to feel this way. Soon after that I started a suicide survivors group, and it wasn't until then that I started to come to grips with it all.

The survivors group helped immensely. I didn't feel so alone any more. I needed to talk about it and meet other people who shared it. I felt that the more I could understand, the better I could cope with it. I went through many stages—shock and denial, guilt that I hadn't seen it coming, and anger—like Kubler-Ross's stages. I hit them all. But what I remember was feeling that I wasn't doing something right. I wasn't grieving right. I had one foot in one stage and one foot in another stage. It took me a long time to understand that that's okay. You can be in denial and still be angry, and reach a kind of acceptance and still be angry. You could be all over the place with the stages. It's not as though you do it neatly and complete stage one and move on to stage two. It's been twelve years now, and it feels very different. It takes time. It doesn't happen right away for people. Time eases a lot.

Early on, somebody said to me, "Some day you'll look back and you'll notice that good comes out of even horrendous situations." I wanted to punch that person in the face. How could anything good ever come out of this? But one thing it did do was make me realize that there are no guarantees in life. I lost my preconceived notion that things would work out the way they were supposed to. And that was an awful loss of innocence, but it *was also freeing. In many ways it opened up for me things I wouldn't have had in life. For example, we never would have adopted our first son, Noah. We had been searching for years for a child to adopt. Then we heard about Noah. He was a part black baby who was HIV positive at birth. With children born HIV positive, we found out, seventy-five per cent of the time they convert and become healthy. If they don't, they usually die by the time they're five. I thought, "Well, there are no guarantees in life, anyway." And thinking about that, I felt free to take a chance. Noah is healthy, so taking that chance worked out this time, although it just as well might not have. Later, because we were already a multi-racial family, we were able to adopt two more boys, who are also part black. So in that sense, good did come out of Simon's suicide. And that is some kind of comfort.*

Ramona

Ramona, who is part Native American, lives in Oklahoma, the home she returned to after her brother's suicide. Since she has no telephone, our initial "interviews" were through letters back and forth. Although she writes beautifully, I finally decided to travel out to Oklahoma to talk with her in person. Her story, then, is put together from both her letters and our personal interview.

Ramona was 31 when her older brother, Jonah, hung himself in a state hospital. She had always been extremely close to him, throughout years of his mental illness, which began when he was fifteen. He had spent his life in and out of mental hospitals, and living an itinerant life in between, working crops or living on skid row in cities. Despite the fact that he had talked of killing himself many times and made half-hearted attempts, his death came as a complete shock. She felt a profound grief, and an enormous anger at the system that had allowed all this to happen.

I always looked up to Jonah and loved him deeply. Even though he was schizophrenic, and I could tell he was very strange, his strangeness didn't scare me or repel me. When I was twelve and he was fifteen, my parents put him in a private institution. It just suddenly happened one day, and everything was different after that. It shook up the world. Before that day the world had been a kind of predictable place. And suddenly it was no longer predictable. He was there almost a year, and during that time we weren't allowed to see him. And when I did see him, he was changed. It wasn't even his body anymore. I felt that they had really done stuff to him. He was in and out of state hospitals after that, about once a year.

We were always very close. My father was a terrible person in a way. That's one reason Jonah and I were so close—we were up against it together. After he became ill, I was afraid that would happen to me. I just wanted to get away from the family, as far as I could. I didn't want to get away from Jonah, but I was afraid for myself in that place. So when I got older, I lived and worked in various places. But Jonah and I always wrote back and forth, and saw each other when we could.

He was a big person, not just physically. Psychically he took up a lot of space. He was wonderful. Once I went to meet him where he was working in a work camp. He had his Bible with him, of course. He told me he was Jesus, and he was here in this camp not to work, though he did that, but to preach, and he did that, too, every evening when they got back to the camp house. The next day we were going to set off traveling together, hitchhiking, and we went back to the camp and got most of his things. He left a second pair of shoes that he had, but he carried his "California suitcase" as he called it—a big cardboard shoebox, tied very neatly with twine. We set off walking down the road, and one of his buddies called out, "Hey, you left your shoes!" He called back, "Keep them for me!" He was like that. There was his bigness in that. Not, "I don't want them, you can have them." He wouldn't pin himself down to never coming back, though he must have known he never would. He left it all open. My brother was as open and wide as the whole universe, and that's the truth. Even the stars spoke to him.

Some people might have found it strange, his saying he was Jesus, or be scared by the oddness of that. But it didn't scare me. I got caught up in it, too. I knew where he was coming from, I guess. We were raised to be so religious that I just took all of that for granted. I thought he was great. And I still do, because it's as if he was really able to see into religious things. He was really able to understand a lot of things I didn't understand.

But I would worry about what was going to happen to him. One time he had a room in Abilene, and I went to see him there. He had an upstairs room in a house with other people, and he must have had a job of some sort. It was a gray room. But he was so proud of his life, and how things were going. He got to talking to me about circles—zeroes. He said whenever he read anything, the zeroes would stand out to him, and they would have great meaning. I remember feeling just worried for him, that he was going to be telling someone else this, and someone was going to think it was very weird. He would be put back in a state hospital. I was always hurting for him and worrying about him.

When he killed himself, I was living in California. That day I had just called a friend of mine and told her that I didn't know why, but I felt very, very sad, so sad that I didn't want to stay at work. Then Mother called and told me he was dead. He had gone back into the state hospital a little while before, and this day he left he left the group on the ward and went into the room where they kept the clothes and hanged himself. I didn't believe her. I told her they were just telling her that. "How do you know for sure he'd dead?" I said. "How do you know that's what happened? They could be hiding something." She hadn't seen his body. Maybe it wasn't true. She talked to me for about half an hour, and finally I realized it was true. It was really true. It was just a complete shock. How could you be prepared?

In the beginning I writhed with the pain and do so yet on some days. It's the worst thing that will probably ever happen to me. I never knew life without him until he died, and he was always the most important person in my life. When he died, I felt that my life also was over. One night soon afterwards, I was lying in bed, with everyone else asleep, and I let myself down into my grief, to take its measure. I felt that I would die, too. In the next few seconds I would have died, and so I know that it is true what people say, that sometimes people die of grief. But then I saw an angel and heard her voice telling me that she would always be with me. Even the light and voice were not the most amazing thing—what was, was how the grief in my heart in an instant had turned to peace, a wonderful, comforting peace. And so I was ready to continue living in this new peace. I still count on it, that feeling. But even so, this life I have now is a separate life. It's as though I died with him and began a new life.

After Jonah's death I took to eating. I gained one hundred pounds in the few years afterwards. I no longer cared how I looked. I never realized before how much being beautiful was for him. Now I try to care how I look for my daughter's sake, and for my mother's, but I don't really care, not the way I did before, when my brother was alive.

For a long time afterwards, I was angry about the whole thing. Two years after he died I was finally able to move back to Oklahoma to be near my family. But I had no job. There were no jobs there. So my mother and I went for an interview at the Bureau of Indian Affairs, because they had something similar to welfare. This was two years after he was dead, but I was still angry. My father's name is also Jonah, and the man who interviewed me, who knew the family a little, turned to my mother and said, "Well, how is Jonah?" I was so angry, I yelled, "HE'S DEAD! THAT'S HOW HE IS!!" I was just that angry. I felt angry at the system, the state hospital. This was done to him ever since he was a boy! And I was angry because he was so poor, for instance, and that made me angry at anyone who had a little more.

I also felt guilty. While he was alive, I was always hurting for him. And when he died I felt relief, too, because it was always like an open wound. And that made me feel guilty. I don't know how many times I had thought he would be better off dead. I had probably even prayed that way, just so he wouldn't have to keep going through all these things. He was beaten at times. He was given shock treatments. Then when he was dead, I felt so guilty. I felt as though I had wished it.

Then one night I saw him in a dream in the middle of many, many separate squares of different colors. He was crying and asking me to forgive him, which, of course, I rushed to reassure him I did. But I was shocked that he wanted my forgiveness, for I felt in need of his forgiveness. I know how much I loved him, but I felt I didn't give him enough, or something. I felt responsible. In the family, too, all of a sudden it just came into focus how we had always believed in his illness, and we were always tense about that. But why didn't we just believe in him? It was so clear how we had failed him.

Jonah's death changed everything for me. Before, I thought that I was doing my life. But after the time when I thought I would die, and God spoke to me, I was willing to keep on living with God in charge. It's as if I had no will anymore. I think when we think we're doing our lives, we are just being foolish. I feel as though my brother already knew these things. Life is basically mysterious and basically God's, not ours. When my brother died, it was as though a new door had opened on top of my head. I understood things I had never understood before. It astounded me to think that that depth had always been there, but closed to me. Sometimes I think that his death was for the purpose of my life, getting it all straightened out.

Now sometimes I dream of being with him again. In the good dreams we walk side by side, our stride exactly matching, both of us strong and tall and well-matched, as we were in life. In the bad dreams, I see him again in one or another of the troubles of his life, and I feel again the despair of that, until I wake up and feel relief that now his troubles on earth are over.

Before I had my daughter, I used often to feel betrayed by him, that he's free now and I'm not, that he left me here. But now I feel different. Now I just miss him and wish he could be with me in person, could share so many happinesses that I feel every day. I know we never know the future, still I thank God every day in my new life. I may just be half of him and me together, but I at least am still here, and I go on with my life, just feel his absence.

Delayed Reactions

Rarely does the reality of a death sink in right away. Like almost all the people I talked with, Joe, Morna, and Ramona had a delayed reaction to the news of their sibling's suicide. Morna, in particular, didn't grasp the full horror of her brother's death until two weeks later, when she understood that it was truly suicide. Joe purposefully delayed his grieving until he had arranged the funeral and taken care of all that needed to be done in the aftermath of his brother's suicide. Now he finds that his grief worsens over the years, as he realizes that his brother will never return, and the hole that he left will never be filled.

Most people I talked with, like Ramona, were stunned by the news and so shocked that they tried to deny it at first. For a time after that, even though they accepted the suicide on some level, they went through a period of days or week of feeling simply numb.

Particularly when a loved one dies suddenly, the survivors normally do react with shock and denial. Kubler-Ross recognizes that reaction as the first stage of grief, whether someone has just been presented with a diagnosis of terminal illness or has just suffered a death. When the death is a suicide, the shock and denial are that much greater. They are compounded by the stigma that surrounds suicide and by the horror of knowing that the victim is also the murderer.

Of all the people who experienced a delayed reaction to their sibling's suicide, Jean's reaction was the most extreme. She was twenty-five when her brother Robert, who was just one year older, shot himself. She had always been extremely close to him growing up. Years of living with an alcoholic father, who abused them both emotionally, if not physically, followed by their parents' bitter and emotionally fraught divorce, gave them a common ground in which they forged a close bond. Jean said, *I felt that we were in this together. I loved him because he was my connection to sanity in this dysfunctional family.*

When she got the news that Robert had killed himself, her first reaction was shock and denial, but she quickly swung into the role she always took on in the family—the clear-headed organizer and practical one. She flew out West where he had been living, sorted through all that had happened, arranged the funeral, and brought home mementos of her brother to share with the rest of the family.

And yet, she told me, *At the same time, I wasn't really connected to any grief. I was sad, but mostly I was still in shock. Four or five years went by, and I didn't really grieve. I think I just didn't understand it. I accepted it and tried to do the best I could, but I was mourning it for my family and not really for myself. I would be in and out of sadness, but it was more a spiritual thing— this was what happened and this was how it was meant to be.*

Not long after her brother's death, Jean became involved with a man who, to her, *seemed totally like my brother. He looked like him, and he was natural and earthy and nurturing like him, so I was really drawn to him. He took care of me for a long time. We took care of each other.*

Jean didn't realize how very much her relationship with her lover was tied in with her feelings with her brother, until she decided to end it. Even though she recognized that it was a co-dependent relationship that she no longer wanted to be part of, she could not separate from him, and finally went into therapy to help her loosen the knot. Working with the therapist, she came to realize that her difficulty in separating from her lover was very closely connected to the loss of her brother. Just as her brother, her only source of comfort and support, had abandoned her, so another strong man in her life was about to leave her, too. As it happened, her therapist was the head of Hospice in Jean's town, and she had helped many people work through grief:

She made me go through the whole process. First, I felt really angry. I was really angry that he did this and didn't let anyone know he was in pain. I was mad at him for killing himself, mad at him for not telling me, mad at him for not telling anybody. I was mad that he left me here to deal with our dysfunctional family by myself. I was mad that he was depriving me of my sanity, because he was the only one who understood anything that went on in our family, and the only one who had gone through all the grief of our upbringing and my parents' splitting up. He left me with no one to talk to. It wasn't the best childhood, but he was the only one I could share the best part of it with. So I was really mad at him for leaving me with no memories, or anybody to relate to from my childhood.

Then I went on to being intensively sad and lonely for a long, long time. There I was, a single mother with this little child, and my brother will never know him. It took weeks. One thing the therapist did, when I finally felt all this grief, was encourage me to say goodbye. She encouraged me to say anything I ever wanted to say to him, after this anger and all this sadness. I was able to say that I was really sad and that I really missed him, and that I was really mad, but it was okay. I forgave him for it. I forgave myself. It freed me up a lot. I felt as though the rock that I was carrying inside my heart was finally lifted.

A Stew of Emotions

Jean's experience in therapy reminded me of an important aspect of grieving: even when a survivor's sense of loss is intense, grief is not a simple emotion. Like Morna and Ramona, most bereaved people also feel angry—at God, at the System, which they feel contributed to the death, or, particularly when it was a suicide, even at the dead person for betraying them. And, even as they feel plunged in grief, many people, like Joe and Ramona, admit feeling relief, as well, which often adds to feelings of guilt they may be already harboring.

Many people I talked to felt confused and troubled by their mixed and conflicting feelings. They floundered in an emotional stew of grief, anger, relief, and guilt. Like Morna, they often felt that they weren't grieving properly, or that they shouldn't be feeling anything but pure loss. The ones who sought therapy or grief counseling, like Morna— who started a survivors group, or Lucy, who tells her story next—felt comforted to know that their mixed emotions were normal.

Lucy

When I talked with Lucy, her older brother Martin had killed himself a mere two and a half years before, and she was still in the process of working through her grief, guilt, and anger. Part of their close bond had to do with the physical and emotional abuse they had both suffered as children, and Lucy felt betrayed and abandoned after his suicide, and angry with him, as well as devastated by the loss of the brother she loved. Despite her grief, though, she feels that her brother's death gave her a sort of gift, by making her realize how precious her life was to her.

When we were really young, my relationship with Martin wasn't that great. We didn't trust anyone. We had learned as children not to trust anybody, not to tell anybody anything. My Dad had a heavy hand when we were kids, and with Michael he was especially heavy-handed. I think we were so terrified as children at what was going on that we had very little communication. We didn't even talk about what was going on in our family with each other. I remember knowing that what was going on was really wrong, being hit the way we were and being treated the way we were. My mother didn't really protect us from it. So all four of us were pretty messed up as kids, and I think as adults we carry a lot of that stuff. I'm an alcoholic and a drug addict, in recovery now. Martin killed himself. My two other sisters seem more stable, but they have their problems, too. My older sister Dinah doesn't trust anyone with much of anything.

We didn't begin communicating with each other until we were teenagers, and then we became very close. We had a shared background that brought us together. At the time of his death, I had just graduated from college and needed a place to live. Martin had just split up with his girlfriend, so he invited me to come share his apartment. We lived together for maybe four months. We were close, really close. We had so much fun together. He got a Nintendo game for Christmas a few years before, and we would stay up playing Nintendo till two o'clock in the morning. We'd play for six hours, and our eyes would be bugging out, and we'd be laughing. He was a good guy, great to hang around with. He had his faults, though! He was a pain to live with because he was a real perfectionist and everything had to be done just so.

Then he injured his back and didn't take care of it properly, so it got worse and worse. He was becoming a cripple and he could hardly walk. He felt like an old man—unbelievable pain. I'd never seen him cry, but he broke down about three weeks before he killed himself, and I knew that there was something seriously wrong. He stopped going to work. He had no motivation to do anything. He was totally broken. But I had no indication that he was going to commit suicide. I just thought he was seriously depressed. He had been to all different kinds of doctors, but there was nothing they could do for him. He had an appointment at another clinic the week after he died, but I guess he felt it wasn't going to help and that the only solution he had was to kill himself.

He was having a lot of trouble sleeping, but the day of his death he seemed to be sleeping late. I thought it was good that he was finally getting some sleep. But finally it got to be afternoon and I thought, "Something is weird." When I went in to wake him, I discovered that his bed was stuffed with pillows and that he was gone. I found a stack of letters under the covers telling us where he would be found, what to do, whom to call in what order. He had gone to a pond outside of town and shot himself in the head. He had a rope attached to his waist to a tree, and by the tree he had his driver's license and another identification, so all the police had to do was pull him out of the water. He had planned the whole thing immaculately. He had left letters to people, and his will, and he had even written his own eulogy.

The investigators, and my family and friends, kept questioning me. Didn't I know? Didn't I have any indication? People seemed to be blaming me for what happened, but mostly I blamed myself. I was full of guilt because I did live with him and I did not see it. And I had a lot of guilt because I felt it should have been me, that his life was more worth living than mine. I'd see how devastated my parents were, particularly my mother, and feel terrible, absolute guilt because I should have done something to stop it.

My whole world had just turned upside down. Not only was my brother dead, but I had no place to live anymore—he had been supporting me at the time. So, in addition to feeling a terrible loss, I felt betrayed. The anger! He left me a note that said something like, "I'm sorry to hurt you. I know you can get on with your life. You'll meet someone really nice and fabulous, and your writing career will take off," and so on. And I think, "How dare you write me a letter like that, and you're killing yourself? You don't know!" For a long time I thought, "If I die and I do meet up with him, I'm just going to punch him!"

The feeling of loss was immense. And there's still such an absence. When our family gets together and he's not there, there still is a void. I thought for a long time that you could fill it with something else, but it's not do-able. And I don't think it ever will be. I thought I could fill it with relationships, and friends, with anything.

Right after Martin died I went into counseling. I did single counseling for a year with a certified grief counselor. Then she started up a suicide survivors group, and I did that for another year, off and on. I'm really lucky to have had the therapy and the survivors group, because I was able to work through a lot of this stuff. Not that it's over. I think that for the rest of my life it's going to be something that I'm going to have to deal with.

I don't think of him every day now, and that's kind of nice. It feels as though I'm kind of getting on with it. In the beginning I couldn't think about anything else. It's nice not to have that looming over my head. I felt *so different from anybody else. I would feel when I was walking down the street that everybody was staring at me, because everybody knew that my brother had killed himself.*

My brother's death and working through the grief and anger has changed me a lot. It's made me really appreciate certain things in life. I don't take things for granted anymore. I don't take my friends or my family for granted. I do a lot more caring, loving things for people. I really worked at my writing, and I stuck with it because I realized my life is precious and that I can do anything I want with it, anything. I save up for myself a lot more now.

I've gained a lot of awareness that I don't think people usually have. I feel old. I was twenty-five then and now I'm twenty-eight, and I think that I've aged in experience considerably, more than most people my age. I feel old sometimes when I'm hanging out with people my age. I feel that I'm way beyond them in life experiences. If you've had a suicide, it compounds life experiences phenomenally. It took me a long time to realize that it was different. To have somebody commit suicide is completely different from any other kind of death. The emotions are compounded a thousand times, particularly the anger. I think that experiencing my brother's suicide and going through all the anger and guilt and grief has deepened me in phenomenal ways.

Can any good come of this?

Immediately after a bereavement, it seems impossible that anything good could ever come of it. Indeed, when someone suggested the idea to Morna, she said, *I felt like punching that person in the face.* But it is normal to try to find some positive outcome in horrific events in our lives and to attempt to salvage our belief that life is more good than evil. So, in the course of living with their loss over time, people looked for some benefit in it, and, often, they became aware that the loss had changed them and their lives in some positive way. Ramona, for example, felt that her brother's suicide led her to a completely new attitude toward life. Morna came to realize that life offers no guarantees, an insight that freed her to risk choices she would not have tried before. Many people, like Lucy, felt that the death had both deepened them and made them value their own lives more.

Lucy's sister, Margaret, also found that Martin's suicide had a positive side. She was about to turn twenty-one when her brother killed himself. Although she was eight years younger, the two of them—the oldest and youngest siblings—formed a strong bond. She told me, *My middle sisters were very close in age, and they made a kind of team, and Martin and I became a kind of team together. We always had a really good relationship. We weren't real huggy or that type of relationship, but it was more that we had a lot of fun together. He did things for me, almost as if he entertained me, and I entertained him. He was really funny. He had a kind of sick sense of humor, like Ren and Stimpy kind of. And I really looked up to him too, and I still do, despite his suicide.*

Margaret was devastated by her loss. After two and a half years, she felt that she was beginning to accept it, and that her sadness was lifting, but, even so, she went in search of a tissue several times as we talked. When I asked her about some of the longer-term reverberations for her, she said, *I think I'm a kinder person since Martin killed himself. I don't want to make anyone feel bad, and I try not to say bad things about people. I really value the people I still have. My relationship with my sisters is even stronger, much stronger, since his death. I'm not so critical of them. We spend a lot of time together, but it's not because they're going to commit suicide. I just really enjoy them a lot, and they're both my close friends. All of us have something in common now, because we all lost the same brother.*

Phil (along with his twin brother Patrick) was only eighteen when his seventeen-year-old brother Mick killed himself in his bedroom. He, too, felt that he had become a richer, kinder person after his younger brother's suicide, and it changed him in other ways, as well. They were just developing a closer relationship after years of sibling in-fighting, and his brother's sudden and unexpected suicide filled him with a deep grief, and a great regret that their new closeness was cut short before ever coming to fruition.

The suicide itself was bizarre. He and his twin had just returned from their high school senior trip, from which Mick, being a year younger, was excluded: *I got the feeling he wanted to go with us, but couldn't. He seemed kind of lonely. The night we came back Mick was upstairs and we were down-stairs, and he came downstairs and went to the bathroom. Then he came in and said goodnight. Later, I thought that was strange because there was an upstairs bathroom. In the morning my brother Patrick woke me up. He came upstairs to the attic where we slept, very agitated, and said, "Mick's dead!" The way he said it I thought he meant he was going to kill him for something he did, so I just said, "Why? What did he do this time?"*

Then I went down to his bedroom. He had shot himself during the night. There was stuff written all over the walls. He must have been up all night writing it. Above his head there was a big tombstone. It took me the longest time to figure it out, but it said, "Not waving, but drowning." He had a quote from Ozzie Osborne, and other quotes from songs, and a quote from the Bible: "Unto thy hands I commend my spirit". It was eerie. We called the police, but we couldn't get in touch with my parents. They were away on a trip and had no telephone, so they didn't find out what happened until they got home later in the day.

Afterwards, even little things reminded Phil sharply of his brother's absence. Letters from college recruiters would arrive for Mick in the mail, or his SAT scores, *which he didn't even wait for,* and Phil would be overcome with the sense of emptiness. For a long time, he said, *Another hard thing was just setting the table. There were always five chairs a the table, and it was hard to remember to just set out four plates. There was this empty chair.*

A few short months afterwards, he and his twin went off to college, which he found very hard. *It bothered me to leave my poor parents. They* had thought they had another year with my brother before he did the same. And all of a sudden this happens, and the house was all quiet. For the next year, Phil was in a fog of mourning, and it was just dominating everything about me. If I went to a party and had something to drink, I'd be an emotional mess. I'd walk alone at night for hours, all upset. I studied a lot about suicide, trying to understand. There were some people to talk to, because they knew what had happened—when Phil starts crying in a bar, they want to know why. Eventually, his grief subsided and turned to a tremendous anger at Mick for what he had done to his parents, an anger that lasted for years.

But over time Phil began to feel that Mick's death had changed his life in many ways, some very positive: My father was a very dominating figure in our lives. He pushed my twin brother and me into the military, so we both did ROTC. He wanted us to go into engineering, so I took engineering classes. The first year I hated the school I was at. I hated ROTC. I hated engineering. So I came home and told my parents that I wasn't going into engineering. I was changing my major to Soviet studies. I told my father I wasn't going back into ROTC. I think my brother's death had a lot to do with that. I wasn't going to waste my life doing something I hated. I've become a real believer in doing things and going out and enjoying life, and I think my brother's suicide is a part of that feeling. It made me grow up quicker, and appreciate things in life more.

Once my grieving was done, my life was so much richer. I consider myself in some ways lucky that this happened, because I appreciate the value of suffering. It's made me a richer individual. I'm much more empathic, and I put much more value on relationships. My whole world got turned upside down, and I no longer take anything for granted. I know people who have never suffered or lost someone, and I think I'm lucky because my life is fuller than theirs. They can't appreciate life as much as I can.

Some people I talked with even went so far as to suggest that, as Ramona put it, Sometimes I think that his death was for the purpose of my life. One of these was Judy, a therapist with a thriving practice who has been very much involved with grief work, both for herself and for several of her clients. Her older brother, Bill, killed himself by carbon monoxide poisoning nineteen years before, when he was forty-four and she was thirty-eight.

When they were children, Bill had been her idol, and they still had a very close relationship as adults. But their roles had switched over the years. Bill was diagnosed as schizophrenic and was drifting aimlessly through life: *He was going nowhere. At the time of his death he was living in the YMCA and had been working in a hardware store selling paint, yet he was a man with an IQ of 140 and a college degree all except for one course. He had been a problem in some kind of way for my parents all of his life. At the time of his death, he was married and divorced. His wife had gotten so frustrated with him for not paying child support and being a poor model for the children, that she had taken the children and moved out West. So, although he had had some of the best psychiatric care that he could have gotten, he still seemed to not be making it in any aspect of his life.*

Judy became the mature, responsible sister, and, since his father would have little to do with him, Bill relied on her to help and support him. Although she would admit that he was something of a burden for her, she said that his situation mostly made her sad for him and desperate to help. When he killed himself, she was devastated:

It's the most significant event of my life. It has changed me more than anything else that has happened, and it's the most tragic thing that has happened in my life. I grieved his death for a good ten, twelve years. It had a far greater impact on me than my mother's death a few years before. She had cancer, and I knew she was going to die. There's no comparison between the effect on me of my mother's death and the devastation I felt after Bill's suicide.

It made me think about my life. It made me think about whether I should take my own life. It made me look at the other tragedies that were occurring in the world or had occurred in the world. I felt very helpless and hopeless. It made me question even more intensely any sort of religious ideas that I had ever had. I planned my own death. I was going to go to Alaska and just go off in the wilderness and die. It didn't matter that I had two little children. I might have died of grief. I felt that if this could happen, there was no point in living.

I feel that he died for me in some kind of way. Because of the manner of his death, there were many rationalizations that went on in the family. They were essentially saying, "Oh, our family is okay. Our family just has a couple of more problems than your average family." Whereas I think his death said, "Oh, I don't think so! I think things are a little more serious in this family. I think there are some very, very serious issues that need to be dealt with and that I need to come to grips with." I felt that if I felt disturbed, or if I had more difficulty handling situations that I think other people handle easily, that was very, very understandable. I felt that my work was really cut out for me if I were going to heal myself. I had a great deal of serious work to do, and I needed to find a variety of ways to do that work.

If my brother hadn't killed himself, I wouldn't have been driven to heal myself in the ways that I have. I would be nowhere near as happy a person as I am today. At least in that sense I feel that Bill has not died in vain. Otherwise, it's just a tragic waste. There are a lot of things that he had to offer, but that he never got to use and never got to give.

Trying to Heal

After the devastation of their loss, people struggled to come to grips with it and searched for ways to heal from their pain. Except for Joe, most of them found that the passage of time itself allowed their original raw wound to heal. Several of them had dreams or visions that gave them some comfort, and also helped them resolve some of their feelings of guilt or the sense of betrayal. Several, like Morna and Ramona, found that paying attention to what their unconscious was saying to them through their dreams allowed the psyche to help them.

Judy, also, told me about a healing dream or vision: *I went through a lot of sadness for a long period of time. Then a wonderful thing happened. My brother came back to me in a vision. He walked into my bedroom, and he was perfect. He was healed. He was whole. He was handsome. He had been handsome in real life, but he was handsomer. He was glowing with health and life, and he said, "I'm okay." And it was perfectly obvious that he was better than okay. He was absolutely wonderful. He let me know that he loved me, and then he disappeared again. And it was then possible for me to let go and for me to realize that wherever he is, he is perfectly fine.*

Those people who had others who were willing to listen to them and share their grief found that being able to talk through their feelings helped them let go and move on. Being part of a suicide survivors group or working with a therapist or grief counselor was similarly of tremendous benefit to the ones who had that opportunity. For the most part, they found that being aware of what they were feeling, even when it was very painful or when it seemed inappropriate, and letting themselves feel it, helped them get through their deepest grief.

Jean's therapist led her through the grief process step by step, through guilt, and rage, and deep sadness, and finally encouraged her to say goodbye. Afterwards, she said: *I was a lot clearer, because I'd said everything I wanted to say. All the confusion that was in my mind about "Why did he do it? Why? Why? Why?" seemed to lift. Sometimes the "why" questions would come up after that, but it was resolved on many levels. It seemed that had to be my process—to find the healing and the way back to life, to let go and get in touch with my feelings, and forgive him.*

Jean also tried to find ways to keep letting go of the past. When she had returned from her journey out west to sort everything out, she had brought back pages her brother had been writing just before his death: *They were all paranoid statements, over and over the same thing. He wrote that he was getting radio messages that people were coming out to get him, and he wrote lists of their names. He just kept writing these names over and over.* She kept the pages for many years and read them often.

Finally, *I felt that I had to let go of him on another level. I lit a candle and burned them in the woodstove. It was in January, the anniversary of his death. I did it out of respect for him, to honor him. I felt that I'd keep needing to let go on a different level. I think it goes on forever, that it will always be unresolved on some level, or come up. When it does, I'm giving it a little more space and honoring it, instead of pushing it away. We need to honor our feelings, whatever comes up, and keep being in touch with our process in order to heal.*

Like Jean, Judy felt that she needed to be actively engaged in healing herself. Her family offered little support: *My father and sister and aunts all responded with, "Buck up. Get over it. We knew this was going to happen, so it's no big deal." I got help mostly from therapists and from a few friends. I joined a group of women therapists, four of us, who met for four, five, six hours every couple of weeks in order to talk about our lives and how we were coping. At that point we were all single parents. Doing that grief work with them has changed me, affected me, deepened me, and helped me understand other people's tragedies. It was that kind of therapy and a few very good friends that I feel saved my life.*

Because her brother had been an alcoholic, Judy also joined Al-Anon and was still in it eight years later. I was surprised to learn from some other people, also, that being in groups like Al-Anon or even Alcoholics Anonymous helped them work through their grief. Judy said, *It really is a wonderful community in which to do grief work. I still would be back where I was eight years ago, which was pretty miserable, if I hadn't been able to get in Al-Anon and been able to talk in that group and feel acceptance in that group for everything that I was going through. That, most of all, has given me the tools to finish the grief work, heal myself, and get on with my life doing what I need to do.*

Because Judy is a therapist, and because she has helped many other people struggling with a loss, I asked her to share with me her feelings about how people could best begin to heal. I will let her have the last word: *To heal from grief, you need to get into it and work with it. You need to face the grief head on. It's important to get outside professional help, and to join a support group like Compassionate Friends or something like Al-Anon. It helps tremendously to have friends who have had some kind of loss themselves, and who have actually dealt with it so that they can understand something of what you're going through. There are a lot of people who may have had tragedies who don't understand, and they can get in the way. But the friends who had fully dealt with their tragedies, and the therapy group, and Al-Anon are, together, what saved my life.*

Chapter Two
"I wish I missed you more"

Not all siblings felt the kind of deep grief upon the loss of their brother or sister that the people in Chapter One experienced, since close bonds between siblings are not universal. Some of them never had a particularly close relationship, either because they shared few common interests, values, or attitudes, or because the family encouraged discord and rivalry rather than harmony and understanding. Others may have been fairly close when they were younger, but drifted apart into different lives and found that they no longer had much in common beyond a shared childhood. For people who did not share a close bond with their sibling, the suicide shocked and grieved them, but did not leave them with a very profound sense of loss.

After the initial shock and horror of my sister's suicide wore off, I found that I didn't feel her absence very keenly. She hadn't been a very big part of my life for many years. We lived far apart, talked on the phone rarely, and got together just once a year for a few days at our parents' summer house. We had always been different kinds of people, and in the ensuing years we followed diverging paths.

As a young child, I very much admired my older sister. She was a complete tomboy and acted as the "leader of the pack" among all the neighborhood kids, boys included. She taught everyone how to play baseball, football, marbles, and other boyish games, and she organized our play, whether it was team games or playing house. I admired her energy and vitality and at times tried to emulate her, but, at the same time, I valued other, more feminine pursuits. I liked playing with my dolls, or exploring our little woodland on my own, pretending to be a deer or watching for rabbits to come out of the burrows. Ann was often protective of me and big-sisterly, but she also made fun of my penchant for "girl" play.

When we got to be teen-agers, I began to notice that my friends did-n't particularly admire my sister as I had, which made me look at her in a different light. I began to see her as rather uptight and uncool—too much the goody-goody, whereas I was being The Rebel. We got along with each other for the most part and had some good times together. I remember times when we would start giggling over something and go on giggling until it hurt. But we didn't share much in the way of confi-dences, and our interests continued to diverge.

There was a period in our twenties, when Ann was living in Vermont, when she began becoming a more interesting person to me. She seemed to be blossoming in Vermont's relaxed lifestyle, and even becoming a sort of "cool" person. I felt at times that hers was a lifestyle I might like to share, and my husband and I used to enjoy visiting her in Vermont. I was disappointed in her when she and her husband decided to move to Houston because, they decided, that was where the money was. Of course I knew that it was financially difficult being an architect in Vermont, but I couldn't respect moving to a place she didn't much like solely for the financial gain. What was the point of earning more money if you were miserable living in the place you had to live to earn it? That was one of the several ways our values diverged.

After her move to Houston, we began moving apart again. Once a year, in the summer, she would come to our parents' Cape Cod house with her two boys, and I would go up with my two children, and we would have a week together. We had a good time for the most part, with very little friction. But I felt I could never share anything very profound with her, so our relationship was never as close as others I shared with my husband or friends. She was never a person I would turn to for support or help with problems or decisions. Her solutions tended to be practical and to my mind rather superficial. I had learned something about feeling through situations from some years of therapy, while she tended to look for external solutions. When my husband was ill with cancer, and then after his death, my sister was one of the last people I would call for support.

In her last years Ann was always too busy with all the aspects of her life that she took on to talk much on the phone, anyway. She was always on her way out the door to Boy Scouts, or Little League games, or this or that, forever pushing herself to do everything and do everything perfectly. It left little time for in-depth conversations, or, indeed, any conversation of more than a few minutes.

My sister was so little a part of my life anymore that it is not surprising that I didn't miss her very deeply after her death. I felt saddened by the tragedy of her death and for the desperation I knew she felt in her last weeks. I felt deeply sad for her children and husband and parents. But I, myself, did not feel a keen loss. It made me feel guilty for a while that I wasn't feeling worse after losing my only sibling. But I understood that that was the way I felt and that one cannot force oneself to feel what one is not feeling. Sometimes I still think, "Oh, I haven't talked to Ann for a while. I should call..." And I do miss being able to talk with her about our shared childhood, since she was my only link to how it felt growing up. But I have never experienced a deep sense of missing her.

Nancy and John, who tell their stories in this chapter, are two of the people I talked to who did not experience much of a sense of loss for their siblings. Neither seemed to feel particularly guilty about not feeling much grief, and both could accept the fact that their feelings were simply what they were. Some of the other people who found that they were not particularly affected by a sibling's suicide (for instance, Vincent in Chapter Six) experienced a good deal of guilt for not feeling much loss, and were sometimes tortured by a feeling of being "wrong". It is my feeling that we do better to accept our feelings, or lack of them, for what they are, and understand that we cannot force ourselves to feel something we don't, rather than torturing ourselves with feelings of inadequacy.

Nancy

Nancy's brother Seth killed himself two or three years before we talked, when he was in his early twenties. She herself was rather unclear about exactly how long it had been or the details of his suicide. Beyond being brought up in the same family, the two had little in common and rarely had much communication. Nancy feels sorry for her mother's loss, but feels little sense of personal loss, largely because Seth was not an important person in her life, and they had no very close bond. It was relatively easy for her to accept his death, and it appears not to have had much impact on her life.

Seth was never really close to me. I don't think he ever sat down to talk to me in a conversation. He and my youngest brother Albert were close, and he and my father were close, because they all had the same interests They all like hunting, camping, and fishing, and they would do those things together. I'm not interested in any of that, and I wouldn't want to converse about it. To me a gun is a gun. Some guns are short, some guns are long. I would rather go out and talk to my horses than talk about hunting and fishing.

I don't really know much about the particulars of his death. He was living with his girlfriend Maria, so he wasn't around very much, largely because she didn't want him having contact with anyone except her. I found out later that they'd been having problems, and it seemed from the letters he left that something had happened between them that made him feel he had to kill himself. He couldn't live with her or without her, he said.

He tended to keep things inside rather than talking about it, so nobody really had any kind of inkling that there was a problem, except Maria, and she didn't have the sense to tell someone. She had a lot of psychological problems herself and maybe didn't realize that keeping a loaded shotgun in the kitchen, which his letter said he did, is just not normal. The rest of the family blames her for not telling us that something was not right.

When Seth shot himself, I was surprised. Just surprised. That, and I was mad at him, because what he did caused a lot of grief for the rest of the family. My mother was devastated, and my father and Albert, so I was mad at him for their sake. But I work in an emergency room, and I see people die every day—old people, young people, suicides, murders, little babies. I tend not to react to death extremely emotionally. I think, "Okay, he's dead. There's not a thing I can do about it." I wasn't angry at him because it upset me.

I was sad for a short while, but I was able to rationalize it right away. I didn't go through a stage where I couldn't handle the fact that he had died. I'm so used to people dying all the time that I can say, "Yup, he's dead. Now I have to deal with other things. I can't get upset over this because there's nothing I can do about it." From the time that I found out he was dead until now I think I cried twice—once when we found out and once at the funeral. I don't get extremely emotional over things. I deal with things in what I guess you could call a logical manner rather than an emotional manner. I have my grief, it's done with, it's over. I don't keep carrying it around with me as excess baggage. I just deal with it, and after that I just have the memories. And, yes, I was angry at him for awhile until we buried him, and then it was over. I let it go because there's nothing more I could do about this. It's done.

Remembering my own feelings of guilt that I didn't seem to feel the loss of my sister as keenly as I might have, I asked Nancy, "Do you feel bad that you don't feel worse?"

No, I never felt bad about the way I felt because I completely understand that not everyone deals with things in the same way. Yes, I loved him. Yes,

I miss him. But to tell you the truth, I think I was more devastated when my horse that I'd known for eighteen years died, because I had to make the decision to put her down. The horse was like my child, so I felt responsible for her. It was my decision. I never felt responsible for Seth. He was a grown adult, and his decisions were his own decisions. As far as I'm concerned, he made the wrong decision, but it was his decision. It was his life to live, and who am I to say that he can't live it the way he wants to? Or not to live it.

John

John comes from a large family of five children. His brother Tim, the middle child, was twenty-one and John a year younger when Tim killed himself. Looking back on his family twelve years later, John characterizes it as an extremely unhappy one with little closeness between any of the family members. His parents' marriage was conflicted ever since he can remember. His mother was often suicidal, and his father was abusive toward her. Both parents tended to favor one of the children over another, and encouraged them to side with one of them against the other parent. In this scrambling for parental favor, the siblings could never develop any sense of kinship or closeness with one another. Although his brother's death was shocking and horrifying at the time, John felt little real sense of loss, never having had much of a bond with Tim, or any of his siblings. He can make himself feel sad by bring up the image of his brother dead of carbon monoxide poisoning in his car, but he doesn't miss him as a person or feel sad at losing him.

We just weren't brought up as a close family. We were just seven people living in a house, like a hotel in many ways, where certain dynamics and economics affected us all, but we just weren't close. We never had a home. I try to make my house a home, but our house was always just a house.

There was never any artwork or anything, and no one tried to make it nice physically. It was just bare and plain.

If we went on a vacation, we'd all just fight. I think it all reflected upon our parents. They didn't like each other. They were married for thirty years, and probably the last twenty years, or ever since I can remember, they were always fighting and hating each other. My mother was suicidal all the time I was growing up. I used to stay up at night with her or fake being sick so I could stay home with her in the daytime. Now that I've experienced love and relationships, I think that my mother really loved my dad, and he never loved her back. My father would throw a bottle of pills at her and say, "Go ahead! Kill yourself!", and she would take the pills. And she used to dunk her head in buckets of water in the kitchen sink. We'd be eating dinner, and she'd get up, fill a bucket of water, and try to drown herself in the sink. It was psychotic behavior. She would scream in the water. I was very protective of her, and I think she would have killed herself if I hadn't been home to take care of things. My father told me recently he really hated me as a kid. And I hated him, too. I was always defending my mom and getting in the middle of them, siding with my mother.

My parents would bait each other and get the kids to take sides. There were favorites. My dad favored my sister, and my mom favored me. When we were growing up, Tim was my father's favorite. He had spinal meningitis when he was little, and my father took care of him. But then when Tim got to be a teenager, he started smoking pot and drinking. He stopped going to football games with my dad, and stopped Little League. My dad couldn't stand him anymore. They found pot in his room and grounded him, but that didn't work. My parents didn't have a lot of control over us. They couldn't even take care of themselves, let alone reprimand us or set rules. Just days before Tim killed himself, my dad got into a big fight with him, yelling at him to get out of the house. I had a fight with my father about that afterwards, and told him it was his fault that Tim killed himself. I think to this day he feels bad about that.

All of us had medical problems, too. I had really serious asthma, my sister had a hole in her heart, my little brother had epilepsy, Tim had spinal meningitis and ended up mildly retarded, and he also had terrible, terrible acne. My parents were never proactive. Their attitude was, "If you have an asthma attack, we take you to the hospital. If you have an epileptic fit, you're an epileptic now, and you take this medicine." But they didn't invest in their children. They just reacted. Tim had cystic acne, and it was really bad. It was terrible for his self image. Kids called him "Pickle" for years, because his nose looked like a pickle. He would laugh, but I knew he didn't like it. Maybe that was why his girlfriend left him, which precipitated his suicide. Do you want to lie that close to someone's oozing face? But my parents never took him to a dermatologist to try to help him. They just let him go around with his face a mess, being called Pickle.

The night we found him, Tim had been gone for days, and no one knew where he was. My mother found what looked like crumpled up suicide note in his wastebasket. I sort of knew that he had done it, but I kind of put on a happy face. I didn't go to work, and my mom and I went shopping. It was weird. It was like years before when I was home as a kid. I kept thinking if it was true, then if we bought Devil Dogs or something, there's now just two siblings in the house, instead of three, to fight over who gets the extra. Another weird thing was that I started digging a tomato garden that night. I was figuring out in my head that this was all probably true, and thinking about what was going to happen next, and digging the garden because that's what my dad and I had in common. What was I thinking? That maybe with his formerly favorite child dead, he'd get closer to me?

Tim had just split up with his girlfriend, but somehow she heard about what was going on. She called me late that night, saying that she thought she knew where Tim was. She drove me out to a kind of secret camping place, and there was the car. It all happened so fast. She hit the brake and jumped out of the car and ran to his car and opened the door. It was a moonlit night, and you could see the car in the moonlight and her headlights on it. She pulled him out, and I could just see from how his body slumped right out of the car that he was dead.

I handle shock really well when it happens, then have a breakdown a day or two later. I got back to my house somehow and called the police. Then I went in to tell my father. He slept in a downstairs bedroom, and my mother slept upstairs. He just kind of sighed and said, "Are you sure?" I told him to go tell my mom. I wish now that I'd told her, but I kind of thought that if anything were going to bring them together, this will. I'll never forget him going up those stairs and hearing her scream in that room. They did sort of come together a little after that, but it only lasted maybe a week or two, and they started pushing apart again.

After we found Tim, I had to sleep on the couch downstairs. I didn't like sleeping in my room in the dark, because his room was right across the hall from mine. I didn't like seeing that. I always believed in ghosts, and I couldn't get the image out of my head of looking over my shoulder and he'd be there. I had terrible nightmares. I'd dream of his body, not him as a person, just this body in the car falling out stiff. I still have nightmares.

But I never missed him. We weren't close. We really weren't. I feel bad for my mother, that she lost her son. I think of a woman giving birth to someone who is a part of her and to lose him before her own death—it's the worst thing that can happen to a mother. I never got very upset about it myself, or missed him.

About once a year, though, I have a serious cry over it. I get an image of that young man sitting in his car, with his lost girlfriend's name scratched in the dashboard, listening to music on the radio as his final thing. At the funeral I saw that one of his hands was all blackened. He must have burned it on the exhaust or something while he was fitting the hose to it. Here he had hurt himself so terribly, but he still went through with this. He got in the car and thought, "That's okay. This isn't going to hurt after awhile."

It's such a pathetic image. When someone takes his own life in the car, the car is dumb. It doesn't know. It just keeps on going. It's idling and idling, and the music's going. If I ever do a movie, I'd use that. It's such a *powerful, pathetic image of this car that's supposed to get you around, and it doesn't know enough to shut itself off to save your life. But it's the image that makes me sad, not missing my brother.*

Chapter Three
"If you weren't dead already, I'd kill you for this!"

Many of the people I interviewed expressed anger at their siblings for purposefully taking their own lives. Earlier, Morna (Ch. 1) talked about feeling extremely angry at her brother Simon for betraying her by walking out on her and leaving her behind, as well as for not being there as an uncle to her children. Jean (Ch. 1) felt angry at her brother Robert for leaving her alone to cope with her "dysfunctional" family. Most of the people I talked with had felt varying degrees of anger at their dead sibling, although it was difficult for some of them to articulate it because they found it hard to be angry at someone so close who is dead.

It appears that it is often easier for siblings to feel and express their anger than for other family members. Parents, for instance, may feel angry, but they are more likely to suppress it, in part because they feel guilty for their possible part in the suicide, and in part because they fear to besmirch in some way the memory of their dead child. Siblings are usually freer to feel angry, perhaps because they are accustomed to it from childhood battles and rivalries. Childhood sibling rivalry and the anger it engenders can, and often does, carry over into adulthood, although people may not be fully conscious of it and may displace it onto a boss, or co-worker, or a spouse. Sometimes, too, as one of the people I talked to—a therapist—suggested, people may have difficulty working out anger at their parents and transfer it onto the sibling, instead. Siblings can feel like safe targets for one's anger, since the risk of losing them may feel less threatening.Among the people I talked to, anger surfaced in two different forms. There were those who felt personally wounded and asked, "How could you do this to me?" Others felt angry for other people's sake and wanted to know, "How could you do this to your family?"

How could you do this to me?

Being angry with the dead sibling because of the personal wound the suicide inflicted on themselves came from two different sources. On the one hand there were people like Morna and Jean who felt that the sibling had betrayed them by leaving them behind to deal with life alone. This is an anger born of love. On the other hand, there were those who felt that their siblings had purposefully hurt them. For several people the timing of the suicide made them feel that the suicide was in some way aimed at them. It is hard not to feel that one's sibling is trying to inflict hurt when the suicide occurs on one's wedding day or on a similar occasion, or when one is sick or in trouble and in need of a sibling's support. This is an anger born of rivalry and conflict, and unresolved issues between the siblings.

Bonnie

Of all the people I talked to, Bonnie was the angriest. She was the oldest of five children, and her brother Ted was the next oldest. Their relationship in the last years before Ted's death had been a rocky one, and when he killed himself—while she was still in the hospital following the birth of her second child—Bonnie was enraged. Seventeen years later, she still sometimes feels angry at him for choosing that moment, of all moments, to take his life.

Ted and I always had a kind of rough relationship. We have home movies from when we were little, and I was always pushing him away from my toys or beating him up. But pretty soon there were three boys and I was really in the minority. I had a brief period of being queen, and then they were just a gang of tormentors to me. The three of them traveled in a pack, and they were always peeking into my diary and coming into the bathroom when I was trying to take a bath.

Ted was always my mother's favorite. He even slept in her bed when he was little. I remember when I was in college, I was taking a psychology course and learning about sibling rivalry, and I asked my mother how I reacted when Ted was born. She said, "To tell you the truth, I didn't notice, I was so happy to have a boy. I was afraid I was going to get stuck with all girls. I was so happy to have a boy, I don't think I even noticed you." My mother always said these great things. They had a really close relationship. The last three or four years of his life, he talked to her on the phone nearly every day. The rest of us would call up every so often, but we were busy living our lives.

In high school Ted and I got along fairly nicely. I went out with some guys who were friends of Ted's, and we double-dated a little bit. Those were kind of good times.

It was when I had my first son that our relationship began to get a tension in it. There was something about the way I was bringing him up that made Ted insane. Once he left a letter lying about where I could see it, talking about how horribly he thought I was raising him. The first time I heard the term "passive-aggressive" was in connection to Ted. I annoyed him somehow. I made him angry and I don't know how, unless it was some sibling jealousy kind of thing. It was like something out of Greek drama.

My mother suggested, on more than one occasion, that his suicide was my fault. She said I always put him down. And I did put him down. He was no academic genius, just a very passable student. Not that I am an intellectual, but he didn't even aspire to it. I used to make fun of him a lot for being a jock, and I made fun of his jock friends, too.

After college, Ted wasn't sure what he wanted to do with his life. He went out West with a friend for awhile and did various jobs, and got a little bit druggy. Then he came back East and bought an island in New Hampshire and lived a sort of subsistence life, doing scalloping and working on lobster boats. That's when we started noticing he was manic-y. He was really a classic manic-depressive. When he was manic-y he was just wild, and he'd talk for hours and hours and hours. He had these great plans—he was going to run for SENATOR OF NEW HAMPSHIRE! And then he'd have a slump and just sleep. He had various therapies, from lithium to insulin shock treatments to EST, but he never stayed very long with any of those things. Shortly before his death, he moved to the city where my brother Jim lived and went to college for awhile. Then he dropped out and was working as a volunteer at a museum, I think.

He used to come and visit my husband and me. We had an old building out back where he would stay. Once when he came we were thinking about knocking down some walls out there and making bigger rooms. Ted offered to knock down walls. But his manic-y, up-and-down states were becoming obvious by now. I said that I wasn't having him out there knocking down walls because I knew he'd probably have a slump the next day and I'd be stuck with a big pile of rubble. We had a screaming fight about it. And sure enough, he did go into a slump. I remember going out there, and he was just sleeping and sleeping the day away. I felt a kind of panic. I started digging him out of bed, and shaking him, and saying ,"You have to wake up. You have to go for a walk. You have to do something! You cannot just lie there!" Of course, he did just go on lying there, and he was angry at me. It was obnoxious on my part, but I couldn't stand his lying around all day. We had a very difficult relationship.

When Ted killed himself, I had just given birth to my second child. It was a difficult birth, and my baby had some problems. There was talk of sending him upstate for some tests. That morning it seemed as though the baby was getting better. I was sitting in my hospital room with the door open, keeping a sharp eye out for the pediatrician. I was separated from my husband, but he was there to help out. He came into the room and closed the door behind him. I started screaming at him to open the door because I had to see the doctor. He told me he had something awful to tell me. And then he told me Ted had killed himself. For the past twenty-four hours my husband had been keeping everyone away from me, and the whole family was in a quandary about how and when to tell me. Later the same day a present from Ted arrived, with a note saying something simple like, "Congratulations."

For years after that I was sure that there was no way that my baby's birth couldn't be connected with Ted's deciding to kill himself. Maybe it's egocentric on my part. But I know I held sort of a special place in his life, a jealousy thing. I can't help feeling the connection. Even if there isn't really a connection, even if he really didn't kill himself because my son was born, he must have known that his timing was going to make me really angry.

My first thought was that every one of my son's birthdays was going to be ruined. In some ways that was true, because my mother, who was always very generous with presents, never, ever remembered his birthday. I kind of tricked myself about the anniversary of Ted's death. In my mind I associated all my anger and grief and whatever feelings I have about his death with Ted's birthday, instead of with my son's birthday.

My anger was incredible. I hated him so much! I remember thinking I wished he was alive so that I could kill him. It was the meanest thing a human being could ever do. It grabbed the attention pretty nicely. Lots of people showed up for the funeral, but very few of them came to visit me. I wasn't recovered enough to go to the funeral, which I was quite angry about, although I probably wouldn't have been the nicest addition to that funeral.

Ted killed himself by throwing himself in front of a subway train. There were eye witnesses. And for some reason that was the thing I most focused my anger on. There were two little children who were looking out of the front window of the train, and they saw him jump. It's the selfishness of it. For years and years I was saying, "I just don't forgive him for being that selfish." There's lots of ways you can be selfish, but the kind of selfishness that is going to have such terrible repercussions on everyone around you is unforgivable.

For the longest time after I was just on fire with rage about him. I used to get in big arguments with my mother. She'd say, "Poor Ted, poor Ted...", and I'd say "Poor Ted nothing!" He had some last wishes, and I said, "Oh, I don't think we should honor them! He's dead! He doesn't have any privileges any more. I'm not honoring his last wishes, because he didn't think very much of my wishes, or of anyone's, so why should we do that?"

Ted had just gotten engaged two weeks before. After he died, my mother got really involved with his fiancé in a way which we all thought was horrible. She was really butting into the fiancé's life. Maybe she felt that she could get her son back by being really close to his fiancé. The fiancé got married not long after, and when she had her first child, my mother put his picture on her dressing table and took down the pictures of her own grandchildren. My mother was really a pretty sick person. After Ted's death, right up until she died eight years ago, she rehashed and rehashed everything about Ted's life forever, all the details of his life from when he was in her uterus. My father cried at the funeral and then said, in effect, "That's the end of it." So for the rest of their marriage they just couldn't talk to each other. He was angry and silent, and she was just crying and babbling and feeling guilty.

My anger has softened now, because I realize his life must have been pretty miserable. And who am I to say he was too selfish? I know how I feel when I'm depressed, as if I'm down in the bottom of a Vee, and I can't remember ever being happy or imagine ever being happy again. In his suicide note to the family, he said something like, "The good times were too few, and the bad times were too frequent." I think when he was down in his deep depressions, he just had no perspective, no sense of it's ever being better.

Mostly now I just sort of feel sad about him, but every so often I'll still feel a little anger. I think if I still felt angry, I still wouldn't feel guilty. I never felt guilty. I felt justified. I think it's a natural feeling to feel, and I don't feel guilty about feeling that way.

Jim

Bonnie's brother Jim was two years younger than Ted. Their relationship, although affable, was not a particularly close one, because they didn't have much in common, especially when they got into their twenties. It fell to Jim to identify Ted's body, and that experience helped fuel the anger Jim felt at Ted for inflicting this on Jim himself and on the rest of the family. Jim felt that his brother's suicide was very destructive to the whole family, and he still feels angry and resentful, although the passage of seventeen years has tempered those feelings somewhat.

Ted and I didn't have a particularly close relationship. We would get together when our paths crossed, usually at family get-togethers. When I was in medical school, I would sometimes see him on weekends or up in the country. He lived in the city for a while when I was in training here, and I might see him every so often. We did sports and things like that together when we were younger, but after he got out of school, he had a very different lifestyle than I did. I'm sort of a nose-in-the-book person. I went straight from high school into college, and then straight into medical school, while he and my other brother lived a peripatetic life, living in different places and trying different things. In retrospect I see his restlessness as an index of his discontent. Ted could have done a lot of things, but he was unable to look at somebody who might put on a coat and tie and go to work from nine to five without scorn. He was a round peg in a square hole, and I, on the other hand, was following a linear trajectory, studying to be a doctor.

When he lived in the city, he would come over to visit sometimes, or I would visit him. I was aware that he was depressed and that he had sought help. I thought my role with him when he was depressed was just to be supportive, just to hang out with him rather than to be diagnostic or try to steer him.

The day he killed himself I got a call from my father saying that he had a call from the police that Ted had thrown himself in front of a subway train. My father lived an hour or so away, so I had to go down to the morgue to identify the body. You go into a room that looks like an old dilapidated school room. They have an area with a bay window over on the side, and the morgue is underneath. They put the body on a slab and push the button and the body rises up. It's very eerie. Of course, the body was all black and blue. I could make out his face, but there was a lot of damage. I'd seen lots of bodies before, but seeing my brother's body was very different. It was just very, very bizarre. The violent way he killed himself, and the fact that he'd had a fiancé, and the timing, and what it did to the whole family, all compounded my anger and resentment.

The timing was terrible. Not only was Bonnie still in the hospital with her new baby, but it was also just before my younger sister's birthday and right around my parents' forty-fifth anniversary. And he'd just gotten engaged. There were a lot of symbolic events right around that time. His suicide, and any suicide, seems like the ultimate narcissism.

When I see death in my practice, when people get old or die of disease, sometimes for the rest of the family that can be a unifying thing. It kind of brings everybody together. It's the closing of a chapter. But how opposite it is when there's a traumatic, self-inflicted death like this. It's a very divisive event in the family in its effect on the relationships between the family members.

I was very angry, and Bonnie was even angrier, and this perpetuated arguments within the family. Some people, especially my mother, were feeling sympathetic and saying, "Oh, poor Ted, poor Ted," and I just wanted to put on boxing gloves and go ahead and spar with someone over this, rather than just kind of sugar-coat it. It just stirred up angry, angry feelings.

I was angry right from the beginning. In some way, suicide seems like the easy way out, so I felt a sense of scorn and resentment about that, that he had chosen that particular course. And more than that was anger and frustration and helplessness that I couldn't save my own brother. If you can't save your brother, who can?

Ted's death in a way made him immortal. My mother, especially, immortalized him, carrying on about what a wonderful son he was. He took his life, and he had this problem, and he was depressed, and it's such a tragic loss. She was forever heaping praise and concern on him. And the rest of us siblings felt, "But what about us who are living?" It wasn't the kind of thing where he's kind of taken off the top and everyone else moves up one step or moves into his empty chair. His chair was "retired". It's like a baseball player, where his number gets retired. He becomes famous and nobody gets to use his number again. My parents felt very guilty, and my mother was always talking about her regrets and what happened and why.

It's been seventeen years, so I have had time to soften my stance and look at Ted's suicide as the act of someone with an illness. But it's hard for me to be objective and look at it that way, without feeling some kind of scorn or blaming him. I still harbor the anger and resentment, although it's been tempered somewhat just with the passage of time. I can let go of some of the anger now, but it's not an easy letting go.

"How could you do this to your family"

Many of the people I talked to may not have felt angry for what their sibling's suicide did to them personally, but did feel various degrees of anger for the pain it inflicted on their parents or other family members. Phil (Ch. 1) talked about how painful it was for him to see his parents' pain, and how his feelings of anger at his brother outlasted his feelings of loss. He was surprised at how protective he felt toward his parents and at the anger he felt at his brother for hurting them. I found in talking to other people that feelings of protectiveness toward their parents were very common, and that anger toward their sibling for wounding their parents followed almost inevitably. Over and over people said that their parents were good people, who tried the best they could to be loving, good parents, and didn't deserve to suffer the pain and guilt their child's suicide left as a legacy. A very few people felt that their parents perhaps did deserve it in some way, and felt angry at the parents rather than at their sibling. Feeling angry for the parents rather that at them, however, was far more common, if not completely universal.

I still find it hard not to feel angry at Ann for my parents', particularly my mother's, terrible pain and loss. Even though I understand Ann's feeling of despair and her feeling that killing herself was the only alternative, and even though I don't think she was really thinking about anyone else's feelings very much or really grasped how devastating her suicide would be to her parents or her children, I was angry at her from the beginning and, even now, find myself seething at my sister when I see my mother's continuing grief.

Probably the hardest thing I have ever had to do was call my mother and tell her that her daughter had killed herself. When my brother-in-law called and told me, he said, "I can't face your mother," which was understandable given how angry my mother was at him already. I was the only one who could break the news. I paced around the house for half an hour trying to pluck up the courage, trying to find some way to say it that might ease what was going to be a devastating blow. But there is no good, kind, or easy way, so I picked up the phone at last. I said, "Mother I have something terrible to tell you…" Oh, God, I thought, she knows what it's going to be. "Drexel just called, and…Oh, Mother, Ann killed herself!" I will never forget my mother screaming, "Oh, God! Oh, God! No! No!" Thinking about this, even after all these years, still brings tears to my eyes.

After that awful call, I found myself pacing back and forth, ranting at my sister, "You stupid idiot! Look what you've done! How could you do that!" That anger only increased in the days and weeks afterwards. My father was too old and frail to go to the funeral service out in Houston, so my fiance and I flew out with my mother. She was, as always, outwardly stoical, but I could feel her pain inside and knew that it would only get worse as it all sank in. After the service she lingered for a long time in the church, looking painfully, pathetically small. "I just want to listen to the music," she said. "Ann, Ann, Ann," I thought, "How could you do this! Look what you've done."

Some days afterwards, a portion of my sister's ashes arrived at my parents' house, and Marty and I went down to help bury them. My mother wanted to put them in a small flowered tin she had found and bury them under a flowering tree in the backyard. She couldn't bring herself to open the box and see the ashes, so I took them into another room and poured the ashes into the tin. My mother stayed out of the room. I had had to deal with my first husband's ashes four years before, so it was not as hard for me as it might have been, but still it was pathetic to see the paltry ashy remains that had been my sister. I kept thinking of her beautiful long, red hair. Then there was the problem of what to do with the empty box and the plastic bag that had contained the ashes, still dusted inside with a film of ash. I couldn't leave them with my mother. She wouldn't know how to handle them. Finally, I snuck them outside and hid them in the back of my car. The next day I threw the box and the plastic bag in my garbage, a horrible thing to do, but at the time I didn't know what else to do with them. Perhaps it was a symbolic way of expressing my anger at my sister.

My mother and I walked out to the tool shed together to get a trowel to dig the hole. It was a few days before Ann's birthday, a beautiful day in October. My mother said, "It was just this kind of day when I went into the hospital to have Ann." She nearly broke down, but then, in her usual way, she pulled herself together. I felt tremendously sad for my poor mother, and, at the same time, deeply angry at my sister. After I dug the hole, we brought my father outside and sat him in a chair near the tree. It was an awkward little ceremony, because we hadn't really planned anything. My father was nearly blind and deaf and didn't seem very connected to what was happening. Afterwards, my mother said to my father, loudly so that he could hear, "Harry, we buried Ann there." He said, "What?" So, her voice nearly breaking, my mother shouted it again. This time he heard. "Ah!" he said, "What kind of tree is this?" It was a heartbreaking scene, seeing my mother, having just lost her daughter, also, in a sense, losing her husband, too. He was not really able to take in what had happened. He was focused on simply surviving, himself, and he was no longer able at that point his life really to share her grief or offer much in the way of support. Seeing my mother's double loss made me doubly angry at my sister.

My mother wanted to hold a second memorial service for Ann in their home town, and began planning dates. She had forgotten that Marty and I were about to get married in three weeks, and we had to remind her and help her find a date after the wedding. This was one moment when I felt angry at Ann for myself, for killing herself just before my wedding. I thought, "What did she care? She didn't like Marty, anyway. Dammit, Ann! Thanks a lot!" After the wedding, which both my parents attended, they came through the reception line. Tears were standing in my mother's eyes, and she hugged me and said, her voice trembling, "I hope you'll be very happy." It was terrible to see my mother trying to be happy for me, and at the same time grieving for Ann. Our wedding could have been a purely happy event, but it was very much darkened for everyone in the family. Had my sister thought at all about my upcoming wedding? Probably not, but I still felt angry at the terrible timing.

Nine months later, my father died at the age of ninety-five, leaving my mother alone in their big house. A minister came over to help her plan the memorial service. The two deaths were so wrapped up together in my mother's mind, that she talked more about Ann and her memorial service than she did about my father. It was sad to see how hard it was for her to even begin to let go of her feelings about her daughter's death. I felt angry all over again at my sister for abandoning my mother.

Then came summer. My sister used to make a yearly pilgrimage to my parents' summer house on Cape Cod with the two boys. This summer was the first that my mother would be alone in the house, her husband recently dead, and no Ann coming to visit. Marty and I drove her up and stayed a few days, but we had already planned a trip for the period when the boys would come, and we had to leave, although my older half-brother came later to help with the boys. All the time we were away, I kept picturing my mother alone in that house, with Ann's kids coming to visit. Just the boys. No daughter. It seemed the ultimate cruelty to my mother. I mentally harangued my sister about it over and over.

I was, at the same time, very angry at my sister for what she had done to her children. They had not really suspected that anything was wrong. My sister was able to keep up a facade of normalcy, so they really had little inkling of her trouble and certainly none that she would kill herself. I was, and still am, very angry at Ann for leaving such a legacy to her children. For them, the message her suicide sent was, "Terrible things happen suddenly out of the blue, for no reason, and there's nothing you can do to stop them." I talked to them about that several times, when they would come to visit my mother. I tried to reassure them that we usually get warnings, that horrible things don't usually happen out of the blue, and that it wasn't their fault that they didn't know or see what was happening to their mother, because she was such a good actress. But I don't know if my words can ever have the power to deflect what they experienced in real life. Ann's suicide taught them otherwise.

All these years later, I still sometimes have internal conversations with Ann where I carry on at her for doing such a cruel, thoughtless thing. I called my mother on my sister's last birthday four years after her death, and we had a long conversation about death and loss. She said, finally, "You know, my friends all tell me, 'Time heals, time heals,' but you know, Sara, time does not heal. It just gets worse and worse." It was incredibly painful to hear that, and to know that my mother will never get over Ann's suicide. I keep thinking, "Ann, Ann, look what you've done. Oh, Ann, I don't know if I can ever forgive you."

Chapter Four
"The guilt still burdens me"

When I was talking with Margaret (Ch. 1), I asked her how she felt her experience of her brother's suicide might be different from that of, for instance, her parents. She answered, *I don't have any guilt, and I'm sure my parents do because they formed him*. But Margaret, I found, is very much in the minority. Almost every other sibling I talked with felt at least some guilt over the sister's or brother's suicide, and some were almost overwhelmed by it.

I felt guilty about my failure to call my sister and talk to her about what she was going through. I felt that I understood very well what she was feeling, because I had been there myself. Afterwards, I beat myself mentally that I hadn't overcome whatever fear and reluctance I was feeling about calling her. I thought I should have overlooked her telling my mother not to let on to me that anything was wrong, and just picked up that phone. I could have told her about my own experience of despair some years before and how I had come out the other side with the help of therapy. I could have told her, "Ann, you don't believe it right now, but you can be happy again." But I didn't.

It seems very natural for the surviving sibling to feel guilty. For some there is the feeling that in the game of life, laden already with rivalry and competition, they came out on top, which in itself creates feelings of guilt. Some feel guilty simply for having survived, while the sibling has not. Others felt guilty that they felt relief at not having to deal any longer with a troubled or mentally ill sibling and the burden that placed on them. Many people felt that because they were the sibling, they should have done something to avert the suicide and that, simply by virtue of their siblinghood, they should have seen it coming. Almost everyone felt burdened by, as one person put it, "the woulda-shoulda-coulda's". A few agonized over whether they had themselves in some way caused their sibling's suicide. The people who share their stories in this chapter are only three of the many people who talked to me about their feelings of guilt and self blame.

Ellen

I heard about Ellen from Bonnie, who had been filled with rage over the terrible timing of her brother's suicide. Ellen's older sister Leah killed herself on Ellen's wedding day, an act that seemed to me to be, if anything, even crueler. When I went to talk to Ellen I expected her to express the same kind of anger over the timing of her sister's suicide. I was completely taken aback to find out that, on the contrary, Ellen felt nothing but self-blame for a very long time. Some anger came up when she got into therapy some time later, but still, twenty-one years after her sister's suicide, it is not her predominant feeling.

It's hard for me to say this, but some part of me feels that my sister never really liked me. She probably resented the fact that I ever was born. I think from early on that it was probably obvious that I was my father's favorite, and she probably resented that, even though she was my mother's favorite.

I just looked up to her. To me she was beautiful. She knew how to do her hair just perfectly, and she knew how to do her eye make-up perfectly, and I didn't know how to do any of that. I was a real tomboy. I just loved to watch her. She was my older sister! I just loved her, and I wanted to be just like her and look like her. She was very small, only five feet tall, and I was always big, and I felt like a huge ungainly thing. I was always very shy, and when my mother's friends came over, Leah would always talk to them. They always felt that she was so animated, and a great storyteller. To me she was somebody to look up to.

I wanted to emulate her, and she just couldn't stand me. She would always say, "Get her away from me, Ma!" If she started to sing a popular song, and I tried to join in, she'd say, "Can't you shut up? Shut her up!" Or, when she didn't want an outfit anymore, she would throw it in the garbage rather than give it to me. I'd have to go and ask my mother, "Can't I have it?" I would want her hand-me-downs, but she didn't want me to have them. This is the way I remember her, knowing that no one is ever just mean. There must have been good times, but I, for the life of me, can't remember any.

When I was eleven, my father moved out, and Leah moved into my mother's bedroom with her. From that time on, from when she was fourteen until she married at eighteen, she slept with my mother. She took over my father's closet and his dresser, and lived in his bedroom. They kept their bedroom door locked. Leah became like my father's stand-in. She took over the father role and became my mother's ally. She acted like a bossy, critical father, always siding with my mother against me. My mother was the Divider. She was always fomenting rivalry between us sisters.

My mother and sister were like a charmed circle, and I kept trying to break into it. They used to shoplift a lot—they even stole Leah's prom dress. I wanted to do it just like them, so I shoplifted for a while. I guess they didn't know that I knew that they shoplifted, and when they found out I had stolen something, they, very hypocritically, called me thief, and told me I was bad. I was really confused, because I wanted to be in with the "in" crowd, and there was nothing I could do to get in.

I always thought Leah was better than me, that she had everything going for her. She had a great husband, a handsome, brilliant guy. I didn't think at the time that eighteen was very young to get married. Not long before her suicide she broke up with her husband and was living with someone else. I don't know what happened. She never really shared herself with me, so I really don't know how she felt or what she was about. She sometimes threatened to kill herself, and my mother would say, "Why don't you just go ahead and jump off a building or something, and get it over with?" Nobody really took her seriously.

Charles and I were going to get married on Thanksgiving, which fell on November 22nd that year. Twenty-two was Charles' lucky number, and we were both twenty-two, so it seemed like the perfect time. We wanted just a simple wedding and a little party afterwards for just our friends and very close family. But our parents wanted a big reception for all their friends, so they were planning it for two days after the wedding and our little party. We had a kind of planning meeting about the reception, and Leah began fretting over which man she should bring to the wedding—her estranged husband, whom I liked, or the man she was living with. I just told her that whoever she brought was fine with me, and to do what felt most comfortable.

The day of the wedding, everyone was there, and we were ready to start, but Leah wasn't there yet. I wasn't surprised by that at first. Leah was always theatrical, and she liked to make an Entrance. She loved being the center of attention. But it got later and later, and the Rabbi was getting anxious because he had another wedding to go to. I went outside to ask my mother whether we should wait any longer. She was on the porch with my father. It struck me as very odd that, even though they despised each other, my father had his arm along the back of my mother's chair and he was looking earnestly at her. I asked my mother if we should keep waiting, and she said, "I don't think Leah is with us any longer." But it just didn't penetrate. I thought she just meant that Leah wasn't coming for some reason. So we went ahead with the wedding and then the little party afterwards.

The next day we and a lot of our friends were going to play football at the beach near Charles' parents' house. We went to the house to pick up the football, and when we rang the bell, Charles' mother and sister came to the door. They didn't look at all happy, and I didn't know why. We had just gotten married! I thought maybe she was upset because our wedding was *not exactly what she had wanted. We went into the kitchen, and Charles and his mother went into another room. I thought he went to get the football. He came back in with it and asked if I was ready to go. We walked out on the porch, and Charles said, "I have something to tell you." And then I just heard myself screaming. It's as if I must have known all the time. Everything clicked—my mother's words the day before, the way Charle's mother looked when we walked in, the fact that Leah never showed up, the fact that for months she had been talking about killing herself. It just went click, click, click, click.*

The reception was cancelled, and people came to the house, instead, where we were sitting shiva. They came bearing gifts, which was awful. I didn't know most of these people, but because they were invited to the wedding reception, they all felt that they should go to the shiva house. They'd come in and come up to me and give me these wedding envelopes. I'd have to smile and say thank you. It was just bizarre.

For the next several months I was sort of stunned and confused. I felt somehow responsible for Leah's death. I kept thinking that she obviously had a lot of trouble around the idea that I was getting married, and I felt terrible about that. I felt somehow also that if she hadn't had to choose which man to bring to the wedding, she wouldn't have killed herself. I felt as though my wedding was somehow a jinx, and that if I hadn't gotten married, Leah would never have killed herself. And I also felt really guilty that my phone had been disconnected for some reason right before the wedding, because maybe she was trying to get in touch with me.

It was really my first major death, and I just didn't expect it. You think your parents could die, or your grandparents, but you never think that your sister could die. I didn't know how to deal with it. I started reading a lot about it, which helped, and the fact that I was married to Charles really helped a lot. Psychologically, he's always been one hundred per cent there for me.

That whole first year I think I was in shock. I was trying to deal with it with Charles, but I didn't really know how confused and horrified I was until around my first anniversary. It was 1973—the hippie days—and I was selling rugs or something on the college campus, and someone offered me a joint. I didn't take too many tokes before I was Way Out There. That was the first inkling I had that anything was amiss. I feel that whatever is going on in your head is exaggerated when you smoke grass, and I guess I really wasn't very aware of what was going on in my head until I smoked that joint. I wanted to get across the street to where my younger sister was working, so she could help me, but when I walked to the curb, I was afraid to step off it. I was afraid that I would step in front of a car and kill myself. Somebody had to walk me across the street.

That happened just before my anniversary, and it all started to come down on me. I was becoming more aware of how awful I felt as my anniversary approached. I didn't know whether I was supposed to feel sad, or happy, or guilty. All those feelings were happening at once. Around that time I started to feel a little anger, because I realized that this was going to happen to me every year. It wasn't just my wedding itself that was ruined, but every single year, as my anniversary came, she would be there again, doing it to me again. That's when I started to get in touch with the anger.

I went back into therapy, and that helped a lot. The therapist tried to help me experience the anger, and I do feel angry, but it's sort of intellectual anger. I feel that I'm entitled to feel angry, but how can I feel angry at somebody who's dead? She was really messed up. She's the one who lost out. She's the one who didn't realize she could come through the other side. She's the one that gave it all up.

A lot of the reason I blamed myself so much instead of feeling angry at Leah had to do with the way I was brought up. It's just my M.O. I remember having long discussions with my father when I was little those times when Leah was being mean to me. He'd say, "You have to understand that Leah must have had a bad day at school. You have to be understanding of how she's feeling." So my natural tendency is to excuse people's behavior and try to figure out what might have motivated them. Also, when I was young, I was always made to feel blame for what went on in the family. Leah was always right, according to my mother. I even got blamed for things Leah perpetrated. The other thing was wanting to be part of that charmed circle, and I tended to identify with their point of view. My mother favored Leah so, and I wanted to be part of that, too. Being angry at the favored one was a kind of dangerous thing to do, and it was also not allowed. I located the blame for anything that happened in myself, instead.

And how could I be angry when I felt that it was somehow my fault? I think, "I'm still alive. I have a wonderful marriage. I have wonderful children. She's the one who lost out." So it's hard for me to be really angry. Every now and then as a sort of exercise I say to myself, "You have to get in touch with your anger about your sister." So I'll punch the bed and say, "Oh, I'm really angry, I'm really angry." But it's more like an exercise. I feel more pity than I feel anger.

One thing that helped me deal with my anniversary came out of a talk I had with my Rabbi. He suggested that I use the Jewish calendar to mark my sister's death, instead of the regular calendar. That way I could celebrate my anniversary on November 22nd, and memorialize Leah's death on what's known as the Yartzheit. My Rabbi urged me to think of it as a different day, and that has helped, even though I know that it happened the same day. It's a little trick, but it does help.

I sometimes think around this time of year, if she were here what would I say to her? I think of the idea of spirits coming to the foot of the bed to watch over you, and sometimes I think, "If she really was at the foot of my bed, what would I say?" I would say, "I'm sorry you were so messed up. I'm sorry my existence was so hard for you. I'm sorry that I couldn't have helped in any way. I'm just sorry for you. I don't think I did anything to hurt you. I didn't mean it. I did it without knowing."

Leila

The death of Leila's younger sister and only sibling, Libby, at the age of thirty-six, was not technically suicide, since she died of complications stemming from anorexia. But Leila thinks of it as suicide, because her sister was very self-destructive and seemed to be willing herself to die. Leila feels that her sister's anorexia was an expression of that death wish. Even before her sister's death, Leila felt guilty that she didn't try harder to help her sister overcome her misery and her self-destructive behavior. She felt that she should have tried to get closer to her sister, in part because she is a therapist and in part because sisters should support and help their sisters. Libby had died seven years before Leila and I talked, and, although she still feels a residual guilt, she has been able to let it go for the most part.

Libby and I were really close as kids. She really looked up to me, and I was wild about her. I had wanted a sister very much, and my mother, who had been warned that she shouldn't get pregnant again, had her anyway, because she wanted me to have a sibling. I took care of Libby and played with her. I was very protective of her. We fought a lot, too, but there was really a strong bond between us. I never really minded her being with me and my friends. We were very different, though. I was a healthy, feisty kid, and she was sickly. I had a lot of friends, and she very much stayed close to my mother. Later, in our teens, she was a good girl and really worked to get good grades, and I was a rebellious teen-age brat. She was always very dependent on my mother, but I escaped from the family and made my own life.

After she finished high school, she went to college, but she dropped out. She was kind of lost. She very briefly worked somewhere, but her dream was to get married and have children, and that was all she wanted. She would never tell me how she met her husband, Richard. Maybe she thought I'd be critical. I think it was at that time that we seemed to kind of divide.

She would tell you that it was a good marriage, but it didn't look like a good marriage to an onlooker. They returned from the honeymoon within days, and Richard worked for the first year, but after that there were periods of unemployment. He was sick, and very dependent on Libby, and she was very dependent on our parents. They were like two sick kids clinging to each other. That was when I first saw the anorexia. When they were first married, Richard owed a lot of money, so my father set them up in a really sweet apartment. But Richard was always getting in debt, and they went through a couple of apartments, and each time they had less and less. By the time they were done, they'd sold off almost everything, and all there was left was a bed. It was hard to watch that deterioration. I felt a certain contempt for her. I understood somewhere her pain, but I guess to connect with that would have brought me such pain that it was easier for me to feel contempt.

After seven years, Richard died after a long lingering illness, so Libby moved home. For the next several years she did nothing. She wouldn't leave the house. She never seemed to get over his death. She was full of grief and anger. There was a very bad scene in the house. Libby threw things at my parents and verbally abused them. My father told me to get out of the "infection", so I moved out and found a place of my own.

She was severely anorexic. I saw her lose weight and go down to probably eighty pounds. Then she'd double her weight, and come down again, and up again and down again.. She was terribly self-destructive and seemed to want to die, or at least not to live. She was very, very conflicted. I think that somewhere in her was a big push to be reunited with Richard.

I know I should have been there more for her when Richard died. But I had a lot of negative feelings about him. I didn't see her go downhill until she married him. When he died, I thought that maybe she'd be able to get on with her life. But her life came to a halt. I think I should have done something. I don't know what I could have done, but I should have done something. I was not supportive. I know that. And she never forgot that. She was very angry at me. Maybe she was too angry to accept support from me, or maybe that's just my rationalization. I could do it for a patient. People tell me I'm supportive and empathic and understanding and very much with them. Why couldn't I do that for my sister? I should have been a better sister to her.

I don't know why I had to pull back. I think because it would have been an immersion. Somehow getting close to Libby and helping her would have blown the floodgates wide open. Her life was so empty, and I didn't want to imagine the emptiness and grief she felt. I didn't want to imagine the pain, which is why I kept my distance. I didn't want to let it reverberate inside me, and feel the pain she did.

The night Libby died, she was home alone and felt faint. She called my father to come home, so he was with her that night. She wouldn't let him call the doctor. She wouldn't let him do anything. She said she had trouble breathing, and she was afraid to be alone. Finally she let him call the hospital, and the paramedics came. She died in the hospital soon afterwards.

I felt very guilty for a long time afterwards. I kept thinking that I should have been supportive and understanding. I felt guilty that I had withdrawn from her and her pain. Part of my guilt was that I had broken free from the family. I had escaped, but my sister didn't. So I felt a kind of survivor guilt that I escaped and I'm healthy. It took a long time to work through all that, but I have pretty much let go of the guilt now.

Now I think of her tremendous pain and the tragic waste, because she was a very talented, smart woman. Toward the end she seemed to be finding interests in life. She read papers and books and magazines, and she knew what was going on in the world. She was interested in politics. So it was really sad to see someone with so many thoughts and opinions just throw away her life. Even toward the end there were things that we could share and that she loved hearing about. Even though I think she felt a lot of jealousy toward me because my life was going so well, she could feel happy for me, and when something good happened, she was the first one I would think of calling. There were still a lot of things we shared, bits of gossip and interesting news, and I miss sharing those things and getting her views. There were good times despite everything else, and I miss some of the good times. The guilt is mostly gone, and I'm left with just sadness at her wasted life.

Everett

Everett's younger brother, Justin, killed himself a little over a year before we talked, when Everett was 38 and Justin was 35. Justin was becoming quite prominent in his field, and Everett had mixed feelings toward his brother. Their relationship had always been competitive, although in recent years they had become much closer, and Everett admired his brother's success but felt jealous of him at the same time. After his brother's death Everett felt guilty for having said certain hurtful things a short time before, and worried that he had been one of the forces that pushed his brother to kill himself.

Justin and I didn't get along that well when we were growing up. I felt pretty resentful of him when he was a baby, just because he had come into my life and stolen a lot of the limelight. He was always raring around as a little kid, getting into all kinds of mischief, and my parents seemed to think that was cute. They were always telling stories about the trouble he'd gotten into, as if it were funny, instead of irritating, which is how I felt about it. When we got to be teenagers, there was a lot of rivalry between us. He had a very outgoing personality and always surrounded himself with a lot of friends, whereas I was pretty quiet, and would rather be working on my music or just being with a friend or two, talking about books or philosophy—kind of teenage intellectual stuff. He was also a real jock when he was a teenager, and played football, and baseball, whatever was in season, and was on the Varsity teams and so on. My thing was mostly music. I played the violin and had to practice a lot. My mother wanted me to be a great violinist, and she and I had music in common, so we were pretty close. She took an interest in my forthcoming career, and I think I was kind of her favorite that way. My father couldn't have cared less about music, though. He was into athletics, himself, like Justin. When my brother was little my father was always outside with him tossing balls around and talking about baseball and football and all. Then when my brother was in High School and starring in all these sports, my father would go to all the games he could get to. But my mother had to drag him by the ears to come to one of my recitals. It was kind of painful that my father was so uninterested in me, but I felt my mother was involved in my life and took an interest, so that kind of made up for it. So back then it was my father and Justin as a kind of mutual admiration society, and my mother and me as another little team.

We had such different interests and outlooks, that we didn't get along very well during our High School years. I used to put him down sometimes for being a dumb jock, and he would make sneering remarks about my playing the violin. And there was always a kind of rivalry about whose way was better, not that we ever came right out with it.

Later though, when we were both in college and didn't see each other that often, we began to get along a lot better. He was studying psychology and had some interesting things to say about what he was doing or learning. He was also very adventurous, going on wilderness survival type adventures or taking off in the summer to travel around, and it was kind of fun to hear him tell about those things. He used to bring back weird stuff for me that he thought I'd like, and that was kind of nice. Also, he seemed to have matured a lot in his tastes—or that was the way I saw it—and he would come to a music recital of mine now and then.

Before he killed himself, we had become pretty good friends. He had become a research psychologist and he was working on some interesting problems that he would tell me about. I got to where I really looked forward to hanging out with him, at least when we were alone and not with our parents, because then they would be completely focused on him. They practically idolized him. What was happening was that he was becoming quite famous in his field. He had published a lot of important papers in professional journals, and he was giving papers at various symposia that were very well received. It got to the point with my parents that whenever we got together for Thanksgiving or Passover or whatever, all eyes would be glued to my brother and all anybody could talk about was what my brother was doing.

Of course, my father had never been much interested in my career, but it began to seem that my mother wasn't very interested in what I was doing, either. I know she was disappointed in me, because I had never become the great concert violinist. I played with a fairly prestigious orchestra, but that wasn't enough for her. So I began to feel that I was losing my mother, too, to Justin. Both my parents used to go to hear him present papers, if he were doing something nearby, but they pretty much stopped coming to concerts I was playing in.

So my feelings toward my brother were kind of mixed. On the one hand, I did get a kick out of being with him. We'd go out to lunch or something together and talk about what was going on, and he'd tell me stories about things he did, or we'd talk about current events. But I also knew he had black moods when he would get very depressed, and he would never talk about what he was feeling then. It's funny that being a psychologist he couldn't discuss those kinds of feelings, but he was a research psychologist, so I guess that's different than if he were a therapist. He would avoid me sometimes, and I guess those were the times he was feeling depressed. Other times he'd be up and flying, so maybe he had some kind of bi-polar thing. I don't think anything was ever diagnosed, though, because I can't imagine him ever sharing his problems with anyone, a therapist included. He never talked about feeling suicidal either, of course, and I never knew how depressed he was until after his death.

I couldn't be very supportive, because he never opened up anything much to me. I was afraid to push too hard to get into those dark feelings of his, because he would just put up a wall. I feel guilty about that somewhat now, but the thing I really feel guilty about was something I said a couple of weeks before he killed himself. I was going to be playing first violin in a production of the Berlioz Requiem, which is a really exciting piece, and I invited my parents. I didn't usually get to be first violinist, but it was a pick-up orchestra just for this one performance. We were all together at my parents' house for Rosh Hashana when I invited them, and my mother said they couldn't because they were going to hear Justin give this paper to some group or other. She was so off-handed about it. She said something like, "We'll catch you another time." The thing is, there wasn't going to be another time. So I just hit the roof. I exploded! And I hardly ever even raise my voice, but I started yelling at her for being insensitive and I finally yelled, "And why is little dumb jock Justin all of a sudden Mr. Hotshot Superstar, King of the World, Center of Your Entire Universe?!" Then I just stomped away. My brother had heard all this, of course, but at that moment I didn't care whose feelings I hurt. Mine were hurt! Then I just left and went home. And that was the last thing I ever said to my brother.

I didn't hear a thing from Justin after that, and I was still too hurt and angry about the whole thing to call him. My mother called me a couple of days later and berated me for hurting Justin's feelings. She kept talking about how sensitive he was and how I had really wounded him and that I should be supporting his career, not putting him down. She went on and on about how I had done this terrible wounding thing to my brother, who looked up to me and counted on me. And that made me start to feel really guilty, which was ridiculous in some ways because I was the one who felt hurt by everything that was going on. But another week went by, and I still couldn't bring myself to call him. Then my mother called again and said my brother was feeling really depressed, and she made it sound as if it were all my fault. She kept insisting that I should call him and apologize, and then he'd feel fine again. But I kept putting it off. Then my father called about three days later and broke the news that Justin had shot and killed himself.

I was completely shocked. I literally fell to the ground. It felt as though the finger of God were pointing right at me. The funeral and sitting shiva were awful, really awful, because I felt that both my parents were holding me accountable for Justin's death. They didn't say anything, but just gave me these looks. They were very cold and stiff toward me.

I'm still laying that burden of guilt on myself, even though a part of me knows I was not the reason why Justin killed himself. He only left a short note that said something like "I'm sorry. I can't take it anymore," but we found some things he had written, and they were just frightening in their *blackness. He would write these things when he was in one of his deep depressions, and they were just horrifying to read. It made me feel that he was going to kill himself at some point anyway, because no one could bear what he was feeling during those years of deep depressions. But it was also clear that he was much, much more insecure in himself than anyone had ever known, and had none of the self-esteem he should have had with all his successes. So I kept feeling that I had, in a sense, made him kill himself. Maybe it was just that last thing I said that drove him over the edge, because he felt that I really hated him, that our brotherly friendship was just a sham, and that my true feelings had come out. I really beat myself with that guilt for months and months, until finally I got into counseling. The therapist has slowly been leading me to realize that I was not responsible for my brother's final decision to pull the trigger. There were too many other things driving him to it for it to be my fault. But I think my parents still blame me, and I still have this lurking feeling of guilt. But as that begins to give way, and the grief is coming up, what I mostly feel now is just a terrible sense of loss. I'll read about someone doing the kind of stuff he used to do, and think of some of those stories he used to tell about his adventures, and I'll realize I'll never get to share any of that with my brother again. It's just sad that, after all that rivalry, we had finally really started to become friends, and now it's just gone.*

Alan

Alan's older brother and only sibling, Jacob, killed himself fourteen years before our interview, when Alan was twenty-four and Jacob twenty-six. Their relationship was rather complicated. On the one hand they were best friends, and shared a lot of activities, but they never opened up to each other emotionally. They were buddies, but not confidantes. At the same time, Alan harbored a good deal of resentment at Jacob for the trouble and grief he caused in the family, because, from early adolescence until his death, he was constantly getting into trouble. Alan's feelings after his brother's suicide were also complex. At first he felt a combined rage and relief, but as time went on his primary feeling was guilt and regret that he never tried to talk to his brother about his problems or tried to help him, and that burdensome sense of guilt still remains after fourteen years.

In many ways Jake and I were very close, even the best of friends. But it was strictly on a buddy-buddy, go-to-ballgames-and-go-fishing-together basis. In another sense I would have to say that we were not best friends, because we never opened up to one another, never confided in each other. He was constantly getting in trouble—smashing cars, getting drunk and trashing parties—and he was also extremely anxiety-laden. I used to grapple with what to do and how I could help him. But humanity's good friends fear and ignorance would always conquer. Ignorance of what to do. Fear of trying anything anyway. So I never confronted him after one of these crises. There was not a word until the crisis had passed, and we'd just go on making jokes and hanging out.

Jake was diagnosed with scoliosis at about twelve or thirteen, and that was when the trouble started. But the question for me has always been, was it an aggravating factor or was it the factor? It's sort of a chicken and egg thing. Here he was at the dawn of adolescence, with all the social pressures and the self-esteem problems. But it's not as though he was the Hunchback of Notre Dame. He had bad posture, but he wasn't grotesque looking. He was actually pretty good-looking, but he felt grotesque. He felt crippled, and he became sort of out of step with the mainstream. But I'll never know whether it would have happened anyway, because he was also artistically creative and maybe that contributed to his being different than the mainstream. He painted, he drew, he wrote, and our house was full of his paintings. Then, as the years went on, he destroyed them all with blades and knives. But was it the physical condition that made him so self-destructive? Reduced his self esteem to nil? Caused him to really hate himself and want to die?. Maybe. My mom feels that was it, but I couldn't say for sure.

He was taking anxiety-reducing medication, because his anxiety was just tremendous at times. He had a constant anxiety, and he had a tic where if something was frustrating him, he would bite his hand. That used to scare me, because it was obviously a blatant demonstration of self-destructiveness. Twice before, once when he was twelve and later when he was seventeen, he had tried to kill himself.

He just couldn't handle the whole social dynamic. As one gets into adolescence, there are the peer pressures and the social pressures. They were there for me, too, and I mishandled a good number of them, but nowhere near the way he did. Low self esteem isn't even the term for how he felt. It was a real self-hatred. He became more and more of a fringe person, and slowly over the years he rejected the few decent friends he had.

Right from the start he got heavily into alcohol. Alcohol was really the only drug, or the main one. He would go on absolute binges at times, because alcohol is the best anxiety-reducer, or it was for him. There were a good thirteen years of just one event after another, mostly alcohol related. I always harbored a small but significant anger over the disquiet and worry he caused in the family, and over the unceasing grief he brought to our parents.

My mom tells me that in his times of confession, when he would come back from the incident, the stunt, he would cry and apologize and say things like, "Look at Alan. He has no one to look up to. All he has to look up to is me, and I'm s——t." He was aware that he wasn't fulfilling the big brother role. But the thing is I did admire him as a big brother. Not only was he creative, but also he was mechanically inclined and strong, and he could fix engines, which I admired. But did I ever say, "You know, I really look up to you because you're so creative"? Never. Did he ever create something and I said, "That's fantastic"? No. Because there was jealousy there. I think everybody wants to be creative. Everybody wants to be able to do something that will elicit Ooh-la-la's from people. I wasn't creative. Once I took a required art course, and I thought, "I'm going to be brilliant here." But all I could draw, basically, was stick figures. Everybody has a little child in them that wants to wow people with his work, and to that extent, oh, was I jealous!

On the other hand he was very much a failure. He never really pursued anything. He could have been an artist, but what did he do? He destroyed all his work. For a while he had a job in a liquor store, of all things. It was sort like hiring a claustrophobic to dig tunnels. We were pretty proud of him for a while, because he was made manager. But he was fired, I suspect because he was taking too many free samples. He was unemployed when he killed himself.

By that time I was living on my own, but I used to go home on week-ends to help care for my sick father. The police came to the door looking for Jake. He had collided with another car and was seen running away from the scene. It was only about his twentieth accident, and I thought, "Oh boy, here goes another incident." All the other times over the years when he pulled some stunt, always he would call or come crawling home to Mommy. But the next morning rolled around and no call, no crawl. I thought, "That's it. He's been leading up to this." My mother was in full denial. For a mother hope springs eternal. A mother has a way of hoping that things will work out for the best, even if reality and rationality dictate otherwise, but I felt that it was just a matter of finding the body. It became a lost weekend of missing-persons reports and friends and family coming to the house to lend moral support. Finally, on Monday the police came to the door to report that they'd found Jake. He had hanged himself behind a building less than a hundred yards away from his car. The autopsy revealed that he had almost immediately taken off his belt and hanged himself. The police officers had to hold my mother up, one on either side, while they were breaking the news.

Someone had to identify the body, and I knew my mother shouldn't do it, so I went down to the medical center. You would think that would be hard for me to do, but it wasn't that hard, because I was so mad at him. I was enraged at what he had done to us. It was the culmination of years of these kind of stunts, which had always made me really angry at him. I would think, "What? Are you enjoying torturing us?" And then there was the look of the corpse. I suppose if somebody takes pills, perhaps he looks restful and peaceful, but because he'd hanged himself, there was a violent look to him—the blue face, and the purple tongue, and the injuries. The violence of it just compounded my rage, and I hated him for what he had done. I was very angry about it for a long time, but also relieved because his suicide was something that, slowly over time, I had come to regard as inevitable, and I had dreaded the day when it would come.

Over time the anger and relief gave way to guilt and regret. My mind is clouded by "what ifs" when I think of the numerous occasions when I, in effect, turned my back on him in his times of need, for reasons no better than simple fear and ignorance. In fact, I think I could have dealt directly with his problems in a far more rational manner than our parents did— simply by the very fact that I was his "peer" rather than a parent. How realistically do parents ever relate to their own adolescent children? Siblings can undestand one another far better, because they share so much—the people who raised them and the environment they grew up in. I saw his inability to grapple with life up close and personal, and I saw where the pressures on him were coming from.

Someone might ask me what I think I could have done. I don't know. I know what I did, which was nothing. I was afraid to try, and I didn't know what I could do or say. I'm willing to entertain the idea that there was nothing I could have done and that it was inevitable. But I'm not sure. Maybe my remaining his friend, his mate, his buddy, perhaps that was all I could do, and maybe just by doing that I prolonged his life for all I know. But probably that's just a rationalization. I feel there was much more I could have done.

As his brother, I was maybe in a better position than anyone to help and understand, and the guilt at having not done anything still burdens me. It was a decision, or rather a series of non-decisions, that still fills me with regret.

Chapter Five
"Frankly, it was a relief"

Several people told me that they felt a sense of relief after their sibling's suicide, a feeling that Ramona and Joe (Ch. 1) and Alan (Ch. 4) talked about experiencing to varying degrees. Often people felt guilty at feeling relief after so tragic an event.

People felt relieved for a variety of reasons. Some felt relieved for the sake of the tortured sibling who was now released from torment. It is the kind of relief one feels after a loved one dies after a long and painful illness. Others felt released from the burden of worry and concern that they carried for their sibling; now they could go on with their own lives. Several of these people, at the same time, also felt guilty about feeling freed by their sibling's suicide.

A few people felt relieved because their sibling was a very difficult person to get along with, and now life, including family gatherings, could be far pleasanter. Some people expressed relief at no longer having to worry about taking care of their mentally ill sibling after the parents' death. Others felt relief that they no longer had to worry how their parents would be able to take care of their ill sibling as the parents grew older, and they were relieved for their parents that they would no longer carry that burden. People whose sibling had been troubled, or difficult, or mentally ill, and who had worried for years what the future would bring, felt relieved that the event they had long feared had finally happened, and that the constant anxiety about the future no longer hung over their lives.

The three people who tell their stories in this chapter talk about some of these forms of relief that they experienced after their sibling's death.

Peter

Peter's older brother and only sibling, Vernon, killed himself five years before our interview, when he was forty-five and Peter was forty. Vernon was an angry person, particularly when he had been drinking, and very hard to get along with. Although Peter thought of his brother as his best friend in some ways, he found it hard to spend more than an hour or so in his company. After his brother's suicide, Peter found himself feeling relieved that his brother's angry presence no longer dominated family gatherings, spoiling them for everybody. He felt relieved, too, knowing that he would be able to deal with questions about his aging parents' needs in his own way, without his dominating older brother trying to take over. Peter also feels some self-reproach that he couldn't help his brother better, but he doesn't feel guilty that he feels relief at his brother's death.

When Vernon and I were growing up, we had a lot of nice moments. We played games together and had a lot of fun. We were pretty close. But things changed after he went off to prep school. I don't know what happened to change him. He was doing very well in school, but he got into some kind of trouble and was suspended from school for a while. After that, he became a very angry, difficult person.

Our relationship was, in some respects, extremely competitive, but there were other ways in which we were best friends. He taught me a lot of different things, and gave me an appreciation of a lot of things, like drama and poetry. He was always ready to give advice on anything. Once I wanted to get a pair of skis, and I called him up and said, "I know you know what's the best kind to get." He would read fourteen articles on the subject and analyze to the nth degree which was best. And yet, he was very angry with me, and I'm not sure why.

There was always a lot of tension in our relationship. He resented me because I had a lot of friends and he didn't. He was very jealous of me and extremely competitive. I remember one time when he had taken a psychology course and had taken a test where you had to match the psychologists to the appropriate quotes. He hadn't done very well on it, I guess, and he was sure I wouldn't get any of the answers right. So he made me take the test. I was a psychology major, and I was getting all the answers. He got so angry that he just tore it out of my hands. He couldn't stand my being better at anything. He was a terrible perfectionist, and he couldn't handle not being the best at everything. Once we were out together for the evening, and he got really angry because somebody thought I was the older brother, because I'm taller than he was. He had a constant hard edge. He would always get the discussion into an area where he could end up barraging you with facts or figures and kind of "winning". Win the battle, lose the war.

Vern was always very critical of everybody, including me. I used to arrange it so that I would only spend so much time with him. I planned it so that I would spend about an hour with him and that would be it. I needed to be out of there before it got to a certain point, and we would get into a fight about something.

Christmas was always a disaster. It was a horror to get together. He'd walk in the house, and first he'd want to get a drink. I'd think, "How long is this going to last?" because he was a mean, angry drunk. I would plan exits, saying, "Well, we have to get up to Sandra's mother's house now," and try to get out of there before he got too drunk and started a fight. It was only a question of time before he would get into some big fight with my mother. An explosion would always come.

He felt an enormous anger and hatred toward my parents, more so than they ever realized. He wanted me to join him in damning my parents, and I just couldn't do that. I said, "Don't ask me to do that. You want me to get

into the pot of hate and sit there and throw mud, and I just can't do that."
He was always causing a problem, ever since prep school. He had horrendous fights with my parents, my mother in particular, tearing phones out
of the wall, and making death threats, and causing horrendous scenes to
the point where they called the police.

Vernon was not a happy camper, to put it mildly, although he was very
successful in business. He went into the same business as my father, I think
out of a sense of competition with him, and he ended up being more successful and making more money. But he had a hard time getting along
with people. He was married three times, and he was very abusive physically to all his wives. He had just been divorced at the time of his suicide.
He was just generally miserable.

He was looking for answers in things. He had the Porsche, he had the
house, he had the job. His lawn was manicured to a Tee. He looked for
answers in doing things, like taking a safari, or going canoeing. But the
answers weren't there, and he just didn't get it. He had really painted himself into a corner. I think he really wanted to get out of it, but he couldn't.
Because he had abused his body with alcohol and smoking, he didn't have
the physical strength to overcome it.

The times when we'd get together for lunch or something in the last
years, I felt he was miserable. I wanted to help him, but I could only get just
so close, and he would push me away. If I tried just to listen to him about
his troubles, he would accuse me of playing psychologist. He didn't believe
in psychology, because he thought he knew all the answers—that he was
smarter than any shrink.

When the police called me to tell me they'd found my brother, I was-
n't really surprised. I always knew that he was going to die early. I
always knew it would be a phone call, but I thought it would be a car
accident, because he drove like a maniac. He had gone up to his attic
and shot himself in the head. He always told people he wasn't going to
live very long, and he was living his life that way, drinking and abusing
his body. I was angry at the timing, though. He killed himself right

before my parent's anniversary, and they buried him on their anniversary. They could never celebrate their anniversary again.

Afterwards I felt, not exactly guilty, but somewhat self-reproachful. I felt I should have done more, and been more attuned to what was going on. But he was pushing me away and wouldn't let me help. What could I have done? It was like watching somebody come to the edge of a cliff, and you're at the bottom. You want to say, "Don't jump!" but all you can do is watch, and he jumps. I've come to the conclusions that this is something he had to do.

I also felt very relieved. In a way he kind of did us all a favor, erasing all the tension that he always caused. On Christmas, after he killed himself, we went to visit family, and we just had fun with our cousins and the little kids. After we got home, we said, "Wow! That was about the best Christmas we ever had! No fights! We just had fun!" So it was just a feeling of relief—justifiable relief—and I don't feel guilty about feeling that way.

I also felt relieved because I had been concerned about what was going to happen with my parents. I dreaded what would happen when one of my parents died or got sick, because Vernon would want to control everything, and it would have been very difficult, because he would want to take over. I worried how I would deal with my parents, whether it was a major illness or the death of one of them, because he would have his ideas about what should be done, and I would have mine, so there was going to be a major competition there. I know my mother would not want to be left in my brother's care. So in that respect, too, I was very relieved that I wouldn't have to go through that.

I was sad about his death, too, of course. He really was in many ways my best friend. I was a little bit like rattling in a cage at first. You want to get out. You think, "This isn't real," and you shake the bars. But then you get used to it. Now I've mellowed down a little bit, and I think that that's just the way it is, and I accept it. I do miss him in many ways, but mostly I feel relief at not having to deal with his anger and the fights and all the trouble and tension he always caused everywhere he went.

Daniel

Daniel's older sister and only sibling, Ruth, was twenty-three and Daniel nineteen when she killed herself. Their relationship during their adolescence was somewhat stormy, largely because of the effects of her mental illness, and she was a difficult person to be with. Daniel had worried about what the ensuing years would be like and, particularly, what would happen years down the road when his parents died and the responsibility for his sister would fall to him. With her suicide, that burden lifted, so it is not surprising that he felt relief at her death, along with sadness at losing his only sibling.

Ruth had serious mental problems for many years, but I didn't understand it objectively, because I was just coming of age as a teen-ager. In a way, I perceived her problems as part of normal development, normal problems for someone becoming nineteen, twenty, twenty-one. She was antagonistic toward me, and I remember fighting with her a lot, and not realizing that it really wasn't my problem. It took me a long time to realize that she was a mentally ill person. When she was seventeen and I was thirteen, and she was still fighting with me, I thought, "Wait! You should be a role model for me. You should show some signs of maturity." But she didn't, and it was really crumby.

I looked up to her, to a degree, because she was older, but I didn't feel competitive with her. I just did my own thing, and never felt compelled to show her up. I was a decent student and worked hard, and I was showing signs of having some artistic talent. I think she resented that in certain ways. She may have resented my modest success in life or resented my being normal, but I don't remember competing with her. She was a girl, and I didn't have the same interests.

I didn't need to compete for attention from our parents. It was only later that I learned that she was the favored one when we were very small. She was the first child, and a nice, wonderful little girl, and I don't think I was perceived the same way. But I don't think that had any impact later on with my parents. I never felt any lack of love or attention. My parents were very good people, and they were attentive to me even though they had to devote a lot of time and worry to Ruth. I think they needed me more than a parent of another child that age if the other child had been normal. My father spent a lot of time with me, and I think he got a lot of comfort being with me, knowing that he had a normal child. I don't feel my parents pressured me very much to take on the burden of caring for my sister. I do remember one time when my father discussed her illness with me directly, but I think it was because he was just at his wit's end and just very tired of dealing with her. It's so sad, because they worked so hard, and they were good people and good parents, and to have to deal with this non-sense…Mostly they were very supportive of me and happy that I was coasting along doing fine. I don't think they thought that there was anything I could do for her, except just be who I was and be there as a sibling and not go crazy myself.

Part of Ruth's and my relationship felt like a normal sibling relation-ship, with its fights and rivalries, and the other part had to do with her problems. She was resentful of me or angry at me, more than in a normal sibling relationship. And the manifestations of her illness in general, that didn't have anything to do with me, were unpleasant—her depression and aggressiveness, and her paranoid and schizophrenic behavior. I did recog-nize that she had a lot of problems and that she was difficult to deal with, and I worried how I was going to become an adult with the burden of a disturbed sibling. I didn't want to grow up with her, disturbed as she was.

Ruth was, I think, mildly schizophrenic, but it was mostly depression. She threatened my parents on occasion, and she would threaten suicide and have to be hospitalized. I think it was an organic illness, but it was probably exacerbated by the times. It was during the sixties, and one of the social norms was to experiment with drugs and have a rebellious nature. And there was a glamour attached to mental illness at the time. I think she was partially caught up in that. She never really finished school properly.

She flitted around to three different schools, but never got her degree. At the time of her suicide she was living with a man who wasn't doing much of anything, either. In a way, I looked down on her for not getting it all together, but mostly I realized that it was like someone with a physical illness like diabetes—her mental illness was a physical problem. I really just felt sorry for her that it didn't work out for her. She was sick for a long time, and it just got worse. I think her depression got to the point where killing herself was the only way to escape her misery.

Her suicide didn't happen out of the blue. She had made threats. But we were still shocked when it happened, because you don't believe a person's going to do it, especially the way she did it. She jumped off a building. We had to identify her at the morgue. It was all just devastating to my parents. They never really got over it, especially my mother, who was not particularly strong emotionally. My father was strong enough to continue living and try to get as much out of life as he could. And they had me, so at least they had a feeling of consolation that they weren't complete failures as parents, because their guilt was tremendous—that they may have caused her problems.

I'm a little angry at my sister for doing that, because of what she did to my parents. And then, she didn't see my children or my wife. I'm sad that my parents couldn't see them, but it's a different emotion. I'm angry at my sister about that, because she had control over it. And I'm both sad and angry that she didn't see my parents in their old age. My parents died not too many years later, and I know I can't blame my sister for my parents' death, but I think she was responsible in some way, because her suicide was emotionally devastating. But I don't think she was aware how her suicide would affect my parents. She was young and stupid. I want to say to her, "You were so stupid. So stupid." But I also know that she was really sick, and so it wasn't so stupid.

I grieved at the time of her death, but it wasn't the same kind of grief as when I think about the loss of my father or my mother. I can't assign a reason why my sense of loss for my parents is so much greater than for my sister. It was pretty horrible to lose her. But it was a relief in a way because she was a real problem.

I'm not proud of the fact that I felt relief. It had to do with feeling, "Enough already. I've had enough of this." I think many of us didn't see any way out because the illness was organic, and we saw adults with mental illness who go on for thirty, forty years with that illness. It just doesn't end, and it's just misery. I was aware at the time that I could be a fifty-year-old, with my parents dead, having a fifty-four-year-old mentally ill leech-parasite sister, making my life miserable. I think that people have to take responsibility for the things that happen in life, but it was a real relief to know that I wouldn't have to do that. I don't feel guilty about it. Who wants to deal with mental illness? There's a family gathering we go to sometimes where one of the family has a husband with a drinking problem and, I think, also some kind of mental problem. He's drunk at the party, and it's really unpleasant. It must be embarrassing to the wife, and I'm just glad that I don't have to deal with that sort of thing with my sister.

After my parents died, I inherited some money that would have gone to my sister if she were alive, so in a sense I benefited from her death. But I would have traded half of the estate to have a normal sibling. I would definitely have done that, to have a loving older sister with a good relationship. My wife has an older sister, and she's my wife's best friend. We're very close families, and I think, "I'd do anything to have a good, happy sibling relationship." I so much envy my friends who say, "Oh, I'm spending the weekend with my brother going skiing." I can't do that. I'd do anything to have that. But I'm not so sure that I would have given up half of the inheritance to have a mentally ill sibling.

The question is, would I rather have my sister now with all her problems—and maybe there would have been nice things about having her—or is it better that she's dead? Would I rather have that mentally ill sister? It's sort of like that game show, "Will you take what's behind door number one...? And the answer is, no, I'd rather not have that mentally ill sister.

Emily

Emily's older sister and only sibling, Janet, died from an overdose of barbiturates and alcohol twenty years before our interview. Janet was nearly forty, and Emily was thirty-eight. Emily had admired her sister when they were younger, but as Janet became more and more troubled in her life and her relationships, and increasingly dependent on other people, especially her mother, for support, her neediness became onerous. Emily and her husband Jerry worried about Janet's dependence on her mother and what would happen as her mother aged. Her sister's suicide, understandably, was a relief, because Emily no longer had to worry how her mother would be able to manage caring for Janet or about what role she herself would be forced to take as the years went on.

Janet started out as a very lovely person, and she was very beautiful. She grew up very fast. She developed early, and she looked older than she was, and tended to date older fellows even when she was in Junior High. She seemed very sophisticated, but apparently underneath it all she never was as sure of herself as we all thought. I thought she was great when we were teen-agers. She seemed popular and at ease in all situations. I was painfully shy when I was little, and she always seemed as though she could do anything. I admired her a lot. I don't know if I was truly jealous, though, although of course we argued as siblings do when we were young. We didn't interact with each other much or with the same people, and we were separate in our social lives. She went to a private school and later to a boarding school. I was offered that opportunity, too, but I'm sort of a proletariat type, and I really wanted to go to public school. We lived in a nice area where the public education was fine.

As a result of being in a private school, Janet met people who had a fairly high income, people who were in "Society", and that's what she really wanted. She wanted to be part of Society. My family came from lower middle class families, but my father did very well financially, and they moved into the upper middle class. Both of us grew up in very comfortable circumstances, but she always wanted more. She wanted the family background, too—the Bloodline—and I never cared.

She started dating someone from a big old family, and she seemed to "glom" onto him. She was always very intense in her relationships. After a while it became obvious that he wasn't going to fall madly in love with her. That was the first time she tried suicide, and it was always a history of that. It was always that she got intense with somebody, and they'd go together for a while, but the man never reciprocated. Except once. She did marry once, and it was an absolute disaster. She never should have married this guy. She just wanted to get married.

From the time she was very small, she was always dreaming of a big wedding and being with people who were in Society. The more I think about it, the more I see that she didn't really have any pervading interests. She could play pop tunes on the piano, and she liked to sing. But this wasn't something she was taking lessons to pursue; it was just kind of part of the whole show. I don't really remember her being really into anything. I'm sure she went to plays and things, but she didn't have strong interests. I was really into jazz, and my friends and I used to go to clubs and hear jazz. When LP's came out, I had a lot of jazz records. She got interested in that some, but I think it was because I had it. She read books, but mostly romances. I don't even know now what she wanted to do in life. She thought she wanted to write for a while, but that was just a passing thing. She wanted to Be a Writer, but she didn't necessarily want to write, and she didn't have the discipline for that anyway.

I had no interest in Society or getting married right away. And I didn't aspire to marry someone from a society family. I wanted to be a writer or an artist, and if I were to get married eventually, I wanted it to be to someone I really loved who liked the same things that I liked. I wasn't in a hurry to get married right out of college like my girlfriends. I fell in love with my husband Jerry because we were interested in the same things. We liked traveling and learning about things—music and art and literature. We had interesting friends, not the kind of glitzy Society people Janet was drawn to. So Janet and I were different kinds of people and had different values.

She went to college, but never completed a degree. That had something to do with a relationship she was involved in, too. She worked in the city where we grew up for a while, then drifted out to the West Coast and worked there for a while before she drifted back home. Then she worked in New York for a while and met her future husband. They never should have got married. They were arguing like cats and dogs even before they got married, and they were both alcoholics. He lost his job because of the drinking. She found some kind of work, but he couldn't. Finally, they split up, and not long after that he jumped out of a window and killed himself.

My mother got Janet into therapy with a Freudian and paid for it, but I don't think it did any good, ever. Janet became very dependent on her therapist, and all it did was convince her that my mother was the one to blame. My mother and sister had a kind of funny relationship. It was a very intense one. I always called it a sort of love/hate relationship. They were always arguing, but yet I always felt there was a great dependency, especially on the part of my sister for my mother. My mother kind of encouraged that by always coming through and taking care of her, instead of saying, "No, I'm not going to do this. It's time for you to really try on your own." In her last years Janet couldn't hold a job, and my mother took care of her. She paid for her apartment and her phone bills and so on. My mother didn't know what else to do. She just felt guilty about Janet, and she thought at least she could make sure that Janet had a place to live and that she'd be all right, but it didn't really help. I felt a little angry about that. I was teaching at the time, and wasn't making a lot of money, although my mother did help me get a car and was very sweet to me.

Around the time after her husband died and she got into therapy, Janet used to call us late at night and go on and on. She'd call us both, and we'd take turns talking, because it would be so late. She was in a relationship again, and she'd be saying, "Do you think this will ever work out?" And on and on. She had always been drinking, and she'd repeat things over and over. We'd just have to sit and listen and say, "Yes, that's possible. Maybe. Yes. Well, I don't know." It got to the point where we'd dread that phone ringing late at night, because it would always be her. My mother said she had humungous phone bills. Of course, my mother paid for them.

Not long before she died, Janet returned to the area where we grew up and lived right near where my mother was living. She wasn't working anymore and was pretty much alone, except for being in close touch with my mother. Mother wanted her to go to group therapy, but she wouldn't. She would have had to bare too much. I don't think she ever wanted to help herself a whole lot.

It was a great disappointment to see someone who I thought had such possibilities go the way she went. I didn't admire her anymore. There was more a feeling of disdain. Other people talk about how close they are to their sisters, but that's hard for me to understand. She was the last person I would have called up to talk over anything important or personal. She was always calling me. There was no give and take there. She was always draining from me. I was the one who was supposed to be giving some kind of something back to her so she'd feel better. She'd never ask me, "How are you doing?" It was always "me".

When she killed herself, I hadn't seen her in quite a while. The last year of her life she'd gotten to the point where she didn't communicate as much. There was no one in her life at the time. A lot of her friends had moved away from her, because they were always listening to the same refrain over and over again. She drank a lot. Sometimes when she was visiting people, she would take pills out of their medicine cabinet so that she could use them later. She had taken pills with her drinks when she died, and that's why she was finally successful. I don't know why she picked that particular time. My mother hadn't heard from her for several days, which was very odd. Someone who lived in Janet's apartment building noticed a smell and contacted the manager of the building. He called my mother, and they found her. She left a very garbled note. It was to my mother only. She accused my mother of not understanding her, and not understanding her relationships, and just went on and on.

I think there was relief on everyone's part when it happened. I think my mother felt relief, and I certainly felt relief for her, because there was nowhere that Janet was going. She would have just been this albatross forever. Jerry and I used to talk about what would happen. We'd think about how Mother would be living alone and Janet living alone and how they would end up living together, and we thought, "Oh, how awful!" In a way, it was a blessing that my sister finally succeeded in killing herself, because I just can't imagine what would have happened. My mother is better off without that burden, even though I know she'll grieve forever. How long could Mother have shouldered that? Mother lives in a retirement community now, which she chose to do, and seems happy with her life. She would never have been able to do that if Janet were still alive. She would still be taking care of her.

The other thing that Jerry and I had worried about was what was going to happen after my mother died. We talked about what we would do and how we would handle Janet being dependent on us in the end. Hers was just a slow deterioration. It was a relief to know that we weren't going to be saddled with that.

At first when she killed herself I felt angry as well as feeling relieved. I thought, "You were such a fool. You could have had so much." I was angry because of the uselessness of it all, kind of angry at Fate as well as at her. I think there will always be a kind of disappointment when I think of her, a regret. But I'm beyond the stage where I was angry and thought about all that wasted life and energy and where she put her energy. I see now that she put it in all the wrong places. In a way it's a tragedy of the times—where women were and what their expectations were. When I feel sad, it's for that kind of thing—for the person she was before, but not for the person she was ultimately when she died.

Chapter Six
Reverberations down the Years

Some of the people I talked to experienced long-term effects after their sibling's suicide that were far-reaching. Many of them (as well as others who wrote to me) described their sibling's suicide as the defining event in their lives, one which affected them in ways that went beyond grief, guilt, or other feelings. Many of these long-term reverberations surprised me. People talked about effects on areas of their lives that one might not expect to be affected by a suicide. It appears that siblings, especially teenagers or people in their twenties, can be affected by a suicide in ways other family members are not. Some of those who lost a sibling while they were still in their formative years found that their personality changed, or the way they dealt with life issues shifted. Some found that they related to other people in a different way after the suicide. Others found that their lifestyle or their choice of a profession was altered by their sibling's death. A few developed certain phobias that they attributed to particular experiences around their sibling's suicide. John (Ch. 2), for instance, became claustrophobic. He witnessed the sealing of his brother's casket, then, soon after, found himself in the back seat of a two-door car driving past the cemetery where he envisioned his brother imprisoned underground. Now he finds himself terrified by the very notion of being trapped himself in the back seat of a car. Another woman told me that she became incapable of dealing with closed doors, either literal or metaphorical, which she attributed both to her sister's hiding out in her room with the door closed and to her parents' excluding her after the suicide.

The six people in this chapter attribute their subsequent life path and attitudes to the effects on them of their sibling's suicide. Alan developed a nearly pathological need to please his mother and make her happy, because his brother's life and death had so destroyed her. Ellen finds that her sister's suicide has made her afraid to reach out for her own happiness. Vincent became irresponsible and self-destructive, while Walter, who had been rather wild before his sister's suicide, became suddenly mature and responsible. Pamela developed a lifelong fear of other people in her life dying and abandoning her, and came to feel responsible for the well-being of everyone she came in contact with. Sam took over his brother's personality and interests and lived a large part of his life as his brother. He feels that most aspects of his life have been shadowed by his brother's suicide, including his career path and his relationships with women.

The people who were young at the time of the suicide, perhaps not surprisingly, seemed to experience the deepest and most far-reaching effects. It seems very clear that all of them could have greatly benefited from professional help and counseling, yet, for the most part, none was available to them. The potential impacts on them as siblings of a suicide were largely ignored, often with painful, sometimes tragic, results.

Alan

In Chapter Four, Alan talked about his sense of guilt for not trying to help his brother during his years of self-destructive turmoil. Here he talks about the long-term effects on him of his brother's behavior and subsequent suicide, particularly in his relationship to his mother and his constant need to please her.

After fourteen years, I still harbor resentment at my brother, because his destructive behavior and his suicide had the long-term effect of robbing me of my own identity and burdening me with a self-defeating mission to be Super Son to my mother. I think every dutiful son has a desire to please his parents, and to achieve the things they want for him and present the grandchildren for them to play with. But my brother Jake did it in reverse. He was bent on displeasing the parents, and his behavior and the anguish he caused our parents put me in an unhealthy position. My need to please them, and later just my mother after my father's death, became almost pathological. Every thought, every experience, every decision would be one tenth me and nine tenths my mother. I feel as though I have been stuck in neutral all my adult life.

Going all the way back to when Jake was still living, I have imposed on myself, both consciously and unconsciously, a steadfast need to be a source of consistent happiness to my mother. She is the lone Holocaust survivor from her immediate family. She came to this country with nothing, and married a wonderful man who would later slowly, painfully wither away and die from Parkinson's disease. Her first-born son was brilliant, creative, and talented, only to become tortured, self-destructive and eventually a suicide. And then there's me—her last hope. I have declared myself to be her last hope for happiness in life, so every decision, and every thought and action has been with her in mind. I always think of her before myself, and this has made me, ironically, a major disappointment to her. Yes, I have what might be termed a career, and I'm married to my dreamgirl, who, thank Heaven, my mother adores, but it could be a lot better.

We haven't dutifully presented her with grandchildren, for instance, and I wish I could tell her not to hold her breath. Children are supposed to be the crowning achievement in life and are supposed to be the one true source of life's fulfillment, but I've seen the downside of all that, and it's not pretty. I know my having children would make my mother very happy, after all the death and destruction in her life. She'll tell me about how a child changes your life and your outlook, and I'll say, "Are you telling me

Jake was worth it?" She says, "Absolutely." I hope the day will come when my wife and I just cast fate to the wind and go ahead and have children, but we keep saying, "Not yet, not now." I want to please my mother so badly. If I thought there was a guarantee that it would be all right, I would have children for her. But that's another effect on me of my brother's trouble and suicide—I've seen too much of the downside of creating life.

I'm not sure to what extent it was his life, which was one slow death, and then his suicide that has left me with such a crucial need to please and that has made me so self-defeating. It could be something else in me as well. But certainly all my mother had to do, once during one of the crises with my brother, was to give me a big hug and say, "You're one of the good guys." What a burden that imposed on me! I thought, "Great. Give me an anvil to carry, please." I have never sought to blame any of my own life disappointments or shortcomings on my brother's life and suicide. I hate the whole victimization culture. Yet I do see that his tortured life and eventual suicide did have that long-term effect on my life.

Ellen

In Chapter Four Ellen talked about her heavy feelings of self-blame and guilt about her sister Leah's suicide, instead of the anger that would be appropriate at a sister who killed herself on one's wedding day. Just recently, more than twenty years after her sister's death, Ellen went back into therapy to deal with her ongoing feeling of being deadened in her life, and realized that her problems have long roots into the past, in her childhood relationship with her sister and in her sister's eventual ill-timed suicide.

I went back into therapy two months ago to try to understand why I was feeling kind of dead, like a zombie. I have a wonderful husband, and two great children, and a nice home, and a life I enjoy, yet I feel a lack of vibrancy. What came up in therapy is that it's tied to when I was little. I was the middle sister. My parents had a label for each of us, and I was the "smart one" and the "pretty one". My parents used to call me that in front of my sisters, and it used to upset me when they did that. I was afraid my sisters would be envious, especially Leah. I asked my therapist, "What is envy?" He said that envy is hatred. I realized that I learned not to live up to my potential in order to protect myself against my sister's envy—and hatred.

I'm considering whether to get into analysis to help me understand this and get through it, and talked to the therapist about it. Part of the problem is that it would be very intensive and hard work, four sessions a week, and of course it would be very expensive. I was talking to the therapist about how long it would take, if it even were successful, since there are no guarantees that it would be—such long, hard work that might not even help. All of a sudden I started to cry, something I rarely do. I cried because I realized I have given my life to my sister, because I took her suicide so personally.

Leah always envied me and hated me, so I always played down my successes. Then, once, I dared to be happy and get married and have a joyous wedding. And that is when Leah killed herself, just when I was daring to be happy. Now, even after all these years, I don't dare seize happiness. I feel like a sacrificial lamb. I sacrifice my own happiness because I somehow owe Leah happiness. Even now, as I contemplate getting into analysis to try to reach for happiness, I think it would be too self-indulgent on my part, that I don't really deserve it. In my rational moments I know that I am bright, talented, good with people, good looking. Yet I don't reach out for things I could attain. My life has a deadened quality. All these years later I still find it very hard to tolerate happiness because my happiness made Leah unhappy. I can feel a twinge of anger at her about that, for how her actions have had this destructive effect on my life all these years later.

Vincent

Vincent's younger brother and only sibling, Kevin, killed himself twenty-two years before our interview, when Kevin was fourteen and Vincent was sixteen. After the suicide, Vincent felt cut loose. The adults in his life stopped setting limits on his behavior, afraid of pushing Vincent toward suicide. Everyone excused his subsequent behavior as the effect of his losing his brother, and Vincent became a "goof-off". He stopped trying to accomplish anything serious in his life, and became a drifter with little ambition or self-discipline. He feels that he never lived up to his potential, and is something of a failure, and attributes that in large part to his brother's suicide and its effect on the attitudes of parents and teachers toward him.

I was never very close to Kevin as a friend. We were relatively competitive for attention over the years, and our personalities were very different. My biological father and my mother broke up when we were very young, and my mother was always working when we were little. She got remarried after a few years to a man named Bill, whom I consider my real father, and things were settled and nice for a while, until they split up. I was twelve and Kevin was ten at the time, and I think it hurt him more than it did me. My mother got re-married again to a man with more money who didn't like either of us at all. There was always a rivalry between Kevin and me for attention, especially after my mother re-married for the second time.

Kevin and I had no interests that were really similar. He was a much more physical person than I was, and I was much more mental, so depending on the venue of the day—if it was a physical activity he would excel, and if it was a mental one, I would. We did very little pal-ing around as brothers would. I hung out mostly with older people, and he hung out mostly with other troubled kids. As a teen-ager he was always causing trouble, and I really disapproved of his behavior, but it was never my place to discipline him. I was never looked upon as the older brother who should set the model for him. He would have resisted that anyway. He was having a lot of difficulty growing up and was very frustrated by a lot of things. I think he needed…I think we both needed a father image that we never had.

Before his suicide, Kevin had been in and out of trouble for some time. He had been taking drugs, but nothing really physiologically devastating. He was using grass and taking pills occasionally, probably amphetamines. My mother and stepfather tried various things to straighten him out, but my stepfather was a person who wasn't really interested in or capable of doing a whole lot with his wife's children. Kevin had been visiting my step-father's son, and while he was there he had taken an overdose of pills and had been taken to a hospital. It was not considered particularly serious, as I recall. There was no psychiatric evaluation or counseling. They just sent him home. I think that attempt wasn't a serious one, but more a twisted cry for help because of all the other stuff that was going on.

While he was at home, it caused a lot of distress in the family, especially for my mother. He and I had a fight about his overdosing. I wasn't convinced that his suicide attempt was in earnest. I thought it was just an attempt to get attention and upset my mother. I yelled at him, "If you really want to do it right, you'd use a gun!"

Not long after, the next-door-neighbor called me at my summer job and told me that Kevin had shot himself. People came to get me and take me back to the house. It was very mixed up. My mother was in hysterics, and my step-father was pretty bewildered and didn't know what to do. My stepbrother went to a liquor store to get some fortification for my stepfather and offered me some, but I said no. Then my stepfather's ex-wife came and offered me some kind of medication that she had, and I said no again. Everyone was trying to give me drugs. It was kind of weird. We went away for a few days and just kind of sat around in shock, while my Mom's friends cleaned up the mess. When we came back, his room had been re-papered and re-carpeted. All his stuff had been boxed and put away. And that was that.

After that I went through a combination of teen-age-dom coupled with the ability to do anything I wanted, because I had an excuse. Up to that point I had been doing very well in school, taking Russian and doing all the things that I wanted, and enjoying it. But after Kevin's suicide, I kind of fell apart and stopped doing anything that required any effort whatsoever. I had a lot of guilt about it, about how I was behaving and about what I had said to Kevin about shooting himself. I was sent to a psychiatrist for a while, who was a very strange person. He was going blind, and he would tell me that because of that he felt he could see more. I told my mother, "You're really wasting your money. This guy is nuts." So that was the end of that. I was also put on tricyclic anti-depressants, which are normally given to people who have a psychosis, but they were prescribed by a family doctor who had probably read somewhere that they might help. I was given those without any regard for their affect on me, or whether I should be monitored, or what they would do. I was also given a completely open-ended prescription for Valium, which I immediately began to abuse.

I started goofing off. When I was seeing the psychiatrist, I asked him for a note so I wouldn't have to go to gym. I would go to the library and read all day. I didn't participate in any classes. Everyone said, "That's fine. His brother killed himself." There was no one there to discipline me. My step-father couldn't. He was afraid to at this point. My mother couldn't, because she was a basket case. There was no one else I could look to in my life. No one. There was no one there to say, "You're going in the wrong direction. It's time you wised up." That was really what I needed.

Then I had an episode. I was at a movie called "The New Centurions". In it a policeman kills himself by putting a gun in his mouth. I was with a friend. I saw that, and I got up and walked out of the theater into the street and hitchhiked all the way to the city where my "real" father Bill lived. It gets kind of complicated after this, and hard to talk about. I began an affair with Bill's wife. It's nothing I'm proud of, and nothing that, had I been a rational person, I would have done. But when you're sixteen and you're abandoned…My father Bill more or less felt responsible for himself. I couldn't get anything from him, so I got myself into a situation for a while that kind of gave me some kind of support. Bill's wife was a high-priced call girl before she married him, not a motherly or nurturing person. She wasn't particularly thinking about my welfare, but probably was just looking for the kind of things that a woman in her early twenties wants from a sixteen-year-old guy. Our relationship was just primarily sex. I got into it, I think, because my brother's suicide had freed me of any responsibility.

I was able to use his suicide as an excuse. Anything goes. Without anyone there to straighten me out, I was able to have that affair. I was a mess. Looking back on it, I think having that affair was both a crime of opportunity and a method to punish myself even more. The amount of guilt I felt about what I was doing to my Dad without him knowing made me feel even worse. I needed to make myself feel bad, because I didn't think I felt bad enough over my brother. In a lot of ways I didn't miss him. And when you're a teenager, you think "Ah, I'm supposed to feel this great loss," but I didn't feel that.

I think with a lot of people when someone kills himself, they're left with the shock of it and the "Why?". In my case, I didn't really have a "Why?" feeling. It was something he had tried before, and he was a very unhappy person, and he was unable to adjust to the things that people around him wanted him to do. Part of me thought it was better that he had killed himself. He was out of the picture. My Mom didn't have to be upset anymore. But another part of me felt, "He was your brother, and you were never as close as you should have been with your brother." There were a lot of conflicting things. I think I was just attempting to heap enough guilt on myself so I could start feeling pain, because I felt that was what I was supposed to feel, and I didn't.

I really screwed up that senior year in school and didn't pass anything except English. A teacher offered to try to get me into a good college, but I said "No." And that was stupid. I went to various small, stupid colleges. I never pursued much. I just destroyed anything that had been good and ongoing in my life. I never got a degree. I have enough credits where I could probably take a couple of classes and get a degree. But I never finished up anything after that. I was a professional student for a long time, and then just started working. I never got back into the academic life. I've worked at one thing or another, but never had a profession or very much ambition.

It's hard to say how different my life would have been if my brother hadn't killed himself. Maybe it's just an excuse. Maybe I would be a mess anyway. I believe one's personality is not just made up of one's environment and experiences only, or of one's genes only. It's a combination. Part of my problem is genetic, but my upbringing and my brother's suicide are definitely contributing factors. It was just a bad time for it to happen. There's no good time, but for me it was a time when a young person is met with a lot of decisions, and needs people to point him to get him on the right path. And there was no one to do that then. I was on auto-pilot and just did whatever I wanted. So the effect of my brother's suicide on my life is that it allowed me to destroy myself.

Walter

Walter's younger sister and only sibling, Corinna, killed herself a little over a year before our interview, when she was nineteen and he was twenty-four. Walter feels that his life has been defined by the deaths he has experienced. After his father's death, he became an irresponsible "wild man" for several years. But his sister's suicide changed his path entirely, and, unlike Vincent, he matured, virtually overnight, into a responsible person. Although it is still only a short time since his sister's death, and he doesn't know what other long-term effects he will experience, Walter feels that his sister's suicide transformed him permanently.

Of all the brother-sister relationships that I've ever seen I thought Corinna's and mine was definitely the closest. We would talk on the phone all the time. Any time there was a family gathering, like Thanksgiving or Christmas, we would joke around a lot and just have a good time. We didn't have a lot in common as far as interests or ambitions went, though. I don't think we were competitive, although maybe she was competing with me. We just wanted different things and were into different things.

Corinna had been depressed for many years, since about twelve or thirteen, basically soon after my Dad died. She was pretty young when it happened, and she just never recovered. I think my Dad had something to give her that she never ended up getting anywhere else. As children, we're looking for approval from our parents, and then we rebel against them and hate them, but ultimately we still need that approval. He wasn't around to approve or disapprove or anything else.

My sister had tried to commit suicide about six times in various ways, but they were ways that were more cries for help than serious attempts. I guess finally she just set her mind to it. She dropped out of college and came home. She had broken up with a guy who was, I guess, the love of her life. She sort of went static. She just went baseline—no response, no coherent anything, just dead to the world. For the last six or eight months of her life I was just another moving figure around her. I understand, because I've been prone to depressions myself. I can empathize with not being able to pay attention to or worry about the people around you, because you have your own problems. But it was pretty eerie. For two weeks before it happened my Mom and I must have talked about what we were going to do about Corinna for a total of thirty hours or so.

The night Corinna killed herself was unusual, because, for once, the whole family was there. I was there visiting for the last time before I left for Chicago to live. I was up in my room reading—it was about one in the morning. I heard her come in, and then a little while later I heard a sort of "pop" in the back yard. I got a chill down my spine when I heard that, but then I thought, "Oh, it's probably a squirrel." It wasn't very loud. I thought maybe it was an acorn hitting the roof. About seven the next morning my Mom came in and said that Corinna wasn't in her bed. So we looked around, and I found her in the back yard. She had shot herself in the mouth.

My Mom pretty much collapsed right there. I called 911 and the police came. And then there was sort of a deluge of family. My Mom just stayed in her room with the door locked, even though there were a million people there. I did whatever arrangements had to be done, calling in the uncles and so on. Then, after the funeral, I still came up to Chicago to live about a week later.

It didn't really come as a shock. The one thing that Corinna ever enjoyed doing was being a stage manager. That was sort of her calling. She had stage-managed a number of plays, and she really set the stage for this, too. She had rehearsed so many times. She really stage-managed her own suicide. It obviously came as a tactile shock finding her there and suddenly not having this person in my life any more. But she hadn't really been in my life for a long time. She'd been pretty wrapped up in her own problems.

Corinna's suicide marked a turning point. My life has been somewhat delineated by the deaths in my life. I think I sprang into consciousness around six or seven when my Granddad died. That was when I first really understood that I was an individual in the world, and this man was not going to be in it anymore. Then, when my Dad died, I felt sort of let loose. I could do whatever I wanted, and there was nobody to stop me. My father had been the rule maker; he was a John Wayne look- and act-alike. My mother worked, and she was placed in the rule-making position only reluctantly. I turned into a real wild man after my father died. I dropped out of high school, and traveled all over the country, and did all these Jack Kerouac things. But after my sister killed herself, I became a regular sort of tax-paying citizen. I moved to Chicago, and got a job, and went back to school.

Corinna's death took all the anger out of me, basically. I guess before that I was angry at parental figures—Authority, The Man. I'm not sure what it was about my sister's suicide that changed me. Maybe, in part, it was seeing what it did to my mother. I don't get depressed very much anymore as I used to. I think those depressions were my telling myself that I wasn't happy with my current situation and that I needed to do something different. That was always how I'd break the depression—by jumping on my motorcycle and heading off into the night. That doesn't happen anymore.

Now I'm pretty much settled down here. I've held the same job for a while, and I'm in school, and I feel a lot more solid. That need to get out and get away is nowhere near as strong. My Mom and I are essentially peers now. Once my sister died, there weren't issues about discipline or how children should be raised. We were just two adults, my Mom and I. Now we just sort of call each other up for advice, and she helps out with school bills, and it's very much more relaxed. I can't tell yet what other effects Corinna's suicide may have on me, but I feel that it changed my life permanently. I was beginning to move in that direction, but my sister's death made me mature a lot faster than I would have otherwise.

Pam

Pam was sixteen when her oldest brother Larry, who was twenty-four, shot and killed himself. Although she didn't know her brother very well, since he was so much older and spent a lot of time away from home traveling, his sudden suicide had a powerful effect on her view of life and her relationships with people. Pam developed a deep fear that other people in her life, and even dogs, would die suddenly. Ten years later she still has difficulty letting go of people, and feels accountable for everyone else's well-being, because she is acutely aware that life is short and that she could lose anyone suddenly. Various events and deaths in the family that occurred after Larry's suicide only deepened that awareness. Pam was not the only sibling who was deeply affected by her brother's death; she describes these repercussions for the rest of her family in Chapter Ten.

I don't really remember Larry very well. It's more like remembering someone who was a cousin or something, whom you've met a few times. Throughout my life he was in and out of rehabs or off to follow another dream of some sort—to campaign for some politician or protest a nuclear power plant—so he wasn't home much. When he was home, he was always trying to give me advice, because he'd been somewhere I hadn't been. As an eight-year-old I wasn't interested in hearing about the social ramifications of what the FBI did to the government. He was always very politically correct and involved in political things, and I was too young to appreciate that. So we weren't very close. He was kind of fanatical, always protesting and marching for peace and telling the people around him what was wrong with their behavior. It wasn't that he was overbearing about it—I know that he was well-liked—it's just that those are my most vivid memories of him.

When Larry was growing up, he was involved in drugs a lot. He was really intelligent, so he didn't see a lot of kindness in the world. I think he always saw things in their black sense, instead of seeing the positive. So he would O.D. periodically when I was growing up, and one of my basic memories of him was when I was about eight. He was about six feet, and I was a little eight-year-old girl walking him around to keep him awake until the ambulance got there.

I know my brother and sisters miss him terribly. I didn't really have the opportunity to miss him. I was just part of the family that he destroyed. I was always closer to Adele, the twin that came right after him, than I was to him. I got to see the destruction that his death caused the people I cared about. Even though I cared about him as a brother, he wasn't in my life. He would show up every two years or so and make my parents really happy, my father especially. Then he'd get an idea and go off again.

Larry went to college off and on, but he would quit every time he succeeded. He would get an A in Business Law, for instance, then quit the week before finals. He didn't like to succeed. The last time he was in college, he was getting A's, and he just up and moved out to Montana, to campaign for a Libertarian politician. Everything seemed to be going pretty well. It had been eight years since he'd had any kind of problems where he was O.D.'ing or anything like that. I understand that what happened was that he was going out with a girl, and she left him and went back to her abusive former boyfriend. He got drunk and shot himself.

Our family usually doesn't get together much—we never got along that well—but that Saturday the whole family was here. We were all taking pictures to send to him, but none of us thought to call him. I always felt guilty about that. The next morning the police called with some kind of garbled message. They were looking for Larry's family, but they mangled his name. My mother got really upset and tried to call back, because I guess she had some kind of a sense that something was wrong. It was about seven o'clock in the morning, and my mother woke us all up screaming, "Something's happened to your brother!" over and over. It was a nightmare. We all got wakened out of a deep sleep for that. We had a Labrador Retriever at the time, and she started howling. The whole house was really upset, and I guess she felt it.

When you grow up in a dysfunctional household, you're always waiting for the other shoe to drop, so I figured that was the other shoe. My girlfriend had spent the night before, and I had had a really good time with her, and I guess I felt guilty for having a good time. It was a long time before I wanted to have a good time again. I always figured whenever I had a good time, something horrible would happen, so I didn't want to have good times. I didn't want to be comfortable and happy.

In the years since, a lot of terrible things happened in my family. My other brother Wes went through a lot of drug problems and psychotic episodes and has ended up a homeless person, and my sister Adele tried to kill herself. It seemed that every time I tried to pull myself out, something else would happen that was just overwhelming to a person who was going through puberty at the same time. I was 230 pounds and having a lot of trouble coping. I suffered from depression, and the doctors put me on antidepressants. And it seems as though every April since Larry died, somebody else would die. My grandmother and my grandfather and my other grandmother—someone was always dying. My boyfriend died. I think this is the first time I've had three solid years of not having to go to funerals.

My father has had three open heart surgeries. They're good for about seven years, so everyone in the family kind of ticks down the time since the last one. So I keep waiting for the other shoe to drop. Who's going to go next?

It's a very strange way of thinking, but I'm always afraid someone else is going to die. The Labrador we had when my brother killed himself, the one who howled, was very special to me, and I got extremely paranoid about her after Larry died. I would be in the middle of class in school, and I'd get up and call my mother and say, "How's the dog? Is the dog still alive?" I was terrified that the dog was going to die. Finally, when we had to have her put to sleep, I couldn't stop crying. I've never really gotten over her.

I never wanted another dog, but people keep thrusting these dogs into my arms. The man who gave me this one kept saying, "You'll love him!" And sure I do, but this dog's entire life has been an overcompensation. He's completely neurotic and spoiled, because I know he doesn't have that long to live, and I can't cope with that. I still to this day cry over the Labrador, and I get teary-eyed over the thought of living without this one.

Since my brother died, death has been one of the uppermost thoughts in my life. I treat people differently, because I know that they're not going to live forever. In some ways it makes me a nicer person, but I don't want to be nice to everyone all the time. It's just that I dread the thought of standing over someone's grave and thinking, "Oh my God, I was nasty to him." I feel I have to be nice and supportive to everyone, even people I actually hate. There's a man at work who is suicidal. I really dislike him, but I spend a lot of time talking to him and trying to help him. Even though I hate him, I know what he's going through, and I can't walk away. There's another kid in the neighborhood that I used to spend hours on the phone with, because his mother beat him, and I was always afraid that he was going to try to take his life. I guess I was always afraid that everybody was going to try to kill themselves.

One of my ex-boyfriends called up a while back, because his wife had kicked him out, and he wanted to get back together with me. I had been really devastated when he got married to this other woman, but I was over it and I really didn't want to see him or even talk to him. But I still stayed on the phone with him for an hour and a half trying to help him. I keep feeling that I'm accountable for all these losers that I dated. That's one of the reverberations of Larry's suicide and everything since. I feel I have to take care of everybody. I fell into that role in my family, trying to keep Adele from thinking about Larry and trying to keep my mother from falling apart.

Letting go is really a big problem. I'm still in contact with all my ex-boyfriends. They all find it easy to call me when they have a problem. And I can't throw things out that meant something to me once upon a time. I have a football shirt that one of my boyfriends had, and it's still upstairs getting moth-eaten and falling apart, and I just won't throw it out. For a while I had a boyfriend who was abusive, and he came across an old I.D. bracelet I had that another boyfriend, the one who died, had given me. He kept insisting that I should throw it out, and I refused, and he beat me up. I can't let go of possessions that I think are going to remind me of dead people or former boyfriends.

After ten years I don't think the healing is done. I don't know if it ever will be. I know I don't carry my teddy bear around the way I did when Larry first died, and I don't obsess about the same things. But I know that there is a certain aspect of my personality that is completely neurotic when it comes to death and suicide and losing people. It seems as though every last thing I suffer is even harder. It really is.

Sam

Sam was fifteen when his seventeen-year-old brother and only sibling, Barry, hanged himself in the room next door. Up until then they had not been particularly close as siblings, and they had different personalities and interests. Yet, afterwards, Sam adopted his brother's interests and submerged his own personality in that of his brother.

Twenty-three years later, Sam is beginning to see that his brother's suicide had a profound and long-term effect on his career choices, his own personality, and his relationships with women.

Barry and I were never very close, and I think he resented me for being born in the first place. He never wanted me around when we were growing up, and he wouldn't let me play with him and his friends usually. As we got to be teen-agers things were a little better. He'd let me help out a little when he was working on his motorcycle, or he'd let me listen to a record. We even double-dated a few times.

But mostly he was kind of distant. There were two things he liked to do—work on his motorcycle and read these weird books. He would hole himself up for hours reading books about parapsychology and existentialism and kind of dark philosophy. Everything he read, I realized afterwards, was grim and depressing. After he killed himself, we found out that he kept journals, too, and they were just dark and bleak. Nobody realized how depressed he really was at the time. He was also compulsively neat and orderly. The stuff in his room had to be arranged just so, and when he was working on the motorcycle, he would lay out the tools in perfect lines. He had a method for everything and all these little rules for himself. Looking back, I wonder if he didn't have a real diagnosable illness, but at the time it just seemed as though that was just his personality.

When I was a little kid, I really looked up to him. He was my big brother, and I thought he was great. But by the time we were in our teens, I began to think he was a little odd with that compulsive orderliness he had. I was pretty untidy myself, and his compulsive tidiness kind of annoyed me. We were also different kinds of people. I was more outgoing and into sports, and the stuff I liked to read was more normal, I think, for someone my age—adventure, and action, and thrillers.

I guess it's been said before that hindsight is 20-20, but I think I should have seen it coming. Of course, I didn't know how really dark his mind was, but I did see him reading all this dark stuff, and I saw how withdrawn and moody he was getting. He had a girlfriend for a while, who was kind of an odd person herself. I think they talked about these books and shared a fascination for morbid things. My parents didn't like her at all, because they thought she had a kind of morbid spell over him and that she was a bad influence, so they wouldn't let him see her anymore. That probably depressed him even more. Also, our house was very oppressive. Our parents were not very warm, either with us or with each other. I think there was trouble in their marriage even then, and there was a lot of tension. Also, they had extremely strict rules for us, and in the last few months before Barry killed himself they got even stricter.

Barry hanged himself one evening when my parents were having a party downstairs. I was already asleep, and I awoke to my mother screaming. He had rigged it up somehow so that when he hanged himself, the door to his room would swing open, so my parents would see him hanging there when they passed by his room to go to bed. It was really horrible in every way.

Afterwards, it was really odd. I went back to school a couple of days later, and nobody said anything to me about it. I guess they didn't know what to do or what to say, so everyone kind of avoided me. No one offered me any kind of counseling. This was twenty-three years ago, and I don't think my school even had a counselor except for maybe a guidance counselor for deciding on colleges. There was still a stigma around getting psychological help, and my parents were the kind of people who never would have even considered it, anyway. So I had no kind of support from anywhere. My parents never talked about it, and there was a big shroud of secrecy and silence over everything.

Up until then I think I was being a normal teenager—a little rowdy, a little rebellious—but now I became like a little adult. I became the Good Son. I never got into trouble, never rocked the boat. I became an A student. I think I sensed that my brother's suicide was the last straw as far as my parents' marriage went, and I was trying to keep everything glued together by being very,

very, very good. I never really had a childhood after my brother's death, because I was too busy being a responsible little adult.

The really strange thing that happened after Barry's death was that I, to all intents and purposes, became my brother. I had never been all that interested in motorcycles, but now I had inherited the motorcycle, and I became obsessed with working on it the way Barry used to. I stopped doing sports and became much quieter and more controlled. I was very careful in how I handled myself so I wouldn't upset my parents, and I also took on some of Barry's compulsions. I never became quite as compulsive as he was, but I did develop a need to be very orderly, and I would figure out how to do everything with the maximum efficiency.

I didn't really realize what was happening, and it's only now that I got into therapy that I'm beginning to see how my brother's suicide has affected my whole life since then. I think on some unconscious level I became my brother in order to save my parents' marriage. I think I felt somehow that since his death had weakened my parents' marriage even more, that if I became my brother, that would somehow patch it back up. He would still be in the world, and my parents would therefore be okay. Of course, none of that was conscious at the time.

Another thing that happened about a year or so later was that I began seeing Barry's old girlfriend. She was in my class at school, and we started getting together after school. I knew my parents wouldn't approve of it at all, and it was the one sort of rebellious thing I did, although they never knew that I was seeing her. I never took her out on a date or invited her to my house or anything. The funny thing was that I didn't really like her all that much. She was a pretty strange person, and she had a kind of morbid mind, but I was obsessed with her. We didn't talk about Barry much as I recall. Mostly she talked about her weird thoughts and philosophical theories. She was pale and kind of waif-like, and she had long black hair. I would just sit there looking at her—I thought she was fascinating to look at—but I didn't talk much myself. It didn't last very long, I think because

I must have bored her, and the next year I went off to college and I didn't see her until years later.

When I was in college, though, I kept getting into relationships with waif-like girls with long black hair. I was still being my brother and still being the responsible one, getting good grades and all the rest. Then when I graduated, when I could have gone on into a profession of some kind, I became of all things an automobile mechanic. I felt that I was a kind of nobody, so I worked at this nothing kind of job. In fact, I was a nobody, because I had submerged my own personality and taken on my brother's life and my brother's interests and my brother's personality. I was not myself anymore. The only thing that I didn't take on of his was his fascination with the kind of dark or morbid books he used to read.

I think my life would have been entirely different if my brother hadn't killed himself. I wound up with a faceless job that was not very interesting to me, and I married yet another waif-like, black-haired woman. It was not a very good marriage. She didn't think I had enough drive, and that was true, although I did eventually move up from auto mechanic to a more administrative position. But I never got beyond that, because I think I didn't want to stand out. I felt I had to stay in the background the way I had with my parents after Barry killed himself. Then I got involved with another woman, and my wife discovered it, and that was the end of my marriage. The other woman also reminded me of my brother's old girlfriend, but that didn't last very long either.

For years and years after that my life was kind of just mindless. I didn't know who I was, and I wore a certain face in the world but I was also faceless, in a way. I kept getting involved with women who reminded me of my brother's girlfriend and kept plodding along in a job that was meaningless. Then a few years ago I ran into the old girlfriend and we got back together for a while. She was a little less weird by then, but what was odd was how all we seemed to talk about was my brother. She kept dredging up memories of him, and it was as if I didn't exist for her except as Barry's brother.One day I woke up and realized that my life was intolerable. Being with my brother's girlfriend with her always obsessing about him, and being in a meaningless job, and feeling like a hollow man—it all came down on me. I got depressed and considered killing myself. Finally I was in such a state that I got into therapy about three years ago. Now my only regret is that I didn't do that a long, long time ago. If only I had had help years and years ago when I was still a teen-ager, my whole life could have been very different. Therapy is hard work, but it's helping me to change and become myself. Now I can begin to see what a powerful impact my brother's suicide had, and how it has affected my whole life.

Chapter Seven
Experiences of Very Young Children

In the course of interviewing men and women whose siblings had taken their own lives, it became clear that, as a general rule, the younger the survivor was at the time of the suicide, the more far-reaching its impact was apt to be. All of the people in Chapter Six who described long-term reverberations in their lives were either teenagers or young adults at the time of their sibling's death. Two of the people I talked with were even younger. Reba was ten when her sixteen-year-old brother killed himself. Scott was only seven at the time of his sixteen-year-old half-brother's suicide.

For both of them, the events around their brother's suicide are indelibly etched in their minds, as is often the case with significant events that occur when one is young and still very impressionable. But, because they were so young, there is also an aura of mystery around their brothers' deaths. How could a child so young really make sense of an event so bizarre and incomprehensible? Both were still in a pre-rational stage in their lives, when children's thinking is magical, rather than logical. Because young children are egocentric, they tend to feel that they are somehow the cause of events that happen in the outside world. For instance, when young children's parents divorce, they are apt to feel that it happened because they themselves were "bad". Both Reba and Scott felt predictably guilty over their brother's suicide, feeling it was caused by something they themselves did, although neither knew how.

Both Reba and Scott are aware that their brothers' suicides had far-reaching effects on their own lives. The idea of committing suicide was a thinkable option from very early on, at an age when most children would have no concept of it. Whether to follow suit became a very real question for both of them. Other long-term effects are harder for them to tease out from the effects of other childhood experiences, but both sense that their brothers' suicides played an important role in their later decisions and feelings, and in later events.

Reba

When I interviewed Reba, it was fifty years after her brother Eric's suicide, yet she remembers the event itself in clear detail. She doesn't remember grieving for her brother, yet she did feel an elusive sense of guilt that didn't become clear to her until years later in therapy. She feels that Eric's suicide had many long-term effects on her life, including her choice of marriage partners and her own suicide attempts, but it is not easy to see how much of that is tied directly to her brother's death and how much is the consequence of a quite disturbed early family life. Reba has suffered many losses and troubles over the years since Eric's death, several of them in some way apparently related to it. But over time, her brother's suicide has tended to pale in importance, in comparison to other deaths and difficult experiences Reba has lived through.

My early family life was very cold and regulated, and throughout my childhood my mother was very depressed and withdrawn. I didn't know why she was depressed until I was around fifteen, when I discovered that there had been another son who died two weeks before I was born. I was raised by Polish maids. My father was very authoritarian and controlling, and believed that children should be seen and not heard. There was no warmth between my parents. My mother would sit in a chair after dinner and read a book. My father would go into his study and listen to the news on the radio, or read the paper, or go to the Elk's Club. I think one of the two nights a week he would go to the Elk's Club, he was actually going to visit a mistress. I don't think my parents had a sexual relationship after I was born. They had separate beds, and in the country where we went in the summer they even had separate rooms, but they stayed married.

My entire life was very regulated. I would go to school and come home and do my homework. At dinner I would sit at the table and not say a word. Children weren't supposed to talk. I wanted to eat in the kitchen with the maid. It wasn't until I was a teenager that I saw how other families lived. I was amazed. People would sit and talk with each other. People were informal—they would walk out of the bathroom brushing their teeth. I saw that there was a whole other way for families to be.

My brother was the only one who gave me a sense of value, except for my dog. My sister and I shared a room and fought a lot—sibling stuff. She hated taking me along anyplace. But I really admired my brother and thought he was great. He would let me come up to his room where he had an amateur radio and his balsa wood airplanes. He let me help make them and share in his hobbies. I felt good being with him. He was the only one who was warm to me and liked me.

Looking back, I can understand why he killed himself. When I turned sixteen years later, my life was so regulated by my father that I hated him. He made me work at his store from the time I was thirteen, and I had to get good grades, and abide by all his rules. It had been the same for my brother. There was a long, long list of shoulds. The message was: "Behave!". And then there was my mother. Until the day she died, she never showed any emotion. She never touched us or said she loved us. I can imagine how that affected my brother. She provided meals, and everything ran nicely. We had all kinds of lessons, but it was not a warm family.

Eric ran away from the family the year before he killed himself, and went to New York. But my father hired detectives, and they found him. He didn't want to come back, but it was very difficult for a fifteen-year-old to get along *in the city, so he came back to this regulated, stifling homelife with the dominating father and cold mother. My father and Eric fought all the time.*

He killed himself on a Friday night. My parents were very religious Jews, and we went to temple every Friday. Eric stayed home. After temple, we went to deliver some Girl Scout cookies, instead of coming right home. When we got back, I went inside, but my father went to park the car in the two-car garage, and discovered my brother. The other car's motor was running and Eric was dead on the floor by the exhaust. I was in my room and I looked down into the garage and saw the fire trucks and the police and all the commotion. On the death certificate it was listed as suicide, but my father's pride wouldn't accept that. He went to court to try to have it changed to "accident", but it wasn't changed. My mother thought that it was more a cry for help, and that Eric didn't really want to kill himself. She thought that he expected us to come home earlier and save him, and that if we hadn't gone to deliver those cookies, he wouldn't have died.

Afterwards, I felt guilty. It wasn't until years later when I got into therapy that I understood why. I had repressed the memories for many years, but then remembered that my brother had abused me sexually. He would come into my room when he was thirteen or fourteen, and it was dark, and he would touch me. I never said anything to anybody about it. So, when he killed himself, what was a kid to think? Was it my fault? I thought he killed himself because I did something wrong, and he did something wrong. I felt that it was this bad thing we did together that had caused his death.

I must have missed him a lot, but I can't remember really grieving. I went on with the routine, going to school, taking piano lessons and acting lessons and dancing lessons. I went through the routines as was expected of me. I was a good girl. By the time I was nineteen I developed ulcers. After Eric's death my father became a complete workaholic, and my mother again got depressed. I remember her sitting in a chair and reading a book and never turning the pages. Her depression went on for years.

I was also depressed. I was skinny and wore glasses, but when I became seventeen and eighteen I developed and became attractive. I started to date, and discovered that men gave me a feeling of self-worth. My brother used to make me feel good, and all of a sudden men could make me feel good. I felt more worthwhile. My relationships with men were connected with my brother, and later on I found husbands who I thought were like him.

My life after that was full of deaths and troubles. I got married when I was 23, and two weeks later my father died. My husband had psychiatric problems, and all his life he was seeing psychiatrists and being hospitalized. I had a daughter who was born with brain damage that affected her physically on one side, so she needed a lot of physical therapy. She had an epileptic seizure, too. Right after she was born I went into a postpartum depression. Everyone was saying, "How wonderful that you had a baby!", and I felt, "The hell with it". I tried to kill myself. I think I was somehow imitating my brother, looking back at his way of dealing with life. I put the baby in a room and closed the door, then turned on the gas in the oven. My husband happened to come home suddenly and saved me.

A couple of years later I had a miscarriage and then, finally, another baby. My husband was very controlling and verbally abusive. Finally, after fifteen years, I divorced him and took my two children and started life all over again, I went back to college to become a teacher. But after a year, I went back to my husband, and soon after that he died, in the locked ward of the psychiatric hospital.

I raised my children alone. When my older daughter was in her teens, she ran away from home, and that brought up memories of my brother and fears for her because of him. I couldn't find her, but eventually she came home on her own. At some point she was on drugs, and took an overdose. She nearly died twice from overdosing. It seemed as though history was trying to repeat itself.

Some years later I remarried. The man was very charming and handsome, and we thought we were in love and that we could communicate. But he had had a pattern of dating a lot of women before we were married, and he ended up having an affair with a girl in his therapy group. I found out and told him he had to make a choice. I thought he had given her up, but then I found out he was still seeing her. I got very depressed. I had given up my home, and moved away from my family and my children. I tried to kill myself with an overdose of Valium, but my husband just walked out of the door and said, "I'm going to choir practice. If you want to kill yourself, kill yourself." I decided I wasn't going to kill myself and forced myself to throw up. Again, I think Eric's suicide played a part in my attempting to kill myself a second time.

Some time later my husband died on the operating table, and I became a widow again. I've experienced so many deaths, I can almost order a funeral over the telephone. The worst thing that happened, though, was my daughter's death. She had been living with a man who physically abused her. She had to quit her job at the hospital because she was so battered. She had an epileptic seizure and fell to the floor and died. He was charged with her murder, but was acquitted. The death of my daughter was the most horrendous event in my life, far worse than my brother's suicide or any of the other deaths.

Looking back, I can see that my brother's suicide had some long-term effects on me. I married men who seemed like him, and tried suicide as he had. It had a shaping effect on my life, but it doesn't feel any more like the most terrible thing that happened. His suicide is all wrapped around my whole early family life. It's not just his suicide, but my parents, too, that made me what I am. They're all tied in together. I feel a lot happier in my life now, and I find a lot of catharsis through my art. But I still find that I choose to be alone too much. I think that has to do with my family background and losing my brother, as well as all the other losses. I'm afraid of getting hurt again. I worry that someone will hurt me, or die suddenly, so I'm afraid of getting too close to anyone. So I can see that there are ways my early family life and my brother's suicide continue to affect my life.

Scott

The suicide of Scott's sixteen-year-old half brother, Stuart, was an extremely bewildering experience for a seven-year-old. On the day of the suicide, his family didn't tell him what was happening for quite a while, and when he finally found out from a neighbor child, he couldn't understand why it had happened. Like Reba, he felt guilty about what his part might have been, and thought that he must have been somehow responsible. His brother's suicide has had far-reaching consequences for Scott, who is now twenty-five. Thoughts of suicide are constantly on his mind, and he feels that he will eventually follow suit; what little psychological help he has had does not seem to have helped him very much. As the only surviving son, he feels that he has to carry the burden of living up to his parents' expectations, particularly his father's, even though their choice of a career for him is not what he wants for himself. Stuart's suicide has also had a lasting effect on Scott's relationships with other people. He finds it hard to form intimate relationships, because he fears they will die or abandon him, and he lives in dread of other people he is close to dying. His greatest fear is being abandoned by everyone and left alone in the world.

Stuart and I were close, but not very close. I looked up to him because he was eight years older than I was, but he could find me a bit of a pest or a burden. He could also be great fun for me to be around, and he did some nice things for me. We were too far apart in age to be rivalrous or competitive, although I was a bit of a snitch, as I recall. Even though we were half-brothers—he was my father's son from a previous marriage—we were raised as brothers, and shared a room. My mother was in the process of readying to adopt him as her own son, and I was happy about that.

I remember the day Stuart killed himself very well, but it was also very confusing and bewildering. My father was away on a fishing trip, and my mother and I were supposed to pick up my grandmother, who had spent the night with a friend, and then drive to the airport to pick up one of my two nieces, my older half-sister's daughter. Stuart didn't want to come along, so my mother left him behind to mow the lawn and other chores. After we picked up my grandmother, we all talked about the fact that we hadn't slept well the night before, because we had all had different kinds of bad dreams. When we got to the airport and picked up my niece, there came a call over the loudspeaker for my mom. She went away. Then she came back and was kind of upset. She said, "We're going to have to change what we're doing here," and she pulled Grandma aside. My mom left in her car, and a police car took Grandma and my niece and me. Nobody said anything to me about what was going on. On the way, we stopped at the hospital and dropped off my grandmother, and the police car took my niece and me home.

At the house there were several of my cousins from my father's side of the family, who were all about my brother's age. They kind of encouraged me and my niece to go outside and play. We couldn't figure out what was going on. I don't know if they'd said something about Stuart not being well, or if we just noticed he wasn't there. We were trying to figure out where Stuart was and what was happening. Finally, we got one of the neighbor girls aside, and she said he'd been taken to the hospital because he was sick. I went and confronted my oldest cousin, and he told me that Stuart had shot himself. I think by then he was dead. And then I cried for quite a while.

It was quite a shock. I knew what it was to be dead, from having lost my grandfather and the other sister from my dad's first marriage when I was five. I knew this meant that Stuart was gone, and I had been rather fond of him. One of my first reactions was that I decided his bed should stay the way it was. Sometime in the course of the day someone made the bed, and I went back and re-rumpled it as best I could. And I set out his shoes in front of the bed.

I had no idea why he did it, and my parents didn't really, either, at the time. When my dad found out what had happened, he went into shock and had to be sedated for about a week. *My dad became convinced that it was murder, but a cousin told us that he had been talking about suicide. My parents were very angry that the cousin hadn't told anybody. Nobody really knew why he did it. His mother had been pressuring him to come to visit, which my parents didn't want him to do, so maybe there was something going on there. We also knew that he had been involved in drugs from reading comments in his high school yearbook.*

People told me not to feel guilty about it, that it wasn't my fault. I don't think I ever felt that I caused it directly, but in a magical way I thought that the fact that we did fight quite a bit might have something to do with it, and I felt guilty about that. I had another morbid thought. My birthday was coming up, and Stuart had been telling me for some time that he was working on a special present for me. I used to wonder what the present would have been, and sometimes I thought his suicide was supposed to be the present. My mother thinks I still have guilt feelings over it, and maybe I do feel guilty still on some level.

Not too long afterwards my parents took all the guns out of the house, but sometime before they did, I remember that I was taking a gun that I had found—I don't know if it was the same one—and holding it to my head to see what it would be like to kill myself. I wasn't actually going to do it. It was more out of curiosity about how that felt.

I've been to see a couple of psychiatrists, but only for short periods. In the fourth grade I went into shock because a favorite teacher of mine was leaving the school and had not told me. I read about it in the school newspapaer. My mother decided this was related to Stuart, so they took me to see a psychiatrist. I don't remember most of what we talked about. I don't think I wanted to talk about it at the time. It didn't help very much. Then in high school there was a girl who apparently tried to kill herself. I became really upset over that and had to be taken to the teacher's office. I was crying, and at the same time I felt very angry at her. The only time I can really identify with being angry at my brother is that in the office I kept saying, "Don't you realize how terrible that is to the parents to do something like that?" But I wasn't sent to a psychiatrist at that point. In college I saw a counselor after my freshman and my sophomore years, someone a neighbor had recommended who was basically a child psychologist. Then in my junior year in college I was cutting myself, and the girl I was dating at the time told one of my teachers about me. I got roped into seeing the school counselor, but I really didn't like him, so I didn't attend the meetings.

My mother has an interest in psychology and is always giving me books on survivors of suicide and so on. She keeps looking for guilt feelings on my part, but I've never had anyone professionally say to me that I was suffering guilt feelings. She keeps expecting me to feel angry at Stuart, too. Once in college I found myself writing an imaginary dialogue between me and my brother. I didn't think it was particularly angry, but I said, "During all this time I felt I would give anything to have you back, but now that I think about it, if you could step back into existence today, I wouldn't want it." I showed it to my mom, and she said "Aha! You have this unresolved anger!" But I don't know that I ever really felt angry at him about it.

I'd say I have more identification than guilt over my brother's suicide. There are times when I go off in my head and think that how I would die would be to kill myself. But after all my parents have gone through, I couldn't do that to them. I often think that I'm going to live until my parents die, and after they die, I'll kill myself. I don't know if that thought would ever have occurred to me, or have occurred to me so strongly, if my brother hadn't killed himself. One of my first reactions to any rejection is to think of killing myself. I would say that in some way my brother's suicide sort of implanted the idea, maybe to follow suit, or just that it became an option. If I kill myself, it would be as a sort of memorial to my brother. I guess a lot of that feeling has to do with the way I looked up to him very much as an older brother, and I would be emulating him in a sense if I were to kill myself. I would do it for those reasons, quite aside from any feelings of depression I might have. I get depressed all the time.

I can talk to my family about Stuart's suicide, or to my very closest friends. Or I can talk about it to a complete stranger and be perfectly frank and examine it. But people who are somewhere in between I can't mention it to. I think that's because I feel a kind of sacredness about it. To talk about it with someone I don't know well would seem like defiling it or using it. I'm always afraid I'll use it in some way with another person, maybe for shock value.

After my brother's death, I began to feel responsible for living up to my parents' expectations. I don't know how much hope rested on the shoulders of my brother, maybe not too much, since he was a very rebellious teen-ager. I have allegedly never gone through a stage of rebellion against my parents. I've always had a very good relationship with them, and I'm sure that that comes from not wanting to rock the boat. My father told me that summer, and has often told me since, "Well, you're all I have left now." I was the last male child. I don't know if he said that to put pressure on me, but it did. It would be nice to have a big family of brothers and sisters to get lost in so that somebody else can be the architect, which is what my father wants me to be. I still think about that and that maybe I should become an architect. What I really want, and what I'm pursuing now, is to be an actor. But they were here just last week for a visit, and my father was asking about possibilities for architecture school, which I foolishly brought up in conversation. He also asked about girlfriends. I'm gay, and I haven't told my father. Everyone says that they think he probably knows, and he baits me occasionally. That's another of the expectations of the last male son—that I should get married and provide grandchildren to carry on the family name. Telling him, if I ever do, is going to be rough.

Stuart's death had a lasting effect on all my relationships. There were deaths after that, but that was kind of the culmination of a bad streak for our family. When I think about other people I'm close to, I think, "When are they going to die?" I hate living here so far away from home on some level, because I'm afraid that one of my parents or my grandmother or some older friends that I have are going to die, and I'll be so far away. I think about that all the time. How could I not stick around when someone's going to die? Even though I know they're not immediately going to die, I still think on that level. If someone were dying of cancer, I think it would be just horrible, because I wouldn't be able to bring myself to leave the room.

I hate making new relationships. I'm pretty shy, I guess, and I think I have enough friends where I don't want any more. I'm afraid of losing the people I already have. One of my roommates was going to paint each of us living in this house as our own worst fear. One person's was becoming a vampire, and another person's was having both his legs cut off and being thrown into the river. Mine was being the last person on earth. I have a terrible dread of other people dying. I'm terrible at goodbyes. I can waste hours doing nothing when people don't show up for appointments. I'm always terrified that I will be stood up. I feel betrayed and upset that I can't find out what's happened to the person. When I was a teenager and my parents went out, I would sit at home waiting for my parents to come home, thinking "What's happened to them?" I'm terrified of being left behind and abandoned.

Up until a couple of years ago I don't think that a day went by when I didn't think about my brother's suicide. And every summer still from about August eleventh—he killed himself on the thirteenth—until the fourteenth, my mother and father and myself go into a period of non-existing. We've generally been together during that time. I used not to go into work on the thirteenth. We'd all just kind of mope around the house, not really talking about it, but just waiting for that day to pass. The first summer that I didn't go through that was this past one. I'd been kind of warming up to it, but the thirteenth went by without my thinking about it. It's been eighteen years since my brother's death, but it continues to affect me. It was probably the most important event in my life. My life has been shaped by it.

Chapter Eight
Losing a Twin

I hesitated for a while about devoting a separate chapter to the experience of a twin's suicide, largely because one of the twins I interviewed, Megan, said that for many years being a twin made her feel like a freak. I felt somewhat uncomfortable about compounding that feeling by treating a twin's loss as unique. But the other twin I talked with, Linda, felt very strongly that a twin's experience is different from anyone else's. After her fraternal twin brother's suicide, Linda became obsessed with finding other suicide survivor twins, and eventually did. They, too, felt that their loss was unique.

How could losing a twin to suicide not be different from other siblings' experiences? Twins have been together since the moment of conception, and, in the case of identical twins like Megan, are genetic clones. They often experience a good deal of competition in their search for an individual identity, but at the same time have a closeness unlike anyone else's. Both of the people I talked with felt that twins have a special bond because of being in the womb together and sharing a single birthday. Both of them had a strong sense, just before their twin's suicide, that something was wrong and that something bad was about to happen. Megan feels that most twins have a kind of extra-sensory perception of what the other is feeling, and that, particularly with identical twins, "You literally feel what the other person feels."

Both Megan and Linda were devastated by the loss of their twin. Megan, in particular, felt that she wanted to die. The idea that her identical twin was dead made her own mortality painfully clear. Seeing her own face on her dead sister gave her the chilling feeling that she herself was dead. Linda felt that she had lost a physical part of herself. She became herself suicidal. Both felt very bewildered at losing someone who had always been in their life and was supposed always to be there in the years to come.

Linda

Linda's twin brother Lee shot and killed himself three and a half years before our interview, when they were thirty-two. Growing up, they were too competitive to be very close, and Linda had always felt closer to her younger brother Douglas. But they had become much closer as they got older, and she felt extremely worried for Lee in the few days before his suicide. His death made suicide an option for her, a viable choice in dealing with life's problems, and she was obsessed with thoughts of killing herself for months afterwards. She was also extremely angry at him for dislocating her life and for the devastation his suicide caused the family. In Linda's large family, her four other siblings all have problems themselves, from alcoholism to mental illness, and, knowing the statistics on multiple suicides, she is still waiting in dread for "the other shoe to drop".

Lee competed with me a lot when we were growing up, and he resented my doing better. My mother was very good about never dressing us the same, and we weren't put in the same sections in school. Still, it was a problem for him having a twin sister, and I didn't really know why until eighth grade. We had just had an English exam, and I had got an A-plus, which I usually did. Lee got an A or an A-minus. The reading teacher called me into his homeroom, and asked Lee in front of the class, "Why didn't you do as well as your sister?" I was in shock. It was the first time I understood why he didn't like me.

It was also the age. He had his friends, and he hung out with them and teased me. Lee was also a male chauvinist pig, and I'm a feminist, and we didn't get along for those reasons. In high school it just got worse. He went into Drugville, and I stayed away from it, because I saw the unhappiness it caused in our family. I was a goody-two-shoes and at the top of the class. I wrote a poem after he died, actually a collage. Under my name on one side is a collage of all my awards in high school, and under his name there's nothing. I put my class picture on my side and his receipt for the purchase of the gun on his side, along with his suicide note. On the receipt it says, "Final Sale. No Return." I entitled it "Twin Survivor-Guilt".

Yet, there was always a closeness between us. It was just unspoken. We felt a pride of ownership in our twinship. Later, we went to the same college, and started doing things together. We'd wait for each other after class and go have coffee. One semester we took archery together and had a great time. We won a trophy. That's one of my things that I treasure, because it was ours together.

Just before his first hospitalization, and before he was diagnosed as bi-polar, he lived with me and my husband for several weeks, and we became very close. He was behaving somewhat strangely, but I didn't know what it was at the time. He was an artist and a creative sort. At what point do they cross over? He created a lot of neat things while he lived with us, and we had some wonderful conversations and some hard arguments. Ever since then we had been really close.

Lee lived in another world. He saw things that no one else ever saw. He tried to explain it to me while we were living together. I think he lived in another dimension part of the time, not in the same reality with the rest of us. He told me that when he first picked up a camera, he suddenly had some sanity in his life, because he knew that if he clicked the shutter the picture would be what he saw. It would be real, and he wouldn't have to question it the way he questioned a lot of other things in his life that he saw or *dreamt of. After he was diagnosed, he was on lithium for a while, and it made his hands shake and blurred his vision so that he couldn't carry on with his photography, which was his profession; he was a professional photo-journalist. He had to take himself off the lithium so that he could do his photography, and I understood why it was important for him to do that. But he continued to go through depressions, followed by manic periods where he would go off somewhere.*

On Labor Day, some weeks before his death, my parents had a family reunion, and I saw that Lee was not doing well. My sister Jane saw it, too, but we really didn't know what it was. We thought he was just having relationship problems. He was very obsessed with having children and felt that would be a way of making up for all the grief he felt he had caused my Dad in his youth. His girlfriend had become pregnant, but had an abortion. He supported her decision, but he wasn't able to reconcile it in his mind. Afterwards, the girlfriend split up with him. He was very depressed, but we didn't know the whole story at the time.

Lee decided he wanted to go to Australia, and he called me on Christmas day to discuss it. Going off was his way of trying to move himself out of a depressive mode. I tried to talk him out of going to Australia and into going to Germany instead, because there was so much for a photojournalist to do there at the time. He was very upset that I challenged him. He said, "You don't understand. I really am having trouble right now. I need to get back to roots. I need to go where there's farmland, and life is simple, and people accept you. And besides that, there's only five days left to when I would have been a father." Then he hung up.

I called my sister Jane immediately and said, "Lee is counting days. I think we have a problem." I couldn't go out there to help, because I had a new baby and was very involved in my professional life. I have an historical role in my family of getting on a plane and going and intervening. I told Jane that I didn't want to put pressure on her, but we needed to do something, and asked her what she could handle. My sister met with him and talked with him a few times. We got him past the date that we were dreading, and he seemed to doing much better. He had dinner with her after that, and it seemed that a lot of the signs one looks for in depressive behavior were lifted. Then we kind of forgot about it for a couple of days, with the holidays and everything.

I had a huge project I was working on at work that was nearing its deadline, and I was very busy. But one day I just could not work. I couldn't concentrate. I got an extension of my deadline, and went to visit a good friend of mine at work. We talked for a couple of hours about family history and family problems, and I told her about my brother. I said, "I'm really scared. I think he's really going to do it this time." I had a sense that something was going to happen, and that's why I couldn't work.

When I got home, I tried to contact him on his pager. A few minutes later he called back. He didn't recognize my number and thought he was returning a business call. He was stuttering badly, which was always a sign that he was having trouble. I could feel the humiliation coming through the phone. What if he were really returning a business call, stuttering like that? I had a really bad feeling, but I couldn't keep him on the phone because he was working. That night I called his home and left a big message, saying, "I know you're going through something still, and please call me. Call me anytime. I love you." And he never called back. He killed himself sometime between the first call and Thursday, when I got the phone call from my Dad. As soon as he called, I knew something was wrong. I just asked, "Who is it?"

Lee's death destroyed my life. I remember saying just before, as New Year's was approaching, "This is the end of the year where I've been really busy doing a number of things. I had a baby, did the architecture exam, moved homes. All these things are settled, and next year I don't have any of those things on my plate. Next year is my year to rest and get over it." And two days later my whole life was pulled out from under me.

The first year I was very, very sad and depressed. I was suicidal. Lee's death had given me so much permission. I'd never considered it before, but he'd made such a statement. I went to work that whole year knowing that

the building was six floors tall and that you could get out on the roof.
Before that I used to need a coping day twice a month, and I would call in
sick to work. But that wasn't enough any more. My coping mechanism
became, "I know I can jump off the roof if things get too bad."

I always used to think that my brother was gorgeous. I sort of had a crush
on him. Then, after he killed himself, every love song I would hear on the
radio seemed to be about him. It wasn't about my teenage love. It wasn't
about my husband, anymore. We had never had a sibling sexual relationship
or anything like that, but it felt almost like that. It was almost sexual in terms
of what the songs were saying. I had a couple of sexual dreams about him.
There was really just this pure love. I missed him so much.

At the funeral we all got up and spoke, and I said, "I don't want to take
away from anybody else's grief, but I can't get away from the fact that I was
his twin." I felt as though I'd lost something that's supposed to be there in
my life. I felt as though my arm was torn off. Then, a few months after Lee
died, I felt as though everything was torn apart. My other brother Doug,
whom I had been closest to when we were growing up, began confiding in
me about all the things that had been going on in his life. He was depressed
and obsessive-compulsive, and much sicker that Lee had been. I intervened
and tried to put him in a hospital, and that completely backfired. He
thought I had betrayed him. So another arm went. My husband and I were
having problems because it was so stressful, so there went a leg. I felt as
though I was being literally torn apart.

I became obsessed with finding out how other twins felt. I think a twin's
experience is unique, but it's very hard to articulate that to someone who's
not a twin. I went to a support group for suicide survivors, and the first
question out of my mouth was, "Are there any people here who lost twins?"
I had to talk to another twin, because it was the only way I was going to
feel that I had talked to someone with the same experience. Eventually I
did find other twins to talk to, and they also felt their loss was unique.

I went into counseling right afterwards, but the therapist terminated
me after the sixth session, because I no longer qualified for insurance

purposes as a "crisis situation", even though my family and I had just unsuccessfully been trying to intervene with Doug, and he was blaming me for the betrayal. I tried to explain this to the counselor, but all she said was, "If you're that upset with me you can come back next week, and we can talk about how to terminate our relationship." I was suicidal that day. I drove home thinking I should run into a car, or I could get home and hang myself on the pipes down in the basement.

I was so angry! A lot of it was anger I didn't know what to do with. I was angry at people who were supposed to be kind to me now, because I'd just gone through this. There was just so much pain that I felt the only way to get rid of it was to kill myself. I wasn't permitted to be angry in my family when I was young, because I was the oldest. This was the first time I'd ever experienced a lot of anger, but the sadness and depression were trying to keep it in check. I was still in shock. I couldn't believe what had just happened in my life and that I would ever get through it. It was so much work to get through it. I just wanted people to be nice to me! The only thing that kept me from killing myself was that I knew it wouldn't matter to my therapist if I went home and hanged myself.

At the end of the year, on the anniversary, I went back to close a circle. It felt like a very natural closure. I went through all of Lee's stuff, and discovered awards he'd gotten which I'd never known about, and looked at his photographs. Then, after that, I finally let myself get angry at him. I felt, "If you come back, I'll kill you!" I'm still angry at him, but I don't want to be. I displaced a lot of it on my husband, because it's hard to be angry at someone who's dead. All I wanted to do was go around the whole house and punch out windows so I could hear the sound of glass crackling. A lot of the anger is that Lee didn't get help. My sister Jane and I have talked about how the women in our family are stronger. When she was having a lot of trouble recently, she got herself to a doctor and got herself stabilized. Why couldn't Lee do that?

My husband took care of the kids the whole first year. My son was six months old when Lee killed himself, and I didn't go to him at night for a *whole year. I was afraid to pick him up and be more attached to him. I was afraid of losing anybody else in my life that I loved. I'm mad at Lee for that. He robbed me. That's part of my problem with my husband, too. I don't want to become dependent. I don't want to have any more losses.*

All my other siblings have real problems, and I'm still waiting for the other shoe to drop. My sister Jane has been an alcoholic, and is depressed and angry, and has been suicidal. Doug is depressed and obsessive-compulsive. He told me that he was lying in the bathtub most of the day after Lee's suicide praying to God for courage to kill himself. That's why we intervened. I found out recently that Jeffrey, my youngest brother, has been suicidal, and recently he was out here visiting and he was having a lot of bad vibes about it. My older half-sibling describes himself as manic-depressive and has been on all kinds of medications for years and years. My half-sister has been through depressions, and hospitalized herself once over a marriage that was falling apart. And I've had eating disorders, and have been depressed and suicidal. My sister Jane and I say to each other, "Who's next?" Jane and I promised each other that we would not kill ourselves. Not that promises are all that great, but it helps to articulate fears. We do a lot of checking on other people in the family, always worrying what will happen next. I read a book about multiple suicides and the risks to other people in the family, and grew obsessed with worrying. It could still happen.

I became very worried for my kids, that they were going to have problems, given the genetics. And I had an odd fear that Lee was going to come and steal my kids from me. I gave up working, and we moved to a less expensive place, so I could stay home with my kids. The one thing that I can thank Lee for is that it made me stop the roller coaster lifestyle I had, trying to work as a successful architect with crazy hours, with a new baby and a two-year-old. I realized the priorities had to be different. I felt that my family was cursed. I had to change my lifestyle for the sake of the children, and myself, too, because I was overwhelmed.

Most of what has helped me get through this was the survivor group I went to, and being able to talk to other people who have lost someone to suicide, especially the twins. I didn't call certain people right away, because I had to tell my story a lot. There were people I didn't call until six months later, so I would have a fresh listener.

I had a lot of bad dreams for the first couple of years, but this last year I've had good dreams. Lee comes back and helps me solve a problem. I know he's dead, and he usually dies again in the dream. It's almost as if he's rescuing me. In one dream there were a bunch of "bad guys" chasing me, and he diverted them so I could escape, and they shot him. Sometimes he just comes and talks and helps figure things out. The dreams are reassuring. I still miss Lee immensely, and I still feel some anger toward him, but the paralyzing sadness has lifted.

Megan

Megan's identical twin sister, Melanie, killed herself a few days after their seventeenth birthday, thirty-two years before our interview. Throughout their childhood, people could rarely tell them apart, a problem compounded by their mother's insistence on dressing them alike. Each of them struggled to find her own identity, and their relationship, while very close, was quite competitive, as well. After her twin's death, Megan felt as though half of her had died, yet, at the same time, felt impelled to get out of the small city she lived in and find her own life, since everyone in her hometown saw her only as the twin of a suicide. She felt as though she now had both her life and her sister's to live. Her sister's suicide has had many long-term effects on Megan's life, especially on her relationships with others, because she is beset by fears of others' dying or abandoning her.

Melanie and I lived in the same room all our life, and my mother always dressed us alike. My adoptive father said he could never tell us apart. We were very close in some ways, and communicated a lot nonverbally, but the competition was intense. She used to fight for things, and I had scratches down my arms as a kid. I was the one who constantly gave in.

When I was six years old, I won an art contest. I was supposed to be on TV, so my mother called up the station and told them I was a twin and asked if my sister could be on TV, too. So we both were on TV. I won a doll, and my great grandmother gave my sister a doll—a better doll. After that I just took a back seat. I thought, "Well, if you get better things by being associated with the winner, why knock yourself out?" My mother used to fuss at me all my life, because she thought I was passive. She didn't realize that there was a reason that I was like that.

I dealt with the rivalry with my sister by being passive. She didn't like me taking art. She wanted to take it alone. She didn't like me taking dance with her. She wanted to do it alone. I thought, "Okay, I'll take theater." There was always something else to do. I just fell into that role. I would do anything to avoid the friction, which was just too monstrous to deal with. It didn't seem that important to do something that Melanie didn't want me to do.

Melanie wanted to go to a separate school, and the principal of our school told my mother to do that, but she did not do that. It's better to separate twins, because it's so close anyway. It's better to let them find their own identity. Our relationship was close, probably too close. We did the same on tests; it was a classic twin thing. There was a sixth grade teacher who accused us of cheating—we'd spell words wrong the same way. Teachers in school couldn't tell us apart.

I went through years of not knowing who I was and trying to find my own identity. Just once, though, I got to be on my own. When I was eight, my mother and sister got mononucleosis. Up to then we had always stayed together when we got sick, and we got sick a lot. We had tonsillitis and pneumonia. I think we wanted to die. My mother wanted to die. She was always getting sick, too. But this time the doctor sent me away to my great grandmother's house, a huge Victorian house. I had a huge room and a bathroom with a bidet in it. It was great! I remember being vividly happy.

I was totally on my own. And in the summers we'd go to my grandmother's and get separate rooms. I loved it. My sister, too, kept fighting to be independent, but she just wasn't given that chance.

My mother was not in very good shape when we were little. When we were three, her brother died, and she had been very close to him. That same year my father killed himself, although I was not told about that until after my sister's death. A cousin told me. It was kept secret. The feeling in the family was that if you keep it secret, it won't happen. I thought my father had done some horrible crime. There were no pictures of him in the house. The secrecy is sad, and I think, without a doubt, that it repeats itself. It's like child abuse. When it's kept secret it happens again and again. My mother was depressed during our childhood, often getting sick, and she didn't have much to do with her kids.

During the year before Melanie killed herself, our communication hadn't been very good. She had a serious boyfriend, which I knew had developed into a sexual relationship. Our parents tried to get them to break up, but weren't successful. The weekend before she died, we were on Easter break. She had gone to some people's house with her boyfriend and another couple for Easter parties, and I had gone to an island off the coast with some other people. I knew something really bad was going on, but I didn't know what it was verbally. I spent two days on the beach, building sand people and watching the waves wash them away. It's the way twins do, I guess. I think it's true with a lot of identical twins that you literally feel what the other person feels. I knew that something was really wrong, and I made one of the guys fly me home a day early. My sister came home, and I wanted to talk with her, but I wasn't able to. She had told her boyfriend and the other couple that she was going to kill herself, but she didn't tell anyone in the family, and they didn't tell anyone.

The next evening I had just gone to bed and wasn't quite asleep, and I heard her. We had a bedroom and a bathroom and then a study. I didn't actually hear the gun shot; I heard what I thought was "Help!". I got up and found her. She shot herself in the lung. My parents came running up the stairs and,

I guess to get me out of the room, told me to call a friend of the family, a doctor, so I did. And we had to call the police. Years later my mother told me that the police wanted to arrest me, because they didn't see how she could have shot herself with a rifle. Then they found her suicide note. I was pretty berserk, because they wanted to take her diary, and I didn't want them to. My parents moved my bed downstairs, and I cried for three days.

I wanted to die. I felt as if I, or half of me, had died. Seeing my identical twin dead was horrible. I felt I had died to me—that I was alive, but I was dead. When a close friend or sibling dies, you have to admit that you're going to die. But when it's an identical twin, you know you're going to die.

Then I went back to school. I took a razor blade at one point and tried to make a scar on my face to show the inward pain. I used to put poptops from beer cans on my finger and turn the rough part around until my finger bled. I wanted a scar to show my pain. I didn't want to fool with anyone who didn't know how horrible I was inside, and how I felt that I was evil. I think it's because of the secrecy around my father's suicide and no pictures of him that I felt so ashamed. I felt evil. I felt somehow responsible for what happened, or evil that I had to suffer these things. I felt enormous guilt and shame. After my sister killed herself, my mother freaked out whenever I was around, but what I didn't realize until recently was that my mother freaked out whether I was there or not. I blamed myself for that for years, and thought if I just kept away from her or if I were dead, then no one would have those problems. I thought that by looking like my twin I was triggering that reaction. I had to look in a mirror, too, and it was sort of freaky.

I wanted to be a writer as a kid, but I really wanted to write after my sister died, mainly to tell the truth, or try to. Everything had always been covered in a veil of secrecy in our family, and it still was. They tried to keep the news about my sister off the front page of the newspaper. Another reason I began writing poetry, besides feeling driven to expose the truth, was because no one wanted to talk about what had happened. It really helped a lot, because I felt as if I was in a void, and no one really did understand.

I strongly believe in writing down things in those situations. You get something out, and you get something back.

My parents sent me to a psychiatrist whose son was in my class, which was a mistake, I think. I used to make up dreams to tell him. It was a place to escape to, but the whole time I couldn't understand why I was going and not my parents. I felt that they thought I was the crazy one. There wasn't family counseling then. My mother was actually jealous of my going to the shrink. She'd say, "I know you're talking about me!" I figured it was damned if you do, damned if you don't. I think it was probably better that I went. I resented that they weren't going, too, because it put me in such a bad place when I'd go home, but it gave me an out. And it made me respect myself and my feelings a little more that someone took the time to listen to me for the first time in my life. And I think it was good that the psychiatrist encouraged me to go away to school, rather than saying, "You're so sick, you have to see me a hundred times."

I needed to get out of that city. I'm from an old family there, and everyone was related and everyone knew who had done what. It was creepy. It's also very humid—an incubator for viruses. I think it's an incubator for emotions, too. My sister killing herself was the reason for me to get out of town. I felt I had to in order to survive. People called me her name all the time, but that didn't bother me as much as feeling that I was a fixed item. I liked the idea of being in a strange place and making friends of people for who I was, and their not knowing what I'd come from. And I hate looks of pity. People would look at me feeling, "Oh, poor little thing." It made me want to scream. That's all I was in that town—the person whose twin sister killed herself. My sister died toward the end of my junior year in high school, and I had to take college boards right after. It was hard, but I was so motivated to get out of there, I took the exams and took an extra course senior year. I went off to a college in the north, and that saved my life.

I don't know if all twins feel this way, but growing up I always felt that I had a replacement, so that I would do anything that anyone dared me to do. There was someone just like me, so I could die, and it wouldn't matter. After she died, I felt a new energy and purpose. I had to get out of my hometown, and I had to be tough. It was almost as if I had my life and hers to live.

I think I understand very well why Melanie killed herself. I'm sure she was pregnant, and there were rumors to that effect afterwards. She was up against a brick wall. My parents would have killed her if they found out she was pregnant, and no way they would have had her have an abortion. In 1962 in my hometown girls were not supposed to be sexual, and they certainly weren't supposed to have abortions. I look back now and think about girls who went to France for a year, or went up to the plantation, so obviously people got pregnant and they did something about it. But Melanie was stuck. My mother's attitude was, "Don't ever talk to me about it." My sister had been turned down for everything she asked my mother for. And my adoptive father is very moral, and it would have been hard to bring that up with her father, anyway. What could she have done?

The other way I think I understand why she killed herself is that when I was pregnant, I felt miserable. I couldn't eat or even smell food, and I would get depressed. When I was pregnant with my second child, I became suicidal. My husband came home with wine and flowers one day, and I looked at him and had a vision of jumping off a cliff. It was deep. I couldn't have stopped myself if someone hadn't stopped me. It was chemical, and I think that kind of chemical, hormonal thing with her being pregnant made her suicide all the more likely.

It scared me when I was overtaken by suicidal feelings during that time, because for me suicide was not an option. It was very simple: I didn't want to be a copycat. My twin sister did it, ergo I don't want to do it. I felt, "You had that choice. My choice is not to do it." Even though there have been times I was ready to die, I wasn't going to kill myself. I felt that what I really wanted was to be really alive. If you're not going to die, let's be ALIVE!

I tend to intellectualize suicide too fast and think that it's an option everyone in the world has, and that it's a God-given option. That's what gives us free will. But it's not a benevolent option.

I never could get angry at my sister. I cried. I was upset. But I never could get angry. I kept rationalizing it away, and consequently deal with depression myself, because when you turn anger inward, you get depressed. I did get angry at God, if there was a God. A friend of mine who's a therapist has asked, "Why aren't you angry at her for leaving you? She came into this world to be with you." But I don't feel she had any other option, so it's very hard to feel angry at her. For some reason my mother's recent death brought out a lot of anger. I felt angry at her for not being tougher in her soul. She was a person who would always give in, and never say what she really felt. And that anger at her could be anger at my sister and father, combined, for wimping out, in a way, and for not recognizing their feelings enough to try to deal with them. I'm getting better at it, but I guess I'm also angry at myself for not getting better at it. That's the thing about suicide. It's violent, and for whatever reason you do it, you're hurting people, and that should make me angry. I've always felt sad for my kids that they didn't know their grandfather or their aunt. My kids grew up without any real aunts or uncles. I guess it's as close to anger that I got, that my kids didn't have that.

The effect of my sister's suicide, and my father's, too, is that I always feared other people I was close to would die or abandon me. With my first husband, I used to freak out when he would come home late, because I would think he was dead. And then, when he did come home, I would be horrible to him. Finally, when he used to go off on his own, I'd rationalize it and say, "Okay, he's dead, and he's not coming home, so I don't have to worry about it for the rest of the evening." Right after we got married, he went into the army. I would start crying at work—I was sure he would never come home. After I got divorced, I had to send my kids down to see their father on visits, and I was sure they would never come back. When I leave, my feeling is that I'm probably not going to come back. I don't know how to find a middle ground with separations, in a way, because there never was a middle ground in my life.

I worried about my kids killing themselves. I can't believe I had kids, when I think about it. What was I thinking? There was a period of four years when I was a single parent of teenagers, and it was a terrible time for me. I would let the oldest one drive the car, and it would freak me out. I didn't want to stay up late worrying, so I tried to put them in the hands of the fates. But I felt the emotional rush each time. I'd have to let it go through and breathe it out. Now they're eighteen and twenty-one, and it's a great relief that they got through most of the bad teenage years.

I guess what helped me survive was my belief that even though the body is dead, the soul goes on. Part of me feels she's still around, but I just don't see her. I miss her, but I talk to her as if she's still alive. And also, as a friend pointed out, I tend to twin with people. I have some good close friends, and I'm close to my kids, and I've never felt really lonely. I love living out in the woods where I do. I guess I do believe in the ancestor theory—our spirits are in the land. I can still talk to my sister.

Chapter Nine
Unbidden Thoughts and Feelings

In previous chapters various people talked about certain feelings they had following their sibling's suicide that they were somewhat ashamed of. Some people were disturbed that they felt relief at the death, or they felt ashamed of feeling angry at the sibling. Some of the women experienced sexual dreams after the loss of their brother that most of them were too embarrassed to tell me about. Yet sibling relationships are so complicated, and so entwined with leftover childhood feelings, including rivalry and competition, that it's not surprising that siblings' reactions in the wake of suicide can also be complicated. Unbidden, "sibling" feelings can come to the surface and create feelings of discomfort at having "inappropriate" thoughts. Nancy (Ch. 2), for instance, told me that one of her first reactions when she learned of her brother's death was, "What?! Before he finished my horse fence?!" I had a nasty thought a few weeks after my sister's death as I was thinking about the blood and brains and hair splattered all over the bathroom where she shot herself. It continues to be a hideous image to me, but that day I remembered how compulsively clean and tidy she had always been—a compulsivity I had always felt scornful of—and I thought with a kind of inward snigger, "Hey Ann, bet you wouldn't have done it if you'd known what a mess it was going to make!"

No matter how shameful such thoughts may be, it's important to acknowledge them, although we don't have to be proud of them. We may feel that we "shouldn't" have such thoughts or feelings, yet they do spring up unbidden, and they are ours. Pretending they don't exist in our minds or hearts doesn't make it so. Various people I talked to felt relieved to learn that they weren't the only ones who had unworthy thoughts and feelings after their sibling's death.

"I won"

Particularly when there are only two siblings in a family, they can experience a kind of competition about whose way of dealing with life is better. I unconsciously felt all my life that there was "Ann's way" and "my way", and one of them must be "the right way", even though I knew consciously that there are many ways. Between us there was always an unspoken competition over who was "doing life" better. My sister was a compulsive workaholic. She felt that she had to do and do and do, and she was driven by "shoulds". I remember talking to her on the phone when I was in the first year of therapy and telling her how I was trying to free myself from the oppressive "shoulds" in my life. She said, "You shouldn't get rid of too many of them, or you'll never get anything done." Through years of therapy I discovered another way of approaching life that was different, and more rewarding and fulfilling, than the way we had both been brought up. I gained a sense of my own authority and was able to let go of the feeling of being driven by outside forces to do and do and do.

I felt a certain superiority toward my sister, who seemed stuck in the old way, constantly driven to succeed at everything and unable to relax and enjoy her life. I knew she and her husband were having trouble, because my mother had talked to me about it, but when I talked to her and suggested counseling, she said in essence, "Oh, we don't need that kind of thing. We just have to work out things financially." I felt that she would benefit greatly from therapy, that it would help her get in touch with her own feelings and free her from her compulsive drive to do things unceasingly from morning to night, but she didn't believe in therapy. As I wrote in Chapter Two, in the last years when I would call her up, she rarely had time to talk very long, because she was always about to take her boys to Little League, or off to Boy Scouts, or she was working on a project from work, or about to drive one of the boys to his piano lesson, and on and on. When she did have time for a conversation, it seemed to consist largely of her listing all the things she was doing or had yet to do. I wanted to say, "Why don't you just have fun sometimes?" On the other hand, I had a certain nagging feeling that maybe I *should* be doing some of the things she did, particularly for my children. *Shouldn't* I also insist that they take music lessons, join the Scouts, join ball teams, go to Sunday School?

I was aware that Ann, always a highly competitive person, was constantly competing with me and trying to show that her way was the best way. I also knew that she was jealous of me on some level, although it was only after her death that I found out from her husband how jealous she had been. She saw me as smarter, prettier, more creative, and wittier. I felt that her not wanting me to know what was going on in her last weeks had everything to do with that ongoing but tacit competition between us. She didn't want me to know she was failing and no longer able to keep everything together by sheer force of will. Her way was not working any more.

The day after my sister killed herself, then, I had a sudden, powerful thought: "I won!" It was not a thought I wanted to have, but it was very clear to me that she had lost the competition. Her way hadn't worked, after all, just as I had long suspected.

I mentioned the "I won" feeling to many of the people I talked with to try to find out how common it might be. It was not, actually, quite as common as I had thought. Or, perhaps, people had experienced something similar but didn't want to admit to it. There were a few people, however, who understood what I meant. Peter (Ch, 5), who had had a similarly competitive relationship with his brother, said, *Exactly. I can relate to that. With my brother everything had to be absolutely perfect. And he never had any fun. There's a lot to be said for having fun. I was much more easy going. And he always had to be right, and my feeling was being right isn't necessary. You can be wrong when you're always right. So, yes, I can definitely relate to that. I felt I won, too.*

Another man I talked to, Cliff, who had lost his younger brother and only sibling to suicide four years before, told me that he had had a somewhat similar reaction to his brother's death. His brother lived and worked in their hometown in the Midwest, while Cliff had moved to the West Coast and was a sort of outsider and black sheep in the family. There was an underlying competition going on between them, and his brother tended to side with Cliff's mother in disapproving of his wife, his life style, and many of the choices he made. Cliff tried to talk to his brother about how he was doing, but his brother wouldn't share his problems and, unlike Cliff, didn't believe in seeking professional help. The two were not very close, being very different people and living very different lifestyles. When I told Cliff about my "I won" feeling, he said, *I've had some thoughts like that, too. And you immediately think that's wrong, and you shouldn't think that. There wasn't exactly a feeling of vindication. But there's the fact that I'm still here and he isn't. I have a sense of seeing how my brother really screwed things up, whereas I haven't. So even though I felt that he was a lot smarter than I was in a business sense, he kind of blew it, and I didn't. So there's a bit of that "I won" feeling. It's sort of a guilty feeling, feeling good about having done better. Even though I was an outsider in the family, I felt that what I was doing was better than what he was doing in some respects. I had the sense of wanting to show my mother and brother that what I was doing was okay. And I guess it was, because here I am.*

"Now I'll get more..."

There is another way to "win" when a sibling is suddenly dead. We may think that we have now won our parents' undivided attention, and feel a guilty pleasure at not having to share our parents with anyone else any more. Even between siblings who are very close, feelings of rivalry still lurk under the surface. The battle for parental attention may be open, as it was in John's family (Ch. 2), or it may be experienced as a sort of background hum, but what child doesn't want to be the center of the parents' interest? Even when we grow into adulthood, sibling rivalry persists, although we tend not to acknowledge that we still harbor childish feelings. Even Joe (Ch. 1), who felt the deepest love for his brother, acknowledged that he felt occasional resentment that so much of the parents' attention was focused on his brother during his lifetime.

A few years after her sister's suicide, Ellen (Ch. 4) realized that all of a sudden she was her mother's favorite, something she had yearned for all through her childhood. Her sister Leah had always been the center of her mother's attention, and the two had formed a charmed, closed circle. Her mother refused to mention Leah's name after her suicide or acknowledge that she had had another daughter besides the two now remaining. Ellen's mother didn't approve of Ellen's other sister's lifestyle, so Ellen became the favorite child, the one with the right husband, the right lifestyle, the right number of children. But even though Ellen feels a certain pleasure at finally finding herself within the magic circle she had been excluded from all those years, it is a bitter victory. As she blamed herself for her sister's suicide, so she feels guilty about now enjoying her new status as the favored one.

Often, it's not only parental attention that we fight for, overtly or covertly, but also material things. John (Ch. 2), for instance, said that, as he began realizing that his brother had probably killed himself, he started thinking that there would be one less sibling to fight over who gets the extra Devil Dog or whatever else they had scrambled for. Older siblings, while their brother or sister is still alive, may feel a tension over who will benefit most from their inheritance upon their parents' death, or which one will get a treasured heirloom. When their sibling is dead, they may feel a certain (unbidden) pleasure that whatever they would have had to share before is now theirs alone.

Everett (Ch. 4), who felt a good deal of guilt over his brother's suicide, found that he had something else to feel guilty for—his pleasure at realizing he would now be the one to inherit all the family heirlooms he had always coveted: *My mother had collected a whole library of wonderful old books. Some of them were quite rare. They had a room built just for that library, with temperature and humidity control and everything. I used to love to go in there and just be surrounded by those beautiful bindings. Then when I got older, I began to think of what would become of them and whether my mother would split up the collection between Justin and me. He didn't care about them the way I did, and I figured he would probably sell his share, which upset me a lot. Then after the funeral when we all went back to my parents' house, I wandered in there and looked around at those books, and I thought, "Wow, they're all mine!" I felt a real charge, a real thrill. And then I felt totally swamped with guilt. How could I be gloating over getting the whole collection when my brother had just killed himself? I felt guilty enough about those things I had said, and now I was having these evil, selfish thoughts.*

Scorn

After my sister's suicide and after I had made the terrible call to my mother, I found myself striding through the house inwardly ranting, "God, Ann, that was so STUPID! STUPID! What a stupid solution!" I had imaginary dialogues with Ann for weeks afterwards while doing dishes or driving in the car, in which I ranted at her for the stupidity of her choice. I told her, "If you had only gotten professional help, if you could have understood that it's all right to ask for help, if you had understood that therapy is an all right thing to do, you could have been happy again! You didn't need to kill yourself, you dope! Why didn't you trust me enough to call me? I've been there, you idiot! I could have helped you!"

I realized that I felt a sense of scorn, or contempt, towards her because she wouldn't accept help, and she didn't understand that there could be another way of dealing with her problems besides killing herself. I felt that she was benighted, that her whole attitude toward life, including her fear of getting help when she needed it, was utterly misguided. But at the same time that I felt that sense of scorn, I understood that it was part of her very nature to feel that it was shameful to admit she needed help. Both of us were raised to feel that we were supposed to solve our own problems. Even while I felt disdain that she somehow "just didn't get it", I could understand that that was her personality and that, perhaps, therapy could not have been a path for her. Yes, what she did was stupid, but perhaps there was no other way for her, given who she was. That was part of the tragedy of her death.

Several other people I talked with admitted that they, too, had felt a sense of scorn at their sibling's choice, and some disdain at the way their sibling had dealt with life in general. At the same time, they could understand that the sibling was in such despair that suicide seemed to be the only option. They and I agreed that calling the suicide a "stupid choice", while that was how we survivors perceive it, is unfair, since the sibling's state of mind wasn't rational and wasn't making logical choices. Yet, even understanding that, we still felt a certain scorn at our sibling's inability to find a better solution.

Using it

Earlier, Scott (Ch. 7) said that he found it hard to talk to people he was not very close to about his brother's suicide, because he was afraid of using it in some way, perhaps for its shock value. Some of the people I talked to found that they sometimes did just that, and then felt ashamed at getting something unhealthy out of the fact of their sibling's suicide.

Lucy (Ch. 1), for instance, found herself using her brother's suicide at times simply for its shock value. She told me, *I used to get a kind of pleasure telling people, when the topic would come up, saying that my brother committed suicide. I would get a little pleasure out of that because it would shock people. It made me feel sort of special, too, because I had had this unusual experience, and because I would be suddenly center stage.* She also told me, *I would go crazy trying to make sense of what my brother did. Why? Why? Why? Why? Why? And part of that was that it was sort of an intellectual puzzle. I was trying to figure out the puzzle and kind of enjoying figuring it out, just on an intellectual plane. It would make me feel guilty.*

Linda (Ch. 8) remembers a moment when she used her twin brother's suicide almost as a weapon. She told me, *Several weeks after Lee's suicide I suddenly needed to talk to my sister Jane to make sure that she was still alive, and that she hadn't just done something. I got to a pay phone, and we were talking about my brother Douglas, because he was having trouble, and there was a long line outside the pay phone. I was trying to ignore them. Finally, a woman rapped on the glass and gave me a look that said, "You're so rude to be on the phone that long with all these people waiting!" I opened the door and said, "Excuse me, but I'm talking to my sister. My brother just killed himself!" When I told Jane, she said, "It's really a sword, isn't it?" I was kind of ashamed of myself. I really wanted that woman to go away and leave me alone, but I could have done it more nicely. Sometimes it's really interesting to see how people will react, to see the shock, but I'm not proud of doing that.*

Part Two

Family, Friends, Strangers, Relationships

Chapter Ten
Family Repercussions

The effects on the rest of the family after the suicide of a sibling are often profound and far-reaching, and all too frequently destructive. The suicide rends the family fabric. Some families gradually mend themselves over time. In other families the suicide leaves a gaping hole that is never truly mended, and the family is left in tatters.

The death frequently causes a breakdown of communication among the remaining family members. Because of the guilt and shame surrounding suicide, many family members may find it very difficult to talk about it. Parents, in particular, may be feeling such a load of guilt that they find it extremely painful to discuss or even refer to the suicide. Some may even deny that their child was mentally ill, or they may deny that the death was a suicide and insist that it was an accidental death. Many, if they do talk about the dead child, prefer to speak only about their memories of happier times. Others withdraw into a stoic silence, attempting to carry on as if everything is normal and the event is in the far past. Ellen's (Ch. 4, 9) mother felt so betrayed by the suicide of her favorite daughter that she removed all the pictures of her dead daughter from the house and refused to speak her name again, saying, in effect, "I never had another daughter."

Seeing their parents' pain, the remaining siblings are very often afraid to bring up the subject at all, fearing to add to their parents' grief or guilt. At the same time, they may feel that by not talking about it, they may hurt their parents more by seeming callous or uncaring. Several of the people I talked to felt that the breakdown in communication between themselves and their parents after the suicide was, in part, a generational problem. Those who had older parents understood that, while they themselves felt reasonably comfortable about talking about their feelings and discussing difficult issues, their parents were of a generation that "just doesn't talk about these things." As a result, many people felt that they were walking on eggshells when they were with their parents after their sibling's death, and their relationship with them became awkward and uncomfortable.

After the suicide, family gatherings, particularly traditional family reunions—such as Thanksgiving, Christmas, or Passover—can be very hard on the family, even excruciating. Suicide feels like an unnatural death, and the family often doesn't know how to deal with it. Family gatherings can be uncomfortable and awkward for everyone, with some members trying to put on a happy face and go on as usual, while others feel a need to acknowledge the pain of the obvious absence of one member of the family. Everyone is aware that there is an empty chair. Some family members may be able to look at it and feel the pain of its emptiness, while others walk around it with their eyes averted. Some wish they could knock the chair over in rage.

Different family members may have different, conflicting feelings toward the suicide, which can tear the family apart. The experience of Bonnie and Jim (Ch. 3), for instance, is not uncommon. Both of them felt a tremendous amount of anger and resentment at their brother for killing himself, while their mother felt nothing but immense grief and remorse. She could talk of nothing but "Poor Ted, poor Ted", while Bonnie and Jim ranted at him for what he had done both to themselves and to the family. Their father, meanwhile, withdrew into silence. Less commonly, it is one of the parents who is enraged at the dead child, while other family members feel empathy and understanding for the dead one's pain and despair. Or, the surviving siblings may feel differing degrees of grief over their loss, and those for whom it is hardest may resent the others, who seem to them unaffected or uncaring. In any case, these conflicting feelings can drive a knife into the family's heart. The parents of several people I talked to reacted to their child's suicide with different, opposing feelings, with one parent feeling great grief and needing to talk about it over and over, while the other wanted to leave it behind and get on with life. As the suicide drove their parents apart, the surviving children felt caught in the middle, sometimes feeling a pressure to side with one parent or the other, or finding themselves in the position of mediator while their own feelings were left hanging.

All too often the survivors try to affix blame for the suicide on others, either family members or people on the periphery. Parents, in particular, often need to deny that the death may have resulted in some way from how they raised their child, or that there was something in their child's psyche itself that led to the suicide. Feeling the need to blame something or someone, they begin pointing fingers at friends of the victim who had a "bad influence" or, very often, the girlfriend, boyfriend or spouse. Other family members, too, may become involved in the accusations and finger-pointing. The need to place blame on someone else, or to place blame anywhere, is understandable, since the burden of guilt could otherwise be intolerable, but blaming and finger-pointing creates rifts and discords that only further disrupt a family already in upheaval.

In my own family my parents immediately laid the blame for my sister's suicide on her husband. My mother even said, "He killed her as surely as if he had pulled the trigger." While I can understand that blaming my sister's husband was a way for my parents to protect themselves from their own sense of guilt, and while I feel that it was perhaps necessary for them at their age to do that, it is very sad that it had to be so. Besides straining my own relationship with my brother-in-law, it is a sad burden to lay on my sister's children, who cannot understand why their grandmother and father, both of whom they love, will not see or speak to each other. It also means that I have to be the go-between in arranging the boys' yearly visit to their grandmother and that I have to be there each year to help my mother while they are there, since the boys' father is not allowed in the house. The times when I have tried to soften my mother's stance toward Ann's husband, she only became upset with me for "standing up for him".

Several of the people I talked with felt caught in the middle this way, and often felt forced to take sides in a conflict they did not want to be part of in the first place. One of them, Karen, whose brother had killed himself only six months before, found herself caught in a web of recriminations, anger, and hurt that was destroying the family. Her parents blamed her brother's wife, the wife blamed the parents, her other brother sided with her parents, and she was expected to take sides, as well, which she refused to do. She told me, *The blaming has hurt. No one can grieve, and no one can get over it, because they're too busy pointing fingers. It's been hard for me to get to my grief, because of having to manage what's going on in the family and having to separate out all those things to get to the grief. And, I may have issues with my sister-in-law, but I also ask, "Where's the compassion? She's a widow!" My brother loved her, and he would want for her to have some support. But it's not going to happen. There's too much controversy and too much hurt and anger in the family for anyone to grow.*

Many of the people I talked to described a snowball effect after their sibling's suicide, where other members of the family, including their other siblings, reacted in self-destructive ways that affected everyone else and compounded the original loss. In several families one or another parent withdrew from the rest of the family emotionally, in effect abandoning their surviving children. Some parents turned to alcohol, while some became severely depressed, throwing the rest of the family into turmoil and placing on them the burden of having to care for the parents as well as try to cope with their own loss.

Very often, the surviving siblings, particularly if they are young, become themselves self-destructive or suicidal. Pamela (Ch. 6), who described the long-terms effects of her brother's suicide on her life earlier, also talked about the snowball effects it had for her other siblings: *Within two years of the suicide, my other brother pretty much lost it. He started doing more drugs and involving himself in self-destructive behavior. He ended up sitting in my mother's office one day telling her that Larry was coming to get him. He had been reading the book Larry wrote, which to me is just the paranoid babbling of someone who was totally against the government, and he believed that it was Larry's message to him to engage in the battle of Good versus Evil. They put him in a mental hospital, and he's been in and out of them ever since, having psychotic episodes where he chases butterflies and raves about Good fighting Evil. I think if Larry hadn't killed himself, my other brother would be vastly different, mainly because he wouldn't have gotten involved in drugs so heavily, which is what first induced his psychotic episodes. He couldn't get the coping skills you need to get through something like that. His way of coping was to destroy himself. Now he's homeless and lives in a car somewhere.*

My sister was completely broken up when Larry died and even now can't talk about him. At the time, she had lost her children in a custody battle and had just started dating another man and trying to get her life together. She kind of went off the deep end. The man asked her to marry him and gave her an engagement ring, and she went into the bathroom and took a bottle of antidepressants. Then she handed the bottle to him and said, "Well, I guess I can't marry you now because I'm going to be dead." It was sort of like Larry—something good happens and you need to kill yourself. It was odd. They got her to the hospital, but by that time her heart had stopped beating. They immediately started working on her and installed a pacemaker to keep her heart beating. She still has the pacemaker. She hasn't really recovered yet, and she has psychotic episodes like my brother. But she has tried to get help and better her life through chemical management. My brother refuses to get help. Those are some of the many reverberations of my brother's suicide.

Several of the surviving siblings were aware of subtle or not so subtle changes in the family dynamic. I noticed a slight but significant change around the family dinner table that seemed to symbolize an alteration in my mother's view of my role in the family. When we were growing up, my sister, being the oldest, felt she was entitled to the best of everything—the biggest bedroom, the right to sit in the front seat of the car, and so on, including the right to sit in the "best" chair at the dining table, the one with a view out the window. I got the chair that faced the wall. Now when I visit my mother, she, quite unconsciously, seats me in Ann's chair. Peter (Ch. 5, 9) noticed that he, too, now was seated in what used to be his older brother's place. It feels as though my mother now expects me to fill my sister's role as the Responsible One, the one she can rely on to take charge in any future crises, major or minor. It is in many ways a gratifying feeling to be recognized as a capable adult at last, but it is something of a burden, as well, having to carry the full responsibility for dealing with whatever future events will come and not be able to share that with my sister.

In many families, though, the dead sibling becomes immortalized. Rather than the surviving children "moving up" to fill the vacant role, the chair is "retired", as Jim put it. In Jim and Bonnie's family (Ch. 3) their mother virtually placed her dead son on a pedestal and would speak only good of him. The surviving children felt resentment that their mother was so focused on her dead child that she seemed to have little energy left for the living. After his brother's death, Everett felt very hurt that his parents, who had focused their full attention on his brother in life, continued to dwell on his brother's life and death afterwards, while appearing to blame Everett for his brother's suicide. They seemed barely to care about Everett's life or career either before or after his brother's suicide, and he felt abandoned once again.

While Ellen (Ch. 4, 6, 9) found that she had moved into the role of favorite child for her mother, her mother made it quite clear that she would never love either of her surviving children as she had Ellen's sister Leah. Ellen described a very painful conversation she had with her mother some years after Leah's death that parallels experiences of many surviving siblings whose parents immortalized the lost child: *My mother would often say, "My life is worthless." She wouldn't say, "When Leah died", because she refused to utter her name. She would say something like, "When I lost my child, I lost my life." Once when my daughter Annie was little, my mother came to visit. Charles had taken Annie out for a walk, and I don't know how it came up, but we were talking about Leah, and my mother said, "I have no joy in my life any-more. Nothing makes me happy. I'm just waiting out my time." I said, "Ma, how could you say that? Look how you love Annie. You take so much joy in your grandchild." And she said, "No, I don't. Look, if you or Annie were lying on the sidewalk bleeding at the curb, and I saw you there, I'd step over you and keep walking!" I just sat there as if I were riveted to the chair. I was speechless. She had taken my breath away. I didn't say anything, but I remember very silent tears just streaming down my face. That was the last time she was ever allowed to come visit without a special invitation. It was the most devastating thing she ever said. The odd thing is, she didn't mean it. I guess she feels as though somehow she's betraying Leah if she loves us, because when she and my father separated, she let us know that we children had to choose between her and my father—we couldn't love them both. She probably feels somehow that she's betraying Leah's life and the love she had for her if she loves us. But it was still a horrible thing to say.*

Some people felt that their parents cast them adrift after their sibling's suicide. Vincent (Ch. 6), for instance, was given no limits after his brother's death, and was set loose to do anything he wanted, although he was only a teenager and in need of adult support and guidance. The parents' grief and guilt, together with their fear that their surviving children may also kill themselves if the parents make a miss-step, can make them step back from their responsibility to their other children. Some parents seem even to throw their hands up in despair and give up any hope for the surviving children, but for most, this is only a temporary abdication while they attend to their own grief and seem to forget about the remaining children. I noticed that for a few months after my sister's death, my mother would forget to do some of the little things she used to do for me, things that she also did for my sister, like send us a card or a check on special occasions. It was as if she thought, "My daughter is dead, so I don't need to do that anymore." If I felt hurt by those little omissions, one can only imagine how painful it was for the people who were far more gravely neglected after their sibling's death.

Many parents, on the other hand, become doubly solicitous of their surviving children. After her brother's death, Morna's (Ch. 1) mother whirled her off on shopping sprees, apparently feeling that if she and her husband had provided better for their son financially, perhaps he would not have killed himself. Morna finally put a stop to it, but she did enjoy feeling like a princess while it lasted. Like several people I talked to, Morna found that her relationship with her parents changed dramatically after the suicide. They became extremely concerned about the well-being of their surviving children, and wanted to know everything that was going on in their lives. Indeed, everyone in her family became much more conscious of one another and of one another's feelings, a common phenomenon in the experience of many of the people I talked to. The surviving siblings found this gratifying on some levels, because of the added attention they received from their parents, but they often found it suffocating, as well, when their parents appeared to be hovering anxiously over them and intruding into their lives unnecessarily.

The surviving siblings also fear for their children after the suicide and worry that history will repeat itself in their own families. If their sibling died before they had children, some, like Alan (Ch. 4, 6), cannot bring themselves to take that step at all. Those that do, like Megan (Ch. 8), who lost her identical twin when she was a teenager, find themselves beset by morbid and continual anxiety, and they hover over their children until they finally pass through the dangerous years.

When the suicide is the culmination of years of mental illness, the surviving siblings are constantly alert to signs of the same illness in their children, a well-founded concern in the case of genetic illnesses like bi-polarity or schizophrenia. But even when mental illness was not an apparent factor in their sibling's suicide, the surviving siblings are never free from a heightened concern, and the slightest hint that their children are troubled or depressed immediately raises red flags.

All of the people I talked with who had children struggled with how to deal with the issue of suicide with their children. Ellen (Ch. 4, 6, 9, 10) took special pains to let her children know how her sister's suicide had destroyed her and her family and flatly informed them, "No matter what happens to you, one thing I absolutely cannot deal with is suicide. Don't ever do that to me." But Evan, a man who had lost both his father and sister to suicide, said he felt afraid to tell his children such a thing, because he feared that they would then seal themselves away from him, not share what they were feeling, and so not reach out for help, which could in itself result in their suicide. Vincent (Ch. 6, 10) tries to take a more pro-active approach, which is perhaps the healthiest one. When I asked him how he thought he would feel when his young daughter reached the age when his brother killed himself, he said, *Her mental well-being is not something I'm going to worry about. It's something I'm going to pay attention to. I want my daughter to be independent. I want her to be able to understand her feelings and deal with them in a healthy way. So I'm going to try to guide her in that direction, so that if she does have problems, she understands what they are and knows how to deal with them.*

Despite all of the potentially destructive effects in the wake of suicide, some families survive intact and even grow stronger. Especially in a loving family that is otherwise strong and cohesive, the suicide may lead to greater closeness among the survivors. Joe's (Ch. 1) family, which had always held together despite numerous tragedies and troubles, weathered this storm as well and became even more mutually supportive. Morna (Ch. 1, 10), who had always been much closer to the brother who killed himself than to her other brothers, now tried to create a warmer relationship with them and to try to forgive her father, as well. For Lucy and Margaret (Ch. 1), their already close relationship became even closer as they dealt with their common loss, although they continue to feel angry at their father for not facing up to what they feel is his part in their brother's death. Sadly, though, as Jim pointed out, a suicide in the family is more often divisive than unifying.

Chapter Eleven
Who cares for sibling survivors?

Following my sister's death, family and friends gathered around my parents, my sister's husband, and her children, offering support and consolation. My parents received many, many letters and cards and expressions of sympathy. I don't recall receiving any. Although I wasn't very distressed by these omissions, since my grief was certainly not as deep as theirs, still, it was puzzling that so little support was offered to me as Ann's sister. In the course of interviewing other siblings, I asked about the level of support they had felt after their sibling's suicide. Most had been offered very little, and some none at all. Those who had experienced profound grief at the loss were hurt, bewildered, and frustrated that so few people appeared to recognize the magnitude of their loss or offer consolation.

Ramona (Ch. 1), who felt overwhelming grief after her brother's suicide, told me that I was the first person in all the seventeen years since Jonah's death that she had found to talk to about her brother and her loss. Even when she went out of her way to find someone who would listen to her feelings, she was rebuffed:

After the funeral, when I went back to the place I was living in at the time, I didn't have anyone to talk to. I had people that I had considered myself close to that I had talked to about lots of things, but all of a sudden I couldn't talk to them about this. No one wanted to hear. It was amazing how they didn't want to hear. I was part of a group of women that met to talk. They had taken up money to help me fly home for the funeral, so I knew they all knew. But no one ever said a word to me. Part of the problem was that it was a man, and they had a lot of anti-male feelings, but it wasn't just that. It was also that no one knew how to talk about death. They didn't know how to talk about someone who had killed himself. When I went back to work—I was a secretary at the university—not one of the professors I worked for said anything to me, not even, "I'm sorry to hear about it," or something.

It was one thing that helped me change a lot of the ways I thought of things, because I realized we're not doing very well if we don't work death into our thoughts. I started looking through all the things I could find to read about death and feminism. I found one article about it. I took it to my group, and I was ready to talk about death. No one was able to deal with it. That made me feel I was ready to break away from that group, because we had to think about death. Maybe none of them had lost anybody, and they just didn't know how to deal with it. Maybe it had something to do with their being city people. It was one of the reasons I had to come home and be with country people. Out here in the country you're aware of every death, and every birth, and every illness, and everything. You might not be intimate about it. You might not get to talk from your heart about it, but at least it's in the plan. At least you have your community around you.

I invited one woman to come talk to me, because I had such a desire to talk about it. I just wanted to let someone hear anything I wanted to say. I wanted to say it over and over, the same thing. She came that one evening, and she listened to me, but she was doing me a favor. She never came back again to listen. I never did have anyone to talk to.

Linda (Ch. 8 &9), who lost her twin brother, did find some people who were willing to talk with her, but she, too, found less support than she needed as a surviving twin:

Relatives sent condolence cards to my parents. That's where all the flowers and so forth went. People at work were, for the most part, supportive, especially the ones who had lost someone. But there are general issues about suicide. First of all, people think you're contagious. Suicide is very frightening to some people. And many people don't know how to deal with any death if they haven't had a loss themselves. I certainly didn't appreciate death until after this—any kind of death. Afterwards, there were people I called and said, "I'm really sorry—I don't think I was a very good friend when your dad died of Alzheimer's. I really appreciate more now what you went through."

People just don't know how to deal with it. My best friend in the world, who knew Lee well, just happened to be in town visiting her family the weekend of the funeral, and she came to the viewing. She and I had the first fight we'd ever had after the funeral. I think it scared her, so she couldn't handle it. My theory is that she was having the best year of her life—she was just about to get married, and she'd just had a big promotion in her firm—and here I was going to ruin it. It's a lot better between us now, but it took a while. It took her grandmother dying.

Karen (Ch. 10), whose family was so involved in finger-pointing and recriminations that she had not been able to experience her own grief after her brother's death, also felt little support, as a sibling, for her feelings:

It's odd how the rest of the world responds after a suicide. A lot of people responded to my parents, and there were lots of people who responded to my sister-in-law, because it's obvious what kind of impact that could have. Many fewer have responded to the siblings. Many parents can imagine what it's like to lose a child. It's very profound, and it bonds them with a parent. And they can imagine what it's like to lose a spouse. But there isn't a lot of support for the sibling. For the people I grew up with—my parents' friends—it never occurred to them to reach out or contact me or my younger brother. It's an indication of where people think support is needed. Perhaps it has to do with how people feel about their own siblings.

One woman who wrote to me, Teresa, had been diagnosed with a life-threatening disease shortly before her sister's suicide. She found that very few of her friends could talk to her about the death of her sister, although they could talk about Teresa's illness fairly openly:

People were quite solicitous about my health during the period after Gail's death, but they never talked to me about Gail or about my feelings about her suicide. In fact, people will still ask how I feel physically, even though I am now apparently healthy, but they never bring up my sister. If I want to talk about Gail, I have to be the one to bring it up. The same people have always been solicitous toward my parents, but they seem to assume that a sister does not have strong feelings. Perhaps a part of that is that there is still a stigma attached to suicide. People can talk more openly about topics like illness now, but suicide seems to be still taboo.

What can account for this lack of support for the surviving siblings? It appears, in part, that friends and other family members tend to assume that siblings do not have as close a bond as parents, spouses, or children, and therefore would not be in need of consolation or help. Perhaps this reflects some people's own relationship with their own sisters or brothers. If their relationship with their siblings is not particularly close, they would find it easy to assume that another person's loss of a sibling is not a particularly deep one. It is certainly true that the people I talked with who had felt deep grief after their sister's or brother's suicide were very solicitous of me, and worried that writing a book about sibling suicide would bring up unbearably painful feelings and memories for me. Those same people, and others who were very close to their siblings, would be the ones who would take pains to comfort a surviving sibling.

Yet those who assume that a surviving sibling did not have a close relationship and therefore is not in need of support, may be using that assumption as an easy rationalization for not undertaking the delicate and difficult task of approaching and attempting to understand the feelings of the bereaved sibling. It is hard enough to write to the parents, spouse, or children, and to reach out to them after the suicide. Assuming that the surviving siblings are not deeply affected can be a way of avoiding having to deal with their loss, as well.

Most people have a good deal of difficulty dealing with death, particularly if they have not had the experience of losing someone close to them. How much more difficult it is to know how to approach someone who has lost a loved one to suicide. There is more openness about suicide now, and more acceptance, but the attitudes of the past still linger. While suicides are no longer buried under crossroads and denied a sanctified burial, and while the Roman Catholic Church, for instance, no longer (officially, at least) regards suicide as a sin, yet a sense of stigma remains. That stigma only adds to the discomfort people feel around death and bereavement, and makes them loathe to get close to the survivors and awkward and afraid about talking about it.

Added to that is the sense that, if a family has suffered a suicide, there must be something abnormal or wrong with the family. And, particularly if the deceased was also mentally ill, others may suspect that the survivors, particularly the surviving siblings, may also be "tainted" with mental illness. Even though attitudes toward mental illness are changing, it still evokes feelings of uneasiness and fear, and people tend to distance themselves from it and the people associated with it.

Daniel (Ch. 5), who admits to feeling relief after his sister killed herself after many years of suffering with depression and schizophrenia, feels that most people still fear and avoid contact with mental illness:

Mental illness is the last taboo, I think. Death is not taboo, anymore. There's so much death talk in the media—Life After Death, Reliving Death, Kevorkian. Sex is not taboo. But mental illness is taboo. People don't talk about it. I don't want to tell people, "My sister jumped off a building because she was crazy." I don't tell people that, not because it hurts me to talk about it, but because it hurts other people to talk about it. It makes other people uncomfortable. They don't know how to respond. They don't know what to say, unless they've been through that kind of thing.

Fearing other people's reaction to their sibling's suicide, many people found it difficult even to try to talk to people about it afterwards. They were too afraid of being stigmatized to chance reaching out for support in the first place. Rosemary's younger brother killed himself thirteen years before we talked. He had been bi-polar for several years before finally throwing himself in front of a car on the highway. She told me:

I was always afraid to tell anyone, because I was always afraid that they'd think I was going to be sick like my brother and that the stigma of the mental illness was also on me. I always tell people it was an accident—that he was hit by a car. I guess I'm still a little afraid of that. It was one of the things that I really feared right after the suicide. My husband's family was really nice about it. They didn't treat me like a freak or anything, but I was afraid of it—afraid of people thinking that I might be mentally ill because it might be a hereditary thing.

Alan (Ch. 4, 6, & 10) and his family had an unspoken agreement not to tell anyone, except close friends and family who already knew the truth, that his brother's death was a suicide:

As long as it stayed out of the papers, to the public at large it was a car accident. Most people knew he was a maniacal driver anyway. And that's how it has remained. At this point I really don't care anymore who knows what, but back then it was difficult. It was a two-way thing where I didn't want to put people in the position of having to react to something as bizarre as a suicide, and, conversely, I didn't know where that would put me in their eyes as someone who was from an apparently nurturant environment, out of which came a suicide. When you tell people your brother killed himself, it shocks them and they can't figure out what to say. It's like opening a can of worms. So for ease or for convenience I'll say I'm an only child, unless it's a situation where I need someone to know me better.

The fear of being stigmatized, the awkwardness of bringing up a shocking subject that other people may not be able to handle, and the sense of vulnerability about sharing a deeply personal experience, all contribute to people's fear of talking about a sibling's suicide. Yet most people told me they needed to talk about it to ease their burden, to understand their own feelings around it, and to achieve some kind of closure. When other people couldn't or wouldn't listen, or when their own inhibitions or fears kept them from talking about their sibling's suicide, they felt frustrated and hurt, and their fear of opening up to other people was compounded.

Joining a support group was helpful to many people I talked to, particularly when it included other people who had lost a sibling. One person who had joined a group for suicide survivors, however, told me that the experience had been awkward for her because she was the only sibling in a group made up largely of parents. She was afraid to talk about her anger at her own parents for fear of upsetting the parents in the group, and she withdrew from it after a short time. This is unfortunate, because had she stayed with it and brought out her feelings, other people in the group probably could have eventually used what she had to say, and the reciprocity could have been healing for everybody.

Some other people, who had no formal support group to join, consciously sought out supportive friends who had themselves experienced similar losses, and they were able to talk about their feelings and work through them. Being able to share their experience, even with just one other person, helps free the survivors to move on. Ramona (Ch. 1 & 11) told me that writing to me about her brother's suicide, the first time she had been able to talk to anyone freely about it, helped her immeasurably:

It did me so much good to write about it. I'm not through writing about it. I'm going to write more. When I saw that I had written that I was twenty-five and he was twenty-eight, it really shocked me because I hadn't realized how present I had kept everything. I thought, "That was a long time ago. I don't have to carry it around as so present with me." It's just getting it off your chest—saying it.

The secrecy that surrounds suicide, the stigmatization of the survivors, the fear and discomfort around confronting it—all play a role in a conspiracy of silence that hurts everyone and denies survivors the opportunity to understand and to heal.

Chapter Twelve
Spouses, Lovers, and Others

Losing a sibling to suicide can have a profound impact on how the survivors approach subsequent relationships with friends, people of the opposite sex, and spouses. Our early relationship with siblings is one of our models for our relationships with other people later in life, yet, for the most part, not enough attention is paid to the role of sibling relationships in our adult lives. Traditional psychotherapy, for instance, tends to focus attention on the patient's early relationships with the parents. Therapists will guide their patients to see how those relationships have affected their choice of a marriage partner or their dealing with a boss or co-worker, for instance, often giving short shrift to the ways their sibling relationships have also colored subsequent ones.

Yet, when we focus on our relationships with our siblings, we often see that it was not our father that we married but our brother, or not our mother but our sister. We may find that we relate to a spouse or to a co-worker in the same ways we related to a sibling—competing, perhaps, or jockeying for power. And we may find that we play out our sibling role in our dealings with friends. As we look at it more closely, the significance of our siblings' influence on our later relationships becomes ever more apparent. Little wonder, then, that people who had lost a sibling to suicide, especially when they were younger, found that their relationships with others were often profoundly affected.

Reba (Ch. 7), whose older brother killed himself when she was only ten, felt that his death had a significant impact on her later relationships with men. Her brother, she felt, had been the only one in her family who loved her and gave her a sense of self-worth. Afterwards, her self-esteem was severely damaged. Then, when she became a teen-ager, she discovered that other men could give her the same sense of self-worth that her brother had. Both of the men she married seemed to her to be like her brother. Yet, while she had, in a sense, temporarily regained her brother by marrying men who resembled him, she always feared that they would leave her as her brother had. Indeed, both of them did abandon her, and her fears were realized. Like many people I talked with, Reba feels that she has lost so many people that she has become fearful of trying again. She tends to withdraw from other people and new relationships, and finds herself too much alone.

Jean (Ch. 1) had a long-delayed reaction to her brother's suicide. It wasn't until she was in the process of trying to separate from a man she was living with that she got in touch with her grief for her brother. She realized that she was involved with the man largely because of his resemblance to her brother. Even though she wanted to put an end to the relationship, it was extremely painful for her because it meant, in a sense, losing her brother again—the strong and nurturing man she needed for support. She recognized why she was attracted to the man in the first place, and she was eventually able to end the relationship and understand that her struggle had to do with her delayed grief for her brother. Yet Jean still finds herself being attracted to men who remind her of her dead brother and becoming involved with them.

Many of the women I talked with who had lost a brother when they were still young also found that his suicide led them to seek out partners who were like him and then to feel anxious that their new partner would abandon them as their brother had. This was also true to a lesser extent for men who had lost a sister at a young age. It seems that there is often a sexual attraction between siblings of the opposite sec, although it is often unconscious or unspoken, and the sudden suicide of the opposite sex sibling can drive the surviving siblings to seek him or her out in other relationships, only to find themselves fearing that the relationship will play itself out the same way.

For Sam (Ch. 6), the effect of his brother's suicide on his subsequent relationships took a different route, but with a similar result. After his seventeen-year-old brother, Barry, killed himself, Sam took over his personality and interests. He became his brother. He began seeing his brother's girlfriend for a while and became bewitched by her looks, even though he did not like her much as a person. In later years he continued to be attracted to women who resembled his brother's girlfriend. He married one of them, then had an affair with another, which destroyed his marriage. After he became involved again with his brother's girlfriend years later, he finally began to see the pattern in his relationships with women. Therapy helped him understand that he was always pursuing his brother's girlfriend in various other relationships, even though he seldom really liked the women he became involved with. Like several people I talked to, Sam continued in a sense to revisit the scene of his brother's life and death, and it had long-term effects on all of his subsequent relationships.

Many other people I talked with told me they found it very difficult to make new relationships after the death of their sibling. A good part of that difficulty is the fear of the stigma the suicide lays on them. Pamela (Ch. 6 & 10) speaks for many surviving siblings about their fears when they approach a new relationship:

I never know what to say to people when they ask how many brothers and sisters I have. Do I say I was brought up with five? Or do I say there were five? Do I say there are five? But then that opens the door for someone to say, "What happened?" When you're meeting someone or dating him for the first time, or getting to know somebody, you don't want to dump all your problems out. You don't want to expose too much, because then they back off and think, "Oof! This is a weirdo. I'm not getting involved with her." So it gets kind of bizarre. I kind of mumble that part. I say I was the youngest of five, but I don't say it very loudly.

Pamela also found that when she did get involved in a relationship, she lived in dread of the person dying. She had trouble ending relationships that weren't working out, and she clung to former boyfriends long after the relationship was over. Her fear of others dying, as her brother had, made it extremely difficult to let go.

The fear of a loved one dying or abandoning them was a frequent theme in the lives of many sibling survivors I talked with, especially those who had been in their teens or early twenties when they lost their brother or sister. No one's experience was more severe than that of Scott (Ch.) 7, who was only seven when his brother killed himself. He lives in constant dread of other people dying and abandoning him. Even when other people are late for an appointment, he becomes extremely anxious. As a teenager he couldn't tolerate his parents' leaving him for an evening, for fear they were never coming home. Even now, years later, his greatest fear is that everyone in the world will die, and he will be the last person left on earth. Making new relationships is nearly impossible for him, because it means that he would have one more person to agonize over. He rationalizes his difficulty with making new relationships by telling himself that he has enough friends and doesn't need any more.

Scott's experience is extreme, but it reflects the difficulties other surviving siblings experience in their subsequent relationships. John (Ch. 2 & 9), who felt little sense of loss for his dead brother, nevertheless found that his suicide had a long-term effect on his own ability to get close to other people.

I said once, "I don't want what happened to my brother to happen to me." I was falling in love, and I was afraid that, if the person didn't love me back, I would kill myself the way my brother did. I don't think it was ever conscious. I thought I would never get to that, to let myself fall in love. But I have since fallen in love, and I found I could handle it and being rejected. My brother's suicide affected me in ways I didn't think about until

years later, when I realized that I was shutting myself off to close relation-
ships. It was as if I were saying, "Look what happens when you fall in love.
I don't want that to happen to me."

For Lucy (Ch. 1, 9, 10), as for many people I talked with, her brother's
suicide two and a half years before made her fearful of getting close to
other people, who might similarly abandon her or reject her. She realized
that she would have to work hard to deal with her feelings of abandonment if she were going to have healthy relationships with other men:

My father's philosophy is to get over it and get on with your life. He thinks
one can do that without going through any of the pain, but you have to go
through the pain. If I expect to have any kind of relationships with people in
the future, I've got to deal with my brother's suicide. I especially had a hard
time with relationships after that. I was involved with one man, and it was a
nightmare. I'm terrified of abandonment. I'm terrified of rejection. I was
abandoned in many ways by my family when I was young, and my brother's
suicide just multiplied it. I just started dating a man a month and a half ago
who's really sweet and caring and loving. I have to watch myself that I don't
set myself up in that situation—getting the fear and starting to push. I have
a tendency to push people away and feel, "Don't get too close to me." I tend to
push them away before they have the chance to reject me. And the other thing
is that the anger spills over on other people. Such anger! I don't know how
they did it, but my friends tolerated me so nicely. The anger was unbelievable
and still is. I have to really watch myself, especially when I'm tired, because I
have a tendency to get angry and lash out at innocent bystanders.

Most of the people who described far-reaching effects on their
other relationships were relatively young when they lost their sibling.
Paul is something of an exception. He was thirty-one when his
seventeen-year-old brother killed himself, sixteen years before we
talked. Being fourteen years older than his brother Isaac, he felt more
like an uncle to him than a brother, but their relationship was a very
close one. Before his suicide, Isaac had been getting into trouble with
alcohol and drugs. He showed up drunk late one night at Paul's

apartment, having just wrecked his mother's car for the second time in a matter of weeks:

He was petrified to go home. He was drunk out of his mind, ranting and raving and out of control. He was a big kid, and he was out of control for an hour and a half. One thing led to another, and by the end of an hour and a half, I was fed up. I smacked him, open-handed smacked him. I immediately called my other brother Fred and told him he had to come down there because I couldn't control him by myself. It took my brother about an hour to get there, and during all that time Isaac was berating me for hitting him and raving that I didn't love him. It ended up really badly for us, because Fred arrived, and Isaac kept screaming, "Fred's my best friend!" and "I hate you!" And that was how we ended the whole thing. We took him to my mother's and put him to bed there, and I guess he had to face the music with my mother alone. Two nights later he jumped in front of a semi on the highway, and it took his head off.

For years my brother Fred blamed me, and there was a rift. I know I should have handled it better, but that's the way it happened, and there's no changing it. I've been carrying a load of guilt for sixteen years. I know it has affected me in the way that I carry myself and the way I deal with people. I'm stand-offish with people. I don't really let many people in.

Isaac's death has affected all the relationships I've had, especially with women over all the years, because it has certainly been the central event in my life, other than my son being born. We named him Isaac after my brother. I never thought I would have a kid. He's five now, and now that's been taken away, too, because I'm divorced from my wife. I have always held back from people, and since Isaac's suicide it's much more pro-nounced. Even in my whole relationship with my wife I always held something back, always.

It was having something given to me, free and open-hearted, and then having it snatched away just like that. I never wanted to have that happen again, so as a defensive measure, I don't allow myself to be put in that posi-tion in the first place, where things can be taken away.

If telling my story can do any good for anybody, hopefully enlighten someone who's considering the act, it would be enough. I would urge them to reconsider, because of all the other ramifications and the lives that can be altered forever. Forever. It will be with me until my dying day.

No doubt the other people who felt profound reverberations after their sibling's suicide would agree with Paul that the effects can be life-long. Many continue to seek out their dead sibling in relationships with others, only to live in dread of being abandoned again. Others relive the sibling's life and death by identifying with his or her persona or becoming involved with people who were close to the sibling. Often, surviving siblings find it difficult to begin new relationships, not only out of fear of being rejected for themselves, but also because of the stigma attached to suicide. Many are afraid to get close to anyone again or trust anyone with their deepest feelings, because the fear of having it all snatched away remains deeply etched in their hearts. A sibling's suicide can, indeed, leave a grim legacy for the survivors.

Part Three
Sibling Issues

Chapter Thirteen
Suicide as an Option

Following Suit

Many of the people who had been in their teens or twenties when they had lost their sibling were aware that their parents began worrying about whether they, too, would kill themselves. Their parents hovered over them anxiously, monitoring their comings and goings, or, worse, they stopped setting limits on their surviving children's behavior, fearing that if they imposed any discipline on their other children, they would follow their sibling.

Those fears do, in fact, have a basis. Statistics indicate that surviving family members, including siblings, are more prone to suicide, particularly if they were young when the suicide occurred. Not all the surviving siblings I talked to, of course, became suicidal themselves, but among those that did there were a variety of reasons why suicide became an option for them.

One of the most troubling for me was the urge to emulate the act of an admired older sibling. Scott (Ch. 1 & 12), for instance, who was only seven when his sixteen-year-old brother killed himself, had always looked up to his brother. He thinks often about suicide himself, and feels that his suicide would be a kind of memorial to his brother's memory. The only thing that seems to hold him back is the thought of the devastation for his parents if he were to "follow suit". The experience of Reba (Ch. 7 & 12) was somewhat similar, although she was not at all as suicidal as Scott. She, too, had been quite young when her admired older brother killed himself, and she thinks of her two suicide attempts, years later, as her way of imitating her brother's solution to life's problems. What gives the urge to emulate their older brother its power is that it is largely unconscious, lodged in the magical thinking of early childhood.

Several people felt that their sibling's suicide sent them a message that suicide was a viable option, a way to solve life's problems. Many said that they had never thought of killing themselves until their sibling did. It became, in a sense, a learned behavior: this is what you do when you have difficulties. Many, like Linda (Ch. 8, 9, & 11), whose twin brother killed himself when she was in her early thirties, felt that his suicide gave her "permission": *I'd never considered it before, but he'd made such a statement.* Her grief at her loss, her guilt for not having saved her twin, and her depression all combined to fill her with such pain that she felt *the only way to get rid of it was to kill myself.*

Grief at the immense loss can be enough in itself to make the surviving sibling feel that life is no longer worth living. As Judy (Ch. 4) said, after her beloved younger brother killed himself, *I was going to just go off in the wilderness and die...I felt that if this could happen, there was no point in living.* Other people felt such an immensity of guilt over the suicide that they felt driven to punish themselves by killing themselves, as well. They thought they should have seen signs that their sibling was at risk and done something to stop it. Many felt that if a sibling couldn't help, who else could? Rather than accept the idea that the suicide was, ultimately, their sibling's decision, and unable to blame the dead sibling, they turned the finger of blame on themselves, instead. And, as if the guilt in itself is not painful enough, some people may call down the ultimate punishment on themselves. Many people told me that they became depressed after their sibling's suicide. Unable to acknowledge the anger they felt at their sibling, they turned it on themselves, instead. The subsequent depression can drive people to the point where they see no value in going on with life. When, as in Linda's case, all of these feelings combine and compound each other, the drive to kill oneself can become overwhelming. A further factor in a surviving sibling's own subsequent suicide can be the feeling of identification with a loved sister or brother. Some people may feel that, because they were so close in life, if their sibling chose suicide, then they inevitably must, as well.

Entwined with all of these feelings, if their sibling had been mentally ill, sometimes survivors may share the mental illness that ended in their sibling's suicide. Bi-polar disorder, hysterical depression, schizophrenia, and other mental illnesses do have a genetic basis and do run in families, which accounts, in part, for the higher incidence of suicide in families that have already experienced it. Since siblings are closer, genetically, than anyone, the likelihood that they suffer from an illness like their sibling's is very real, and that can raise the odds of their own suicide.

Although Pam (Ch. 6, 10, 12), for example, did not herself become suicidal, two of her other siblings did. Both seemed to have some form of the mental illness that afflicted their dead brother, and their drug use exacerbated it. After their brother set the example, they seemed to see his act as permission to act on their own impulses to kill themselves. Those impulses may have been already present, driven by their own mental illness, and their brother's suicide may have suggested that suicide was a viable choice and served to trigger their suicide attempts. For Linda (Ch. 8, 9, 11, 13), too, the fear that she or another of her siblings would kill themselves after her twin brother's suicide came fully to the fore. Her brother had suffered from bi-polar disorder for years, and all her other siblings, including herself, had some form of mental instability or disorder. She and one of her sisters acknowledged the strong possibility that Larry's suicide could prompt the other siblings to follow through, themselves, and they went so far as to promise one another that they wouldn't kill themselves. Still, Linda lives in dread of what will happen to her other siblings, and is still "waiting for the other shoe to drop."

One woman who wrote to me about her brother's suicide expressed many of the feelings that can lead to the surviving sibling's decision to follow suit. She had been in her early twenties when her younger brother, who was a paranoid schizophrenic, killed himself. She had been very protective of him, acting as a kind of surrogate parent, and his suicide laid a great guilt on her. She wrote, *I blamed myself for various reasons. I was the only one who could have saved him; I was the last person to speak to him; I was closest to him. I don't think I cried for years about anything, but I proceeded to leave my marriage, become alcoholic, leave a promising career by dropping out of graduate school, and at various times consider suicide myself. It seemed both more an option because of my brother's suicide and also less one—how could I do that to my remaining family? On a simple level, I was telling myself I didn't deserve to live if he couldn't; on another, I think I was almost living his life for him and assuming his feelings—that he couldn't live in this world. Later, after a second marriage that was a new brand of hell, and after having two children, I slipped into a psychotic episode that kept me hospitalized for five weeks. Again, I wonder if I was recreating his life in my own. Somehow, if I had a life like his, I could tell myself I wasn't responsible for his death. I could see myself as much a victim of our early family life as he was, and therefore, not capable of saving him. It took years of therapy before I could let my brother's suicide be his own act, his responsibility, not mine.*

Thankfully, most people do not choose to follow in their sibling's footsteps. Those people I talked to who had felt suicidal themselves, or had, at least, considered suicide as an option for themselves after their sibling's death, had often made a conscious decision not to, for a variety of reasons both philosphical and practical.

Ramona (Ch. 1, 11) had felt at one point after her brother's suicide that she would literally die of grief, but she would not kill herself because she feels that her life is not hers to take: *I think it's very strange when people kill themselves, because, for myself, I feel that I'm in God's hands. I was born, and that's a mystery, and I'll die, and that's mystery, and I just have to know that I'm in God's hands. But when you kill your-self, you've kind of taken it out of God's hands.*

Pam (Ch. 6, 10, 12, 13), whose two other surviving siblings became suicidal after her brother's death, did not, nor did she feel that suicide is a viable choice. She told me, *I just don't understand what at my age would make me take my life. Things get bad, but...I have thought, "Gee, wouldn't it be nice to crash my car so I wouldn't have to go to work, and I'd have a good excuse." But I don't want to die in that car crash. I want to be able to get up. I just don't want to have to go to work. Once I got put in the psych ward for six days. My boyfriend married someone else, and I went into my therapist's afterwards and couldn't stop crying about it. My therapist had never seen me cry. She called my mother and said that she felt that I should be hospitalized because she was worried that I was going to take my own life. It never occurred to me to take my own life, but I don't blame her for that. I know that once a doctor hears that someone in the family has killed himself, they're afraid you're going to do that too. After my sister tried to kill herself—she used the same kind of anti-depressant I was on—my mother hid my pills. I got so indignant and so annoyed at her, because I am not going to kill myself. I am my own person and always have been, and I always thought of suicide as a coward's way out. Once a boy told me that he wished he were strong enough to try to take his life. I said, "Strength isn't involved here. You're more of a man for not trying than you ever will be if you do try."*

Knowing about the statistics on the likelihood of multiple suicides in a family, many people told me that they were especially careful with their own thoughts and feelings after their sibling's suicide. Ellen (Ch. 4, 6, 9, 10), who was filled with self-blame after her sister's suicide, went through an episode a few months later when, spaced out on marijuana, she was terrified that she was going to step in front of a car and kill her-self. Not long after her sister's suicide a woman had come up to her and said, "You better watch out, because it runs in the family." The idea filled her with terror, and that episode when she felt she might step in front of a car seemed like a nightmare about to come true. She told me, *Still to this day, when things feel really bad, I think, "I wish it were all over." Over the years I have thought about that. Not that it should have been me, instead. Never, never that. But just if I weren't around to feel all this, I wouldn't have to deal with it. I'm guessing that most people have suicidal thoughts at one time or another, but right after Leah committed suicide I never allowed myself to think about killing myself. Right after what happened with her I didn't allow myself any suicidal fantasies at all. I felt I had to be very careful.*

Joe (Ch. 1, 10) also feels he needs to be careful with himself. He had been extremely close to his brother Matt, and they had talked about the issue of suicide together. Joe accepted his brother's decision to kill himself as a release from his acute pain. He told me, *I think I may be a kind of melancholy person overall, but I have an internal engine or spirit that constantly propels me forward. I have never been at all as depressed at Matt. I have contemplated suicide, but it was more of an intellectual exercise than literally thinking about it because I want to do it. I've tried to be very careful, because I don't want to make too strong a linkage between my acceptance of the idea of suicide and my emotion for Matt. I don't want to make it too acceptable to me in the sense of its being associated with him, as being a bonding with him.*

Megan (Ch. 8, 10), whose twin sister killed herself when they were just seventeen, had always had to fight to forge her own identity as a person separate from her twin. She had a very definite reason for not choosing suicide herself: *Suicide became not an option. It was very simple: I didn't want to be a copy cat. My twin sister did it, ergo I don't want to do it. When I was pregnant and had suicidal fantasies, what scared me was that it was unconscious. I couldn't control it. I didn't want to do what my sister did!*

Phil (Ch. 1), whose younger brother killed himself when Phil was eighteen, had similar reasons for not seeing suicide as an option for himself: *I think everyone thinks about suicide. I've thought about it sometimes since Mick's death, and the times that I did I felt cheated because I can't do that now. That so-and-so did it before me. If one of us in the family was going to commit suicide, Mick just happened to be the one, and I can't do it now because he beat me to it.*

Like many people I talked with about their feelings about suicide as an option for themselves, Phil had another, better reason for not taking his own life: he had seen first-hand the pain it caused his parents, and he would not inflict further pain on them. He said, *One of my greatest hurts is seeing my parents and what this has done to them. Why would anyone do that when they know the destruction it causes?* His is a feeling people I talked with expressed over and over. John (Ch. 2, 9, 12), for instance, said, *I have thought about killing myself sometimes when things were bad, but I would think, "No, I can never imagine doing that." Part of that was that I'd rather go through whatever I go through here than not know what's on the other side of it. And, second, I can never imagine hurting my Mom the way she'd been hurt so many times. She's been institutionalized. She lost her son. Right before that she lost her brother to cancer, and right after that she lost her Dad to cancer. So she had "Boom Boom Boom" one after another. I wouldn't do that to her.*

Some of the people I talked with were able to deal with their suicidal feelings successfully on their own, but many of them did not feel they could cope with the aftermath of their sibling's suicide without professional help. Given the statistics on the heightened probability of other siblings in a family becoming suicidal, therapy or counseling should be made available to surviving siblings, yet, too often, it is not. Unfortunately, for some people there is still a stigma attached to the idea of needing professional help to deal with life's crises. Several of the people who were young at the time of their sibling's suicide told me that no professional help had been offered, but that it might have helped them immeasurably. There should not be any stigma attached to reaching out for help when we need it. As one man wrote me, *My therapy has saved my life. I cannot impress enough on anyone the value of this work.*

Attitudes toward a Sibling's Choice of Suicide

Their attitude toward their sibling's suicide may, to a degree, also be a factor in whether survivors would choose to do likewise. Among the people I talked to there was a wide range of feelings about their sibling's choice and of attitudes toward suicide as an option in general, from complete acceptance, to ambivalence, to rage at their sibling's decision. That variety in attitudes reflected many things: the kind of relationship people had had with their sibling, the effect of their own background and religion in forming their values, and the nature of the suicide and its causes.

For the most part, people whose sibling had suffered from depression or other forms of mental illness accepted the suicide as inevitable—the only way for their brother or sister to escape the anguish caused by years of mental illness. Joe (Ch. 1, 10, 13), who had been very close to his brother, had witnessed his brother's intense pain for ten years, and his brother's anguish was so great that, for Joe, *His expressions of seeking escape or seeking peace seemed very valid to me and seemed very possible.* Joe felt his brother's eventual suicide was inevitable, and he felt relief that his brother's suffering was over. He feels that his brother simply ran out of strength and did the only thing he could after years of trying to get medical help in vain. Joe said, *Suicide seems to me like a real option. It seems like something I can see doing if you found out you had a terminal illness. I think I would kill myself in that case, or if I found out I had Alzheimer's disease.* Yet, even though Joe can accept the idea that his brother's suicide was a viable solution to his anguish, he wishes his brother could have waited a while longer—that perhaps a cure could have been found—and he continues to grieve for him.

Rosemary (Ch. 11), whose younger brother suffered for more than eight years with bi-polar disorder, feels much like Joe: *I felt Sean wasn't responsible for what he did, because he was depressed, because he was sick. I did wish that I'd had more time to spend with him, that I had known him better as an adult. I wished we had all seen it coming and been able to help relieve his pain. I blamed myself to a certain extent, but I don't know how much we are responsible. I think that he didn't have any control over what he was doing, that he was in so much pain. The only way that I guess I've been able to live with it is that it's like a terminal illness that he had. Maybe he saw his life ahead as one long series of getting better and then having another attack, and then being depressed for several years, and then maybe getting better. And then the illness came back. And that's not so different from when you're sick and you're dying from cancer. I saw it as a release from his pain.*

Like Joe and Rosemary, Evan (Ch. 10) felt that his sister had no other choice besides suicide, given her years of suffering from hysterical depression. Yet he feels somewhat more ambivalent about her choice than they do. He told me: *Valerie had been through all kinds of different programs, different medications. They really experimented on her, as they do on everybody, because they don't know what goes on in the human brain. I think life was very, very difficult for her, and these depressions were severe. I heard once on National Public Radio about someone who did an article on clinical depression. They said it's like being in a hundred and forty degree room with no fan and no windows. Just oppressive. I can imagine that her depression was just hugely difficult to live with. I'm still very sad about her death, and I still wish she were here. But that's really a selfish feeling. For her, she was released from this awful illness she had that nobody was able to treat. And the treatments were, in many cases, worse than the illness. She gained a tremendous amount of weight, and she blew up and got thin and blew up again. It was just horrendous. My sister was a really good-looking woman, and it really was a pity to have her go through all this stuff. The last time I saw her she was in great shape. She was in a great mood. I think that last month must have been great for her, because she had figured everything out, and she figured the next time she went into a bad depression she knew how she would kill herself.*

I'm a little bit angry at her though, because I think it's just terribly, terribly hard for her daughter. Maybe she could have waited until her daughter was a little older. I don't know. I think of that hundred and forty degree room with no windows and no fans. I don't want to be too magnanimous here to my sister. Certainly she made a mistake. She left us all. Suicide is a horrible thing. My father committed suicide when I was fifteen, and I'm certainly never going to get over that. So in a way it does make me angry, because my sister knew what it did. She knew how hard it was, so how could she do that to her daughter? But if you could ask her about that, I bet that she would say, "Yes, but I couldn't stand to be alive for one more minute." And she prepared her daughter for it, as well as one could be prepared. But when I think about my father's suicide and my sister's suicide, suicide is not an option for me, but I'm not a depressed person, either. I would not do that to my wife and my kids.

Several people I talked with took the philosophical approach that their sibling had a right to choose to live or die. Nancy (Ch. 2), who had not been close to her brother and did not feel a great sense of loss after his death, told me: *I just have the philosophy that it's that person's life, and they have a right to decide what to do with it, and who am I to make their decision for them? Of course, the flip side of the coin is maybe they're not completely rational, and don't really realize what they're doing at the time that they're doing it. So, therefore, I would attempt to intervene in that situation and stop them from doing what they're doing. But if they actually do manage to complete their plans and perform what they want, there probably is nothing that could be done to stop it. For me, personally, that's an option I never would have taken, because as far as I'm concerned there's always another solution. But I've never really been there. Seth was in a very different mental state, and he couldn't see any other option. So I blame him for what he did to himself, but in a way I don't blame him, because that was the only thing that he felt he had left to do, and who am I to make decisions for him?*

For Megan (Ch. 8, 10, 13), her twin's suicide when they were seventeen was devastating, yet she could not feel angry at her sister. She tends to rationalize her anger away: *I think I tend to intellectualize it too fast and think that that's an option everyone in the world has, and that it's a God-given option. That's what gives us free will. I'm not making it benevolent, though. The other reason, too, is that I don't think she had another option. What could she have done? I never knew how to be angry at her, because she was trapped.*

A handful of people saw their sibling's suicide as a courageous act, although that did not mean that they would choose it themselves. Earlier, John (Ch. 2, 9, 12, 13) talked about his personal unwillingness to follow through on his occasional suicidal feelings, for fear of hurting his mother still further, but he does see a degree of courage in his brother's act: *When I saw Tim in the casket, his fingers were black and flat. I think somehow he had touched the exhaust on the car, and he burned his hands. That got my head to going. Here he hurt himself so terribly, but he still went through with this. He got in the car and thought, "That's okay, this isn't going to hurt after awhile." What is going on in a head that goes that far…? I think it's the most courageous thing in many ways. It takes such courage to do, because I am so afraid to die in that way. I have a little odd sense of respect for him, almost. He messed up so many things in life that he made this decision, and he followed through with it. I feel if that's what he wanted, that's what he wanted.*

Like several other people, Walter (Ch. 6) felt that his sister made the only choice she could have, and, like John, he respects her courage in following through: *Corinna lived in a full-time depressed state. She was unhappy in this world, much as someone might be unhappy living in an apartment or in a city. My answer to that has always been, you get out. You just get out of the apartment, leave your job, and you go try to do some-thing else. I've lived that way my whole life. I think she was unhappy on this planet, and that's how she got out. I feel if you're in some place you don't like, if you can't do anything to change it, you get up and leave. The faulty link in this argument is that maybe she could have changed. But I don't think she was equipped to be changing. Some people aren't. I don't think she had the tools.*

It is courageous to sit there and have this be the one act of your life that is so definite. It's interesting that she rehearsed so many times, but in ways that weren't going to be, that were not going to work. But then, the one time she thought the stage was set properly, then she did it as though she meant business, and there was no getting around what was going to hap-pen, at that moment. I guess I fall into the camp of respecting that. At least for once in your life, don't sit around and watch TV—do something real. And if that's the only thing she could do, after years and years of trying to figure out what she was going to do, then I have to respect it.

Several people felt just the opposite about their sibling's suicide. When I mentioned to Alan (Ch. 4, 6, 10, 11) that some people felt suicide was a courageous act, he put on a look of disgust, and said: *Argh! See my reaction there? Every now and then some creative person will commit suicide. People have a tendency to glamorize it, or raise suicide above the level of what to me it really is, which is a PATHETIC thing. Suicide is horrible! A while back I answered an ad for volunteers for the suicide hotline. I had an interview, and discussed my reasons, and they never called me back. I finally called the direc-tor, and he said, "It isn't that we thought you were too close to the situation. We felt you were carrying an agenda, that you had too much of an axe to grind, almost to the point of militancy." I said, "You're right. I HATE suicide! It's so stupid!" One of the reasons I was interested in being part of the hotline was my feeling that no matter how methodical someone is about suicide, no matter how at peace they are with this ultimate decision, if you would just string them along a little, if you would just get them to think it out, they wouldn't do it. The chances may be one in a million, and maybe you'll fail, but try!*

Paul (Ch. 12), who was devastated by his much younger brother's suicide and still feels its effects sixteen years later, would agree with Alan: *Having given it some really serious thought over the years, I think suicide is a completely self-centered thing. Shakespeare said it—there's only one choice in life: to be or not to be. And when you come down and make the decision not to be, it's a completely self-centered act, a completely self-centered decision. You don't think about anybody else. How could you? How could you do that and be thinking about the feelings of anybody else? Maybe it's one thing if you're alone, and your parents are dead, and you don't have brothers or sisters, or a wife and kids. But if you've got people around you that you halfway cared about, how could you do that to them? It's just foreign to me.*

Neither Alan nor Paul have experienced the kind of deep depression that drove their brothers to suicide. Bonnie (Ch. 3, 10) was furious with her brother for years for killing himself when she was still in the hospital with a new baby, but she has been depressed at times, herself, so she has come to understand something of what drove her brother to take his life. For many years she felt that *the kind of selfishness that is going to have such terrible repercussions on everybody around you is unforgiveable.* It is only in recent years that she has developed some empathy for the pain her brother experienced by considering how she feels when she is depressed. She said, *When I'm depressed I feel that I'm in the bottom of a cleft, and I can't remember any good times, and I can't foresee any good times. When Ted was down in that cleft, he had no perspective on any goodness in his life.*

Her brother Jim (Ch. 3, 10) was also very angry at Ted for killing himself, and called suicide "the ultimate narcissism". He felt tremendous anger and resentment at his brother for years for taking the "easy way out". Over the years, he says, *I have had time soften my stance and look at it as someone with an illness. But I think that I still harbor the resentment and the anger.*

Most people feel ambivalent about their sibling's decision. Judy (Ch. 1, 13) grieved deeply for her younger brother. His choice to kill himself left her feeling "betrayed" and somewhat angry at him as a result. But, on the other hand, she says, *I knew that his taking his life was the end result of a whole series of events, that it was part of his illness.*

Margaret (Ch. 1, 10), who felt the loss of her older brother keenly, says, *I still look up to him, and his choice was his choice. Even though it hurts me a lot, and my family, that was his choice. I don't know if I respect it, but I know that he had thought about suicide several times, so it was like part of him. I never really hated him for his decision. I'm a little angry at what he did to his family, though. Maybe he took the easy way out. I don't know. I think one thing and then I think another thing. It's hard to know, because I have never felt suicidal myself.*

Phil (Ch. 1, 13) felt in some ways that his brother had a right to his choice, and that his last letters to his family had made suicide seem logical. He understood something about his brother's wish to leave this "grim plane" and go on to another. Yet he felt very angry at his brother for the pain and devastation his suicide caused for his parents. He felt, *he could have waited a little longer. If it's out there, it's not going anywhere. You'll get there eventually. It was very selfish. He never knew the damage and what would be left to the survivors of his suicide.*

Daniel (Ch. 5, 11) felt relief after his older sister, who had been mentally ill for some time, decided to kill herself. He, too, had somewhat mixed feelings about her decision: *I'm a little angry at my sister for doing that, because of what she did to my parents, and for not seeing these children of mine. But I don't think she was aware of what was going to happen to other people in the family. I just feel as though she was young and stupid. I want to say to her, "You were so stupid. So stupid." But my sister was really ill. She was a classically depressed person who killed herself. So in a way it wasn't so stupid of her. It was a way for her to escape her misery.*

Earlier, Karen (Ch. 10, 11) talked about the destructiveness of blaming and finger-pointing in her family. It made her think about the degree of her brother's own responsibility for his act: *Even with this blame, this pointing fingers back and forth, at some point you have to ask, "Okay, where does he come in? Does he get to take any responsibility for this? He was an adult. Did he make any choices here?" I blame him for this, in some ways. He did a horrific thing. But in one way I can't blame him because no one would do something so painful if he was not psychotic. Can you blame someone who's chemically imbalanced? Was he? Who knows? What I do blame him for, and I blame me for it too, was not reaching out. I've gathered from psychiatrists and psychologists I've talked to that he had to have been psychotic to do something so painful. For a long time just imagining the despair he must have been in in order to do that would just dissolve me. It was a magnitude beyond what I've felt. I've been depressed, but it's amplified so many times.*

Like many of the people I talked with, I felt some ambivalence about my sister's decision. I felt scorn at the stupidity of her suicide, because I felt that she did have other options. At the same time, I wondered if she really could have been helped, given her personality and her attitudes towards therapy. I understood the intense pain that drove her to feel that there was no other way out, but, at the same time, anger at her for the great grief it caused the ones she abandoned. On one level I could think of such a final act as requiring courage, but on another level it does seem, as others have said, the "easy way out." In the end, there is no one way to feel about any suicide.

Chapter Fourteen
Am I my sibling's keeper?

In the few weeks before my sister's death my mother, as I already mentioned, called me more and more frequently to share her anxiety, saying, "I'm very worried about your sister." The word "sister" reverberated in me. The word itself created a pressure to do something—a sister should. And, too, I felt that, as her sister, I understood where she was and what she was experiencing, and was in a unique position to help, if she would let me. But would she let me? She didn't even want me to know there was trouble, and I felt she would resent little sister coming to her aid. As Ann's sister, I felt it was incumbent on me to do something, but, paradoxically, as Ann's sister, I could not. I still feel guilty about failing her. For me the answer to the question, "Am I my sister's keeper?" is, "Yes. I should have been."

Most of the people I talked to felt similarly—that it is the role of a sister or brother to at least try to help. Many felt guilty that they had failed even to try. Others who had tried, still felt guilty at not having done enough. Some felt in some way responsible for their sibling's suicide, as if, like Cain, they had somehow committed fratricide.

No one was more conscious of being his brother's keeper than Joe (Ch. 1, 10, 13). When his brother first became ill, Joe took Matt into his home and watched over him for two years. After his brother moved out, he kept in constant touch with him. His brother was always on his mind wherever he was, and they discussed the idea of suicide openly. Having done everything he could to help his brother, and understanding his brother's decision that suicide was the only solution left to him, Joe does not feel guilty about his brother's death. He feels his brother knew the depth of his love for him, and he has no regrets in that way.

But Joe's deep commitment to his brother and consequent absence of guilt are rare. More often, people felt that they had not done enough for their sibling. Leila (Ch. 4), for instance, had always been protective of her younger sister when they were children, but when Libby became depressed and anorexic after her husband's death, Leila kept her distance. She felt pressure to help her sister, in part because she was herself a therapist, but also simply because a sister should. Yet she couldn't bring herself to get that close to her sister's pain, fearing that she might be drawn into it herself and be overwhelmed. She said, *I don't want to imagine the emptiness she felt. I don't want to imagine the grief she felt. I don't want to imagine the pain. Which is why I kept my distance. I think somewhere I don't want to let it reverberate inside of me.* After her sister's death, Leila felt guilty for a long time about having failed to fulfill her sisterly role.

For Linda (Ch. 8, 9, 11, 13), who lost her twin brother, her role as her siblings' keeper never seems to be in doubt. All her brothers and sisters have some form of mental illness or instability, and the siblings are always checking up on each other. Her parents tended to deny that there were problems among their children. Linda said, *There is a code of silence in our family. My sister calls it the big piece of elephant s—t that we use as a coffee table. We eat off it, we put our feet up on it, but we never call it elephant s—t.* With their parents in denial, the siblings had to be each others' support. Linda, especially, was the one who would take over in family crises. But when she realized that her twin brother was in trouble, she was, for once, too busy to travel out to be with him. She had to call on her sister to step in, instead. After his suicide Linda felt guilty that she had not been there this one time for her brother, and she was depressed to the point of considering suicide herself.

Alan (Ch. 4, 6, 10, 11, 13) felt tremendous guilt that he never stepped in to help his brother in all the years that he was getting into trouble. Fear and ignorance, he says, kept him from following through, and then, suddenly, it was too late. He said, *Am I my brother's keeper? Did that ever have an answer? I think that we are our sibling's keeper because, even if there's a wide difference in age, maybe even five or ten years, I think there's enough commonality that siblings share that they share with no one else. We should be one another's keeper, because everyone else—parents, friends, everyone we relate to—they all have their own agendas. They all have their own use for us. But our use for each other is something unique.*

I think a sibling is in a better position than anyone to help and understand, and yet how often does a sibling apply that position to its maximum benefit? Probably rarely. There's always fear of backfire, of rejection. Even if you know that desperate situation exists, you think, "Better to do nothing than to do more harm than good." And I think we fear rejection from a sibling more, because it would devastate us more than rejection from anyone else. I should have been my brother's keeper. I don't know what I could have done. But I know what I did, which was nothing. That weighs on me.

Not everyone agrees with Alan and the others about the degree of their responsibility to their sibling. Nancy (Ch. 2, 13), who felt little sense of loss over her brother, feels no guilt, either: *I never felt responsible for Seth, because he was a grown adult, and his decisions were his own decisions. I couldn't run his life, and I wouldn't have wanted to. I think he made the wrong decision, but it was his decision. It was his life to live...Or not live.* Jim (Ch. 3, 10, 13) felt extremely angry and resentful toward his brother for killing himself, but not guilty about his role in his brother's life: *I think parents probably perceive themselves as being responsible for their offsprings' well-being. If they let the fox into the chicken coop at night, and the chickens are gone, it's their fault. Parents are supposed to be protective. I don't see my role as the primary protector or responsible for my siblings, so there's not a need in me to preserve whatever overwhelming sense of guilt that people might have.* Walter (Ch. 6, 13) voiced similar thoughts about his role toward his younger sister: *I don't feel guilty about it. I was not my sister's keeper. I never was, and I never sought to be, and she never sought that from me. I think about how things might have been different, but I don't have any guilt about my sister's suicide.*

Sharon arrived at her answer to this question only after many years of looking after her sister, and a good deal of soul searching. Her sister Hilary, older than Sharon by six years, had made repeated suicide attempts since she was twenty-one, and Sharon was expected by her parents essentially to devote her life to watching over her sister. When we spoke, Sharon was forty-two and Hilary, who was still alive, was forty-eight and still suicidal. Two and a half years before, Sharon had cut off all contact with her family. It was a difficult, but, she felt, necessary decision to make.

Hilary had a breakdown when she was seventeen and I was eleven, after our grandfather died. That's the first time she started acting weird. In between seventeen and twenty-one she became a hippy and started doing a lot of drugs. She had another breakdown, and then the pattern after that was breakdowns that were signaled by suicide attempts. She's been diagnosed with lots of things, including schizophrenia, but bi-polar disorder seems to be the most current. She goes back and forth from cutting to overdosing. It feels to me as though it's been something like ten tries.

I was only sixteen when this started. A lot of my anger stems from the fact that I was a teenager and very much in need of my parents' help and participation and guidance in my life. But my parents' attitude was that she was the needy one, so I got very little attention as a teenager. I think the way they see it is not only is there not enough room for both of us, but that it's really distasteful of me to be asking for anything or to be focusing my attention on anything but my sister. She, obviously, is the needy one and the one with problems, and I'm supposed to take on a parental role and all of us pull together in devoting all our time and attention to my sister. It was very clearly conveyed in words and in action and in overall attitude that there was something expected of me, and that was to share the responsibility. If I didn't, I was just really not a good person.

Not only was I supposed to share this responsibility, but I wasn't supposed to get any kind of satisfaction in my life. At that point I was clearly not enti-tled any more to my own enjoyment. For a long time I would go see my sister in the hospital and draw her pictures and write her poetry. It was almost like being a spouse or a lover. I was really trying to reel her back and give her the will to live. And more and more I came to resent that responsibility and that role. I realized more and more that I had no life of my own.

As I gradually began to withdraw from that role, and complain about it, there was a lot of negative response to my trying to relate to Hilary in a healthier way. There was a lot of yelling and screaming. "How could you do this to your sister? You have so much more than she has. How could you be so selfish? You're healthy. You have a job. You have an apartment." I felt totally guilty that I had a job and an apartment and a cat and occasional-ly a partner. My basic feeling at that time about being the healthy one was that I would allow myself to have only so much money. I was keeping myself somewhat marginal, so as not to be overwhelmed by this kind of survivor's guilt. I felt I really should take care of her because I have so much. If I had a really successful job, and owned my apartment, then I would have to take total care of my sister. The guilt would be so unbear-able if I reached a certain level of success, and I would feel that I'd have to take a more active role because I had so much. I'd have to invite her to come sleep on my couch: "Aaaagh! I can't even buy a new couch!"

I still do feel guilty about withdrawing from this situation. It's a regular internal battle for me. One of the last things that happened was that my sister had voluntarily put herself in the hospital again, just about three years ago. I was at a point in my life where I was just in a panic about the whole situation. I was in a panic about her being at home, so dependent on my family, not functioning, not doing anything at all. She wasn't going to any kind of day treatment center. She was sleeping a lot, going shopping with my mother, eat-ing. My mother also has deteriorated emotionally and physically, so they were just kind of doing this together and clinging to each other. She and my sister were companions in this TV-watching, eating, and sleeping thing.

My parents were in their late seventies, and my sister was getting no closer to any kind of functioning, and I was totally freaking out, thinking they're going to die, and I was going to be my sister's keeper for ever and ever. I didn't have any sense at the time that I had choices about that. I felt that I had to make them do what I knew was right to do, and I was afraid of my own future. My sister had decided to go into the hospital, and I was really supportive of that. She was going to spend some time there and then have them get her into a structured housing situation. I really wanted to support her, and I felt my mother and father sabotaging it. Even my father was sabotaging it, because he doesn't particularly want to be alone with my mother. He'd prefer to have my sister there as a buffer.

So here were these people totally sabotaging what felt to me like my sister's sincere effort to try to change things. I went out to have dinner with her in my attempt to be supportive. It's a pretty far trip to the hospital, about a two hour trip by train and then bus. I got out there to find out that she was coming home the next day—that she had decided it wasn't working. This was very upsetting to me. And it was also upsetting that she knew she was coming home. The three of them had decided, without any input from me, that she was coming home, a decision that had an impact on me. When I confronted my parents about that, they said, "Oh, we never thought about that. We were just hoping that you might make her feel better." It was so painful to see how absolutely they disregarded me as a separate person, how they could justify my taking that long trip just to make my sister feel better. It was as though she was the center of the universe, and I was just a satellite.

It was shortly after that that I withdrew from the family. The whole situation was so destructive, and it was absolutely bankrupt for me. I think the decision was an obvious one to have had to make, yet it was a very hard one. I feel guilty because I was conditioned from early on to feel a responsibility for my sister's life.

My greatest fear when I made the decision to leave the family was that before the year passed she would attempt suicide and that she would succeed. Last year she took a massive overdose, but she didn't succeed. I was very relieved that she didn't, and I think having experienced her trying and not succeeding took a lot of that fear from me. I don't feel as superstitiously responsible any more. My parents did a lot of blaming. For a long time my mother felt that my sister's first lover was responsible for all her problems, and then I took on that role, when I became less and less willing to take on the role of parenting.

My parents called to tell me Hilary had tried to kill herself, and I stayed in contact with them about what was going on, on the phone. I didn't see her. When she was physically stabilized I cut back to the way it had been. I got a letter from my sister a few weeks after that, basically telling me that I was responsible for her suicide attempt. She said that by abandoning the family and abandoning her I had caused her such an excess of despair and loneliness that she inevitably had to kill herself.

All these unsuccessful attempts are like her saying, "You'll be sorry when I'm dead." I felt very much like a puppet. She wanted my attention. "Pay attention to me!" And then when I didn't respond by coming to the hospital that must have been very hard.

I think eventually she will kill herself, that she will eventually give up all hope and do it seriously. I don't see the situation getting better. I don't see my parents having the motivation and the resources to help her get other resources. And I don't see her having the strength or ability at this point of her own deterioration to find her way without help. I think she will kill herself, and I hope I'm wrong.

Maybe when she does succeed, it will be aimed at me somehow, as it seems to have been this last time, but I still don't regret my decision. I couldn't go on sacrificing my life to my sister, when the whole situation was bankrupt and going nowhere. The repercussions of making such a decision have been challenging, but I sure feel better than before I made it. My life is a lot better now.

A few months after our interview, Sharon called to say that she had run into a cousin on the street who had offered her condolences on the death of her mother and sister. This was how she found out that her mother had died during the Spring, and her sister had killed herself not long afterwards. (Much later, Sharon found out that her sister had actually died of natural causes stemming from her physical deterioration.) Sharon didn't want to talk about her feelings at that point. She was still rather numb, and didn't seem to know really what she felt. When I talked with her a few months later, Sharon still didn't want to talk about it much, except to say that a sense of guilt was not uppermost in her feelings. Mostly she was feeling grief. She wanted her sister—not the sister of her last years, but the sister she might have had if things had been different. Even though she had withdrawn from the family and was not expecting to see her sister again, and even though she felt that her sister would at some point kill herself, it still came as a shock and has led to real sadness and a strong sense of loss.

There is, of course, no ultimate answer to the question people in this chapter have pondered. Certainly, those who did not feel responsible for their siblings' fate did not suffer from great guilt after the suicide. The rest of us, who felt we were or should have been our sibling's keeper, felt varying degrees of guilt about our failure to protect him or her. That guilt is natural, but, as Megan (Ch. 8, 10, 13) told me, guilt may be something of an "ego trip". There is a limit to our responsibility toward our siblings. No one has that much power completely to control another's life or decision to die, and we have to accept the fact that, ultimately, the responsibility for a sibling's suicide rests with the sibling, not anyone else. Taking over total responsibility for a sibling, as Sharon did for so long, and sacrificing one's own life in order to help, support, and watch over a sister or brother, is too large a burden to bear and can only be destructive, in the long run, to everyone involved.

Chapter Fifteen
Were you thinking of me?

Many of us harbored a nagging question after our sister's or brother's suicide. Did we have anything to do with our sibling's death? Were we in our sibling's thoughts at all? It can seem like an egocentric question, and yet...

I wondered whether Ann had me in her mind at all, perhaps unconsciously, simply because she had so pointedly excluded me. She had made it clear to our mother that I was not to know anything about her troubles, which, as I have said, seemed to be a clear reflection of her ongoing competition with me as her younger sister. She didn't even include me in her suicide note. I did not feel that her suicide was aimed at me. If it was aimed at anybody, it was her husband, at whom she was very angry and who would, she knew, be the one to find her. But I knew that Ann always had a feeling of being on trial, with everybody else acting as judge. She always had to appear competent and confident, no matter what was going on inside. And I, as the younger sister with whom she always competed, was a "judge" for her with more power than most. I doubt that she was consciously aware of me when she killed herself, but I do suspect that I was there in her unconscious mind, as one who sat in judgment and found her wanting.

Her timing also made me wonder. Did she remember that I was going to be married soon? Did she give any thought to what effect her sudden death would have on what was supposed to be a happy event? She didn't approve of my fiancé, and her own marriage was falling apart. Was she aware at all that she was sabotaging her sister's upcoming wedding? Even if she wasn't, and even if the timing was purely unintentional, it still seemed to me like a mean thing to do.

The timing for Bonnie (Ch. 3, 10, 13), still in the hospital with her new-born son when her brother killed himself, and for Ellen (Ch. 4, 6, 9, 10, 13), whose sister killed herself on Ellen's wedding day, does seem to suggest that the suicides were in some way aimed at the sibling. Bonnie felt angry for a long time afterwards. She said, *For years after this I was sure...that there's no way that my son's birth couldn't be connected with him deciding to kill himself...Maybe that's very egocentric on my part.* Given the nature of their relationship—Bonnie's often disparaging remarks about Ted, the anger and jealousy he seemed to harbor toward her, the fact that he was critical of how she was raising her first son, and the fact that she was happy with a new baby while he was miserable with his ongoing depressions—all of that suggests that Ted's suicide at such a moment could well have been intended as a message to his older sister. It was almost as if he were saying, "You're happy while I'm miserable? You're getting all the attention? Well, watch this!" As Bonnie pointed out, "It grabbed the attention pretty nicely."

It is hard to see how Bonnie could not feel that her brother's suicide was aimed at her, at least in part. The quality of sibling revenge appears even more striking in Ellen's case, although she always denied that her sister meant to hurt her by killing herself on Ellen's wedding day, and could never seem to feel angry at her sister's act. Ellen felt that her older sister Leah had never liked her, and, indeed, from what Ellen told me Leah was a mean and even spiteful sister. Leah was already depressed and had talked of suicide before, and her own marriage had disinte-grated. And here was her younger sister, whom she had always seemed to resent, about to embark on what looked like a wonderful marriage. Added to that must have been Leah's need to be center stage. Certainly she was not going to be the center of attention on her sister's wedding day, unless...It is almost impossible not to see intention and sibling spite in Leah's suicide. It has had long-term reverberations for Ellen, particularly a fear of daring to be happy, yet Ellen cannot summon the rage that would be completely appropriate toward her sister. She had been raised to blame herself for everything, including her sister's ill-humor, jealousies, and unkind acts.

Of course, no one can ever know what went on in a sibling's mind just before the suicide. Many of us wondered whether our siblings could have been thinking of anyone besides themselves and their own pain. Evan (Ch. 10, 13), for example, thought of his sister's depression as feeling like being trapped in a 140 degree room with no fan and no windows, and he felt that she could give no thought to anyone else or the consequences for anyone, only her own need to escape. Morna (Ch. 1, 10) for a long time had an unconscious feeling that her brother's suicide was an act of betrayal and that he meant to hurt her. That she had been feeling that inner hurt became clear when she had a dream in which he assured her that he would never try to hurt her. She also remembers being suicidal herself several years before, and realizes that she was not thinking about the effect on anybody else if she killed herself. Other people I have talked to who had at one time or another felt suicidal also remembered not really considering the effect of their death on other people, or, if they did, thinking that they might be doing their families a favor by relieving their family of the burden of dealing with them.

Yet, despite their feeling that their sibling was probably turned inward and not thinking about anyone other than themselves, many of the people I talked with still pondered what part they themselves may have played in the ultimate decision. Phil (Ch. 1, 13), who with his twin brother was only a little older than his brother Mick, who killed himself at age seventeen, always wondered if Mick was finally pushed over the edge because he felt left out and left behind. Phil remembers Mick watching disconsolately from the stoop as Phil and his twin drove away for a camping trip at the end of their senior year, from which Mick, as a mere junior, was excluded. He felt that his brother felt left out in some ways as the older twins gained certain privileges that he could not yet share. And soon the two older brothers would go off to college and leave Mick behind. Phil's musings may not be out of place, since Mick set up his suicide so that his brothers would surely be the ones to find him.

Peter (Ch.5, 9, 10), who felt a certain relief when his difficult older brother killed himself, sometimes wondered if his brother's feeling of jealousy toward him contributed in any way to his decision. He mostly felt that, if it had been aimed at anybody, it was aimed at his parents, since his brother had been very angry at his parents and the suicide occurred right before their anniversary. Yet he knew that his brother was always very competitive with him and hated seeing him do better, and he wondered if his own good fortune, and even the fact that he had just rented a mansion much larger than his brother's house, could have fueled his brother's jealousy even more and added to his sense of failure.

Paul (Ch. 12, 13) feels a lingering sense of guilt that he wasn't more responsive, and in fact lost his temper, when his fourteen-years-younger brother, Isaac, came to him in his last crisis. The boy had just wrecked his mother's car for the second time, and was drunk and raving when he came to his brother's door. After an hour or so, Paul lost his temper and struck him. This final scene, with Isaac berating him for hitting him and screaming, "I hate you!" has haunted Paul for seventeen years. As a much older brother, he had always felt like a supportive uncle to his little brother, and he carried around a load of guilt that his own loss of control may have made his brother feel that he had lost his last support and contributed to his final despair.

Some people, like Everett (Ch. 4, 9), worried that something they had said or done might have helped trigger their sibling's suicide. Everett and his brother had a very competitive relationship during their youth, and, while they were now much closer, a rivalry persisted. Everett resented the attention his brother received in the family because of his skyrocketing career, and when his parents turned down Everett's invitation to an important concert he was playing in, in order to go to a presentation his brother was making, he lost his temper and yelled some damaging and spiteful words he later regretted.

Even though his therapist tries to help him see that his brother's suicide was his own act, and even though Everett knows that his brother was deeply suicidal, he still worries that his angry words may have given his brother the impetus to kill himself. He wonders if his brother was so sensitive and had such low self-esteem that he felt wounded to the core by Everett's angry remarks. And it is possible that Everett's brother cared more about Everett's feelings toward him than Everett knew, and that his self-esteem was so low that that was all it took to drive him over the edge. What plagues Everett, and other people who may have said or done something wounding, is that they can never know how significant what they said or did was to their sibling and whether it helped cause the suicide in any way.

Teresa (Ch. 11) worried that her own recently diagnosed illness had somehow influenced her older sister's decision to end her life. She and her sister Gail were both in their forties when Teresa was diagnosed with non-Hodgkin's lymphoma, a life-threatening disease. Her sister, a nurse, was not usually particularly warm or supportive, and the sisters apparently had never had a very close relationship, but when the diagnosis was made, her sister became Teresa's greatest support. Teresa wrote: *Gail really came through for me. She faced it squarely and gave me much support and advice. I was amazed at how helpful she was and how she threw herself into researching my disease and trying to help me see the optimistic side. However, I once overheard her on the phone during this period saying something like, "If I had it, I'd kill myself." I was never sure if she was talking about me, but she did not know I was in the next room and heard what she said. When she killed herself with an overdose, I was completely shocked and devastated. I could not understand why she had done that at a time when I really needed her and when she was really my only strength.*

For a long time I have wondered whether my illness had anything to do with Gail's suicide. She didn't say anything about it in the note she left, which was not addressed to anyone. It just said, "I've been depressed so long I'm tired of fighting it. The time has come." I always wondered why she chose that time of all times. I kept thinking that she had somehow stepped aside for me. Gail was always our parents' favorite, and I wondered if what she did had some kind of altruistic motive about getting out of the way so my parents could focus on my problems. It is an odd idea, because she had never been that way before, but I keep thinking that maybe being a nurse had something to do with it. The other thing I worry about has to do with what she said on the phone, because I thought maybe she made a connection between my possibly fatal illness and the idea of suicide—perhaps she had a feeling about "fatality" that suggested the idea of killing herself. Of course, I will never know the answer to these questions, and they will always hang heavy in my heart.

Even Walter (Ch. 6, 13, 14), who feels that his younger sister's suicide was her own decision and even respects it in some ways, nevertheless wonders about his connection to her death. His sister had been depressed for some time, and had paid little attention to him as a person in recent weeks. He felt that, as a theatrical person, she had stage-managed her own death. But why, he wondered, had she chosen to kill herself outside his bedroom window, out of all the places in their large backyard? His mother's and sister's bedrooms were at the far other end of the house: *It was as close as she could possibly get to me. The only "What if" for me was, what if she had just walked out the gate and come to my window and said, "I have a gun, and I don't know what I'm doing." I would have known how to handle that, which is why I guess she didn't.* Walter will always wonder why his sister picked that spot to kill herself, and whether she had singled him out as the one who might stop her.

Sharon (Ch. 14) had good reason to fear that her sister's eventual suicide would be connected to her as the younger sister. She had always had a peculiar relationship with her sister Hillary. It was tinged with jealousy on her sister's part, and there was a sense of too-close-ness in her sister's dependency on Sharon. As time went on, Sharon began to find her sister's neediness disturbing: *I remember somewhere in that long line of attempts of my sister's that I went to see her in the emergency room at one or another hospital, seeing her with tubes and more tubes, and I said to her, "Are you glad you survived?" or something that conveyed that message. She just shrugged. But the next day she said, "I thought about your question, and I decided the answer is yes, because I get to see you." It made me uncomfortable, and I didn't realize at first why. At first I thought, "That's so loving and so nice." But then I began to think, "Why me?" There was this whole feeling that fits in with the whole sibling thing, this unnatural focus on me that was certainly making me feel in a position of responsibility. It also had something to do with the whole competitive thing somehow. I think that's when I started my withdrawal from the situation, because something about that comment felt almost sinister. It was too close. I felt, "If you want to have the will to live, go ahead and have it, but don't look to me. I won't always be here. I have my own life to live."*

Then there were times my sister would call about near attempts. She was sort of thinking about thinking about it. She would say, "I just put my fist through the window" or "I'm thinking of taking the knife out of the drawer," or something like that. What began to frustrate me more and more was that there were people she could be calling who would really know what to do with this information. There were professional people all over the city who were specifically trained and available to help her with her particular problem. But she wanted my attention. It became clear to me that this problem and this crisis was not something that I was appropriate to solve. It became clearer and clearer that she didn't so much want to solve the problem, but that she wanted my attention and involvement with her. I was really trying to solve the problem, and that wasn't really what she was asking me to do.

Later, after Sharon had withdrawn from the family, and her sister made another suicide attempt, Hillary wrote to her saying that Sharon was responsible for it, because by abandoning her she had driven her to unbearable loneliness and despair. Sharon felt that if and when her sister did eventually succeed, that her suicide would very possibly be aimed at her.

It is, of course, impossible to know in any individual instance to what degree a sibling is involved in a person's suicide, but, at least in some cases, a sibling may have more to do with the suicide than people realize. Bonnie's brother and Ellen's sister may, indeed, have been acting in part out of spite toward their sibling. Phil's brother's suicide *may* have been driven to some degree by his feeling of being excluded from his brother's ongoing lives. Paul's younger brother *might* have felt that Paul's hitting him took away his last support. Perhaps Peter's brother's suicide *was* connected to his jealousy over Peter's life and his feeling of being a failure in comparison. Maybe Everett's angry last words were, indeed, the final blow to his brother's shaky self-esteem. It is not impossible that Teresa's sister did feel an altruistic urge to step aside so that her parents would turn their attention for Teresa's needs, or that some superstitious feeling did make Gail perceive Teresa's possibly fatal illness as a sign that the time had come finally to kill herself. Suicidal people are often superstitious and look for signs that the time is right. Maybe Walter's sister *was* conveying a message to him in her choice to kill herself under his bedroom window. Sharon's sister *did* seem to be unhealthily over-aware of Sharon, and did, in fact, blame her latest suicide attempt on Sharon's abandoning her.

But while we can be aware of such possible connections, we should be wary of taking on excessive responsibility for a sibling's suicide. Rather than laying an unhealthy and inappropriate burden of guilt on ourselves, it is important to bear in mind that other influences, both internal and external, may well have played a greater part.

Chapter Sixteen
Can a sibling understand it best?

After my sister's suicide, I felt that no one understood what had driven her to it as well as I did. Of all her friends and family, I felt I was the only one who could really "get" it. Ann's friends were completely bewildered. To them, because she wore a persona of calm and capability, her suicide was a bolt out of the blue. My parents singled out her husband, and his actions or failures to act, as the direct cause of her death, and they did not seem to want to see the role that her own internal demons had played in pushing her inevitably to her ultimate decision. I understood that they could not allow themselves to look at that closely, because it would make their own guilt unbearable if they began to contemplate the root causes of their daughter's final despair. Her husband probably understood a good deal more of what had driven her, but there was still a way in which he could not fully understand that, faced with what she saw as her utter failure, Ann would almost inevitably choose suicide. If he had really known what failure meant to her, he would have surely have had her hospitalized. He had taken her to a psychiatrist the day before, but the psychiatrist failed to sense the gravity of Ann's situation and allowed her to go home.

I myself was too far away to see first hand what was happening, and it was only after my sister's suicide that I saw how inevitable it was. Almost the moment I got the news, I felt it made perfect sense, and I could feel the forces that drove her to do it.

We were both raised with similar pressures, expectations, and attitudes. Success, for instance, was important in our family, and Ann, especially, was very competitive and ambitious. Our family also placed an undue emphasis on the opinions of other people and how they saw us. Both of us tried to live up to other people's expectations of us as we perceived them. We strove to do well at life more because we "should" than out of love for what we were doing, and our motivation was, to a large degree, extrinsic. The "shoulds" drove both of us, and the fear of failing in other people's eyes was omnipresent.

There came a point in my life when I felt on the verge of mental collapse. I felt like a failure at life, and my life seemed flavorless and dead. It was then that I found a Jungian therapist and began six and a half years of work. I began to give form to inner figures. There was a huge Judge, who sat on a throne in the middle of the room and looked on me with disfavor for everything I did. There was a Driver, who ran after me with his whip, lashing at me and yelling, "Faster! Faster! More! More!" As I recognized them and saw the power they had always had over me, I learned how to keep them in their rightful places. (The Judge, for instance, had to sit over in the corner.) At the same time, I began to recognize other figures, helpful and enlivening beings, who now stepped forward, and gradually helped me feel empowered. I was eventually able to shed the heavy shoulds, and life gained a flavor it had never had.

I am sure that my sister shared many of the same inner demons, particularly the Judge and the Driver, although she might have called them by different names if she had ever had the opportunity to become conscious of them. In any case, Ann never saw the value of therapy for herself. She continued to be driven by the need to impress others, and to "should" herself into doing and doing. She had to do everything and do everything perfectly. She invested men, in particular, with great power, but she felt judged by all of Them Out There. I do think that both her inner judge and her inner driver were harsher than mine and ruled with a heavier hand, but I still feel that therapy eventually could have helped her become herself, not their puppet, and she could have been happy.

I believe I had at one time felt very similar to how my sister felt at the end. I had experienced the terrible dread of failure and the same sense of being judged by the whole rest of the world. Being competent to do men's work in the world was immensely important to my sister, and when she found herself failing there as well as in her marriage, she saw no other options for herself than to kill herself. Added to her shame at failing in the world of work was the shameful idea of having to go home to Mother, as well as the humiliation of having her little sister be the one who would come out to rescue her and take her home.

I do not blame my parents for any of this, because they did the very best they could for us, but I am aware that the circumstances of our mutual childhood and the values and attitudes we were raised with helped create the inner demons that plagued us both. Several of the other people I talked with felt something similar—that being raised together and sharing the same upbringing gives us a window on our sibling that others cannot quite share. Siblings are, in a sense, raised in the same "room", even though we may have had our own rooms in the literal sense. We live through our childhood together and share common experiences and a similar upbring-ing. Our personalities are different, and we differ in how we take in our experiences, but we still share certain common grounds—our parents, our circumstances, the times, the community—that in conjunction make up something that is unique to us.

Among the people I raised this topic with, the vast majority also felt that they could understand their sibling's suicide better than other peo-ple, simply by virtue of being a sibling. Alan (Ch. 4, 6, 10, 11,13,14), whose older brother and only sibling killed himself when they were in their mid-twenties, and who felt a good deal of guilt that he had not been his brother's keeper, agreed that because of their shared childhood he understood his brother far better than anyone. He saw that both of them had experienced the same pressures growing up: *We grew up in an upper middle class Jewish community. Most of the people we knew were way above middle class. The fathers were doctors, lawyers, or Wall Streeters. The mothers were society women and club women. As we got older, the children developed that same kind of mind set. Our parents were school teachers, and they weren't right up there. I think the values that our parents imparted were somewhat different. The other parents were very aggressive, manupulative people, and I think that they conveyed that to their children who were our peers. We both experienced a good deal of social unacceptance, he to a far greater degree, but I did, too. I was able to handle it, and he didn't. I didn't view myself as a physical geek. He did. I wasn't full of creative, driving energy. He was an artist. An artist generates outlooks on things that are uniquely his own, and it gives him that ability to create things. It involves looking at things differently, so in that respect I think that, while the social pressures of adolescence and eventually young adulthood were very trying and taxing on me, I more or less handled them. They ripped him apart, and everything would snowball.*

I think I can understand him and his suicide better than other people. I saw his inability to grapple with life up close and personal, and I also saw where the pressures on him were coming from, where the guilt was coming from. Some one else might just say, "What a mess you are!". They wouldn't see the torture that I saw and the battling influences. I saw that he had the desire to please people, but there were things that he was unable to conform to and please people with. I saw how he just couldn't do it because of how he viewed himself, and I understood the very unique pressure he felt from our parents, particularly from my mom. My mom's a Holocaust survivor. Sometimes if there were troubles, she would go on verbal tirades where she would say, "It's like the Nazis all over again. It's like when my parents were deported all over again." Which was all we needed to hear. It's all he needed to hear, especially. As if he weren't miserable enough without knowing that he was making her miserable. The pressure that came from her I think was too much. It was as though that Holocaust-induced need for achievement back-fired, and it became defeating because everything else had him so tied up in knots. *He was a failure. I don't think there was a lot of alcohol in his system when he hit that parked car. He just decided "This is it. I can't take this any-more." And then he went and hanged himself.*

Rosemary (Ch. 11, 13), who lost her younger and only brother when she was in her mid-thirties, also felt that their shared childhood put her in a unique position to understand her brother's suicide: *Partly I feel that because I tried suicide myself once, I know the pain that it takes, and I felt I could understand it that way. And there were the pressures growing up. My father died young, and that was very hard. Jimmy was only two, and I was seven. Then there was the new stepfather, whom nobody liked. We thought that he took the place of our father, and I think that my broth-er felt that really keenly. He didn't like the new stepfather—none of us did. He had never been married, and he didn't understand young people. The problem was that there was a family friend that my brother was living with, who had dated my mother all the time we were growing up, and we all really liked him. But our mother married this other man.*

I think she's made a good marriage for herself. They travel a lot. But the thing is that she has withdrawn herself from her family. I don't see her that much. I don't think she cares about me that much, because of her remar-riage. I think Jimmy must have felt that way, too. She lives three hundred miles away from me, and so many times we want to go visit her, but, Oh, she's got this or that. She'll say it's not convenient because she thinks maybe she'll be having company then, or something. I don't see her that often because I don't feel welcome over there. I get angry and upset, and I'm sure my brother felt the same way. Abandoned. I'm sure that was part of the problem, along with his bipolar disorder. It's a way I can understand my brother's suicide better than other people. We both grew up in the same sit-uation with the same mother and stepfather.

Megan (Ch. 8, 10, 13, 14), whose twin sister killed herself when they had just turned seventeen, felt she could understand her sister's suicide better than others in part because of being her twin, but also because she felt the same oppression in their family and community: *I think it's*

*true with a lot of identical twins that you literally feel what the other per-
son feels. . . And I'm sure my sister was pregnant. When I was pregnant
with my second child, I was so suicidal. It wasn't conscious. My husband
came in one day and had wine and flowers in his hands, and I looked at
him and a vision went before my eyes of jumping off a cliff. It was deep. I
couldn't have stopped myself if someone hadn't stopped me. It was chemical, and I think if my sister were pregnant, it would have made her suicide
even more likely.*

*She was also up against a brick wall. My parents would have killed her
if she'd been pregnant, and no way they would have had her have an abortion. The small city we grew up in was oppressive and repressive, and
everyone was related to everyone else. And everyone knew who had done
what. It was creepy. I hated it. It's also humid. It's an incubator for viruses. I think it's an incubator for emotions, too. Between our family and the
secrecy and their being unable to talk about things, and the community as
a whole, I know my sister felt that she was just stuck. And there was maybe
the chemical thing, which I have also experienced, which just exacerbated
it. These are things no one else could understand about my sister's suicide
the way I can.*

Evan (Ch. 10, 13, 15) was in his forties when his younger sister and
only sibling killed herself after suffering for years from hysterical
depression. He feels that his mother never understood his sister as he
could, and that he alone can really understand what drove her to suicide: *My sister had stopped speaking to my mother years and years ago.
That upset my mother a lot, but it was a release for my sister. My mother
was controlling, and she expected people to be what she wanted them to be
instead of what they were. I think that was a huge burden on my sister,
because my sister was who she was, and she had enough problems to deal
with, with her condition, and then to deal with my mother pestering her
all the time, wanting her to be what my mother wanted her to be. My
mother was always mad at my sister, and concerned, because, she said, my
sister couldn't hold a job, and she couldn't do this, she couldn't do that. My*

sister didn't want to hold a job. She wanted to be a writer. My mother couldn't accept her for who she was.

I knew my sister a good deal better than my mother did. I don't think my mother understood my sister at all. I remember one tiny thing. My sister had very, very tightly curly hair, and I think a lot of people are unsatisfied with their hair. If they have curly hair, they wish it was straight. If they have straight hair, they wish it was curly. My mother would always complain about my sister's hair. When she was a teenager, it was unruly, or she had a huge Afro, or she was trying to straighten it. And my mother never agreed with anything that my sister did with her hair, and she would constantly complain at my sister about it. It would make my sister crazy. People need to be accepted by their mothers, but my mother couldn't accept my sister as how she was, right down to the way her hair was.

The way I feel is, if you can't accept another person's faults, you better kiss that person goodbye. And if you like the person, then you better accept their faults. I think I understood my sister and saw her and accepted her for who she was. I understood her deciding to kill herself, too, because of her terrible depressions and not being able to escape any other way. Even though I don't get depressed that way, still I understand how she felt and that she just couldn't wait anymore.

Judy (Ch. 1, 13), who had become her older brother's protector and who was very close to him, was in her thirties when he killed himself. She, too, felt that she was the one who best understood her brother's suicide: *I understood what was going on inside him and what he felt, because of being his sister. I understand in a way that I don't think anyone else could understand. His suicide made me aware of the effects of our family, not just for him but for myself, and it drove me to try to come to grips with those issues. I was very close to my brother and I saw his pain. He was mentally ill and a failure. Yet, it looked as though his dreams were about to materialize, success was almost in hand, and it was at that point that he decided that he couldn't go on. That terrible fear of success. But I could understand that, and understand his killing himself. Since my father and my brother didn't get along at all well, and my father was very angry at my brother and very disappointed in him, a lot of the responsibility fell on me, and I was with my brother a lot. I could see that he was gradually deteriorating, and that things just continued to get worse and worse for him. Nobody else in the family was as close to him as I was or saw it all, and his pain, so clearly. No one else could understand his suicide the way I can.*

Ramona (Ch. 1, 11, 13) had been very close to her older brother Jonah. She felt that, despite his mental illness, she understood him deeply. She felt that his thoughts and feelings, and who he really was, were clearer to her than to anybody, and that she is the one who can best understand his suicide: *I feel that I understand why Jonah killed himself and how he felt. He was tormented, and I see it as a product of that. I used to get right in there with him. Things that were tormenting him, I'd get in there and be tormented, too. I do know how his mind was. The difference was that I would keep going away and getting away from it. I could. He couldn't. That was the difference. I could get caught up in it with him, but by myself I wouldn't get caught up in it too much.*

I think my parents just saw it as part of his mental illness. I had a different idea of his mental illness than they did, I think. They just saw it as a disease that he had, whereas I'd get in there with him. I could see his questions. One thing we had experienced was the Void. I know what it was like when he experienced that, because I had experienced that a lot. There's a way in a brain...there's something you have to deal with mentally sometimes. He and I called it the Void. We both knew about that. We both knew about a lot of things. I also was really careful not to be too religious. I didn't want to get off the deep end as he was about it, and I still kind of watch myself, but it's not necessary because I'm not him. It never was necessary, because if I had been like him I couldn't have avoided it. But I was enough like him so that I watched myself closely. I felt that he couldn't keep living, and that's why it happened when it did. Another part of it was that he thought he was Jesus sometimes, and Jesus was thirty-three years old, so how could Jonah keep living and become an old man?

Not everyone I talked to was so confident that they understood their sibling's suicide, or understood it better than anyone else. Reba (Ch. 7, 12, 13), for instance, who was only ten when her brother killed himself, could perceive, when she became a teenager, how her brother's life must have been, which gives her a window into what might have driven him to kill himself, but she is not sure that she necessarily understands it better than anyone, because she was so young when it happened: *My father was an authoritarian, controlling, domineering person. At dinner none of the children said a word. He was extremely domineering to the point where, when I was sixteen and eighteen, I hated my father because he wouldn't let me do anything I wanted to do. He made me work at his store twice a week from the time I was thirteen, and I had to get good grades, and all these rules were there, too. It was true for my brother, also. He had to work. He had to get good grades. He had to be Bar Mitzvahed. He had to go to temple. All the shoulds—a long, long list. Behave.*

The other thing was that my mother until the day she died never showed any emotion. She never touched you. She never said she loved you. She never learned to share emotions. She was very cold. Now, how that affected my brother, I don't know. I know how it affected me, so I can imagine how it affected my brother. She provided meals, and very good cooking, and everything ran nicely. We had all kinds of lessons, and the house ran well, but it was not a warm family at all. We had a domineering father and a cold mother, and we were so regulated. I was very depressed by the time I was in High School, so I can understand why my brother was depressed.

I'm not sure that I really understand that well why he killed himself, though. I was only ten and he was sixteen. I can see that he was in a similar family situation that might drive him to do something like that, so in that way I can understand it better than, for instance, my father or my mother. I think my sister understands it quite a bit. She's a social worker, and she has a lot of insight into these things, so I'm sure she's done some thinking about it. Maybe she's the one who understands it best.

I raised the question with Linda (Ch. 8, 9, 11, 13, 14), whose twin brother had killed himself when they were both thirty-two, because I thought that, as a twin, she would feel she understood her brother's suicide best, but she was not entirely sure that she did: *I have a very strong theory about what it was, and I also had a very, very strong need to feel his pain that led to pulling the trigger. Because I do feel it's pain, emotional pain, that led to that. It took me a long time to figure out, but I finally accepted the idea that I can't feel his pain, and if I ever were able to feel his pain, I'd have to do the same thing. It's like eating the apple in Eden. Once you've crossed the threshhold, there's only one thing that's going to happen. The pain has to be that bad. And for me to understand him, and to really accept it because I understand, that would be useless because I'd have to do the same thing. Do I understand it better than anyone? I think pretty much everyone in my family has a strong theory, or opinion, or rationalization that they have adopted in order to not feel guilty, to be able to talk about it, with the exception of perhaps my dad. Really to understand it would mean just feeling the sureness that he was really on the edge. I saw it coming, but just in fleeting statements. But I also had not seen it coming.*

When I put this question to Walter (Ch. 6, 13, 14, 15), who was in his early twenties when his younger sister killed herself, he was somewhat ambivalent about whether he could really understand his sister's suicide best: *Right after it happened my mind went into overdrive trying to connect all the dots. I guess when most people hear about a suicide, even when it's someone close to them, it's sort of a "Wow, that's terrible. So what's for dinner tonight?" It's not that big a thing, unless they're in your family or a close friend. But I would consider myself to be pretty much at the epicenter of the blast. It was definitely something that changed my life.*

So, yes, I do sometimes think I understand it better than anybody, although I'm not sure. In my family it seems as though everyone's going to have their private rationale that they're going to trot out, and, of course, I'm going to think that mine's better, and I'm going to scorn everyone else's. I'm sure if I were to call up her psychiatrist, he would have a very textbook rationale—*"Well, when the dendrites are not reacting properly with the synapses, it results in a condition of symbiotic whatever..." See, that's the rub. Everyone comes up with their theory, and I guess because I'm more given to philosophy and literature I sort of have more romantic thoughts about why these things happen. Maybe I understand it better because we were closer. We were really close growing up. But it's my mom who must feel nothing but guilt, and she has her own understanding of why my sister killed herself.*

Finally, there were a small handful of people who felt that their being the sibling did not put them in a position to understand their sibling's suicide better than other people. Phil's (Ch. 1, 13, 15) younger brother, for instance, who killed himself when they were both in their teens, had left an explanatory note that Phil took at its face value. He felt it explained his brother's suicide clearly to everyone in the family, and that his understanding was not necessarily greater. Indeed, because his brother used to talk to his mother a good deal, as he never talked to Phil, he thought that perhaps she was the one in the family who could understand it best.

Cliff (Ch. 9), too, whose younger and only brother killed himself when they were in their forties, felt that he did not have any special insight into why it happened. He had moved away from the family years before, while his brother stayed in their home town and lived near their mother, and he rarely saw him or spoke to him. His brother never confided in him, and his suicide came as a total shock. Cliff still does not entirely understand why his brother killed himself, and feels that his mother, who saw him more often, had more insight into it that he does.

Finally, Jim (Ch. 3, 10, 13, 14), the doctor whose older brother suffered from a bi-polar disorder and killed himself when they were in their late twenties, disagreed with the underlying premise itself: *That implies that there was something from your environment that made it more likely that suicide would take place. I don't know if I necessarily go along with that. Nature versus nurture. It's very difficult to know how much of it is chemical or how much is psycho-dynamic, learned patterns of behavior which are self-destructive. And our family is a perfect example of five very disparate courses in life, and we're all very different.*

But of all the people who contemplated the question of whether a sibling is the one who can best feel and understand what underlay the suicide, most felt that they were in a unique position to understand their sibling's psyche because of their shared childhoods. They had been molded to some degree by similar forces and experienced similar pressures and expectations, and had been brought up in similar ways. For the most part, it was the people whose siblings had suffered from some form of mental illness who did not necessarily feel that they understood the suicide any better than other people, because they felt that their sibling's state of mind made them too different from themselves. Yet even many of those felt that they could still understand it best.

Conclusion
Siblings in the Wake of Suicide

What was striking as I talked to people about their lives in the wake of their sibling's suicide was the immense variety in their experiences and their feelings. As there is a great gamut of relationships possible between siblings, so there is a great gamut of feelings possible after a sibling's suicide. One experience, however, was nearly universal among the people I talked with, and that was their perceived lack of support from other people for them as a sibling.

Surviving siblings may themselves feel confused about their own feelings and reactions, since sibling relationships are seldom simple. Yet, paradoxically, it is that variety of sibling relationships and the consequent variety in siblings' feelings after the suicide that seem to lie at the root of the lack of support they often experience. It seems that often other people do not know what the relationship between the siblings was and therefore cannot tell whether the surviving sibling needs support. Since it is more comfortable to assume that the siblings were not particularly close and therefore that the survivor is not in need of support, little is offered. Yet siblings often grieve deeply and need consolation and a willing ear. Other surviving siblings may have more conflicted feelings, and they, also, need support and the opportunity to talk through and work out their feelings.

From listening to surviving siblings tell their stories and share their experiences, it becomes very clear that there is no one experience that can be labeled the "sibling" experience of suicide. The experiences of sibling survivors depend very much on the kind of relationship they had with their brother or sister before the suicide. Sibling relationships run the gamut from extreme closeness and acceptance of one another, through varying degrees of competition and rivalry mixed in with love, all the way to coolness and distance and even, at times, extreme friction and anger. One can hardly expect, then, that the feelings of surviving siblings could be any more homogeneous. In Part One people described a wide range of feelings after their sibling's suicide: overwhelming grief, little feeling of loss, anger, guilt, and relief. For the most part, these feelings are intermixed, and a sibling's experience of a suicide can be immensely complex and often conflicted, with lingering feelings of sibling rivalry often an ingredient in the stew.

During the course of working on this book, I asked myself often how a sibling's experience of a suicide might be different from that of other family members or of friends, and I posed the question to some of the people I talked with. Again, there is no single answer, but there are certain threads that weave through people's experiences. As I noted in Chapter Three, for instance, siblings may find it easier than others, particularly parents, to acknowledge their anger at their brother's or sister's act. For many people anger at a sibling is a familiar emotion. We remember our squabbles and conflicts as we were growing up, and venting anger at a sibling often seems natural, and easier than allowing ourselves to acknowledge our anger at other people in our lives. Some of the "unbidden thoughts" of Chapter Nine seem, also, to be unique to siblings, since they seem to spring often from deep-seated jealousies or rivalries rooted in a shared childhood. Who but siblings could feel that they had "won" after a suicide, or feel that they would benefit by now getting their parents' undivided attention or, even, be the sole recipient of family goods or treasures?

How the suicide affects siblings has a good deal to do with their age at the time, and younger people often experience deep, long-term reverberations. Their sibling's suicide when they were in their teens or early twenties can leave survivors with a deep-seated fear of abandonment by others, a fear of getting involved in other relationships, or the fear that they will take their own lives. Some take over the dead sibling's persona and bury their own personalities, while others, feeling now abandoned by their parents, act out self-destructive rebellions. Some may take on a nearly pathological sense of responsibility for the well-being of their parents and subsume their own identities in their need to please them and make up for the grief their sibling caused them.

The family dynamic may also change and have any number of effects on the surviving siblings. Some may find that they have suddenly "moved up"; they may find they have now become the parents' favorite or that they have new responsibilities in the family that they may or may not welcome. Or they may find that their parents have immortalized their dead sibling, and they feel abandoned by them. They may become resentful that little attention is paid to them as a surviving child. Conversely, some surviving siblings find that their parents now hover anxiously over them, or ply them with presents, which can be sometimes gratifying, but also sometimes irritating when they feel smothered by their overly-solicitous parents. Some surviving siblings may find that their life in the family has been permanently altered, whether positively or negatively, and that can have long-term effects on their subsequent lives.

Some of the people I talked with suggested another way that their experience was different from anyone else's. As Ramona (Ch. 1, 11, 13) put it, *I know my experience is different from anyone's. My mother, for instance, was probably twenty years old when she had Jonah, so she can remember life without him. For me, he was always there, and that's why it feels so strange not to have him now. I told that to my mother. I said, "You don't understand. You had a life before you had him. He came into your life and he left. But how can I have a life without him when I've always had him?" It doesn't seem to have changed her life that much as it did mine. She's still living the same way she was living before. But my life changed completely.*

Rosemary (Ch. 11, 13, 16) also shared this feeling: *Losing a sibling is more long term. You're close to this person. You grew up with him. I was only thirty-five when my brother died, and I have to live with this for the next forty or fifty years, whereas my mother is going to die and anybody else that was close to him. They're not as close as a sibling who lived with him and grew up with him.* Neither Ramona nor Rosemary would want to downplay the impact of their brothers' suicide on their parents or other family members, but they do feel that their own loss is unique to them as siblings, because their lives were inextricably connected with their brothers' from a very early age.

As I pointed out in the previous chapter, siblings, in effect, grow up together in the same "room", and even if they have drifted apart, there is a strong, lifelong bond between them. That bond is not a simple one, however. It is often a complicated braid of many strands complexly woven together, which is why siblings' feelings and experiences after a suicide are so varied and often complex. But that bond, forged in a shared childhood, often gives surviving siblings the feeling that they are the ones who can best understand what drove their brother or sister to suicide. The expression, "I know where you're coming from" can be literally true for siblings.

Many people, particularly if they have no other siblings, feel cut off from their childhood after a sibling's suicide. That would be true however the sibling died, but the fact that the sibling purposefully and suddenly severed the connection makes the loss more acute. Siblings share memories of childhood experiences that are unique, and they experienced that time in their lives from a similar vantage point. It is bewildering suddenly to find that no one shares those childhood memories anymore, and, even if their relationship was not a particularly close one, losing that connection can make the surviving sibling feel alone and lonely.

One truth came out over and over in my interviews with surviving siblings, and that is that they need to talk about their feelings and experiences with a willing listener. Many of them realized that our interview was the first opportunity they had ever had to share their feelings and explore with another person the impact the suicide had on their lives. It was moving that many of the people I talked with felt relieved finally to be able to explore and express their feelings, but it is also sad that they had up to then felt little support from other people. I was struck again and again by the importance of support for surviving siblings of suicide.

The fact that surviving siblings felt that they received so little support points to a larger issue: little attention is paid in general to sibling issues and sibling relationships. Our siblings are inextricably entwined in our lives from an early age, and our relationship with them colors all our other relationships, yet the effects on us of our sibling relationships are rarely taken into serious consideration. If therapists and lay people paid better attention to how their own relationships with their siblings have affected their lives, people like those in this book would not suffer from the lack of help and support they experienced.

Perhaps the most important lesson to be learned from the experiences of the people in this book is that surviving siblings need to seek out people who will listen to them and encourage them to share their feelings. When, as is too often the case, friends and family cannot fill that role, then grief counseling or therapy can greatly help people work through their grief, or anger, or guilt, and come to understand their often complex feelings in the wake of a sibling's suicide.

THE END

CPSIA information can be obtained
at www.ICGtesting.com
Printed in the USA
LVOW10s1521220217
525092LV00003B/517/P

9 780595 095230